THE BRITISH EMPIRICISTS

LOCKE

John Dunn

■■■

BERKELEY

J. O. Urmson

■■■

HUME

A. J. Ayer

Oxford   New York

OXFORD UNIVERSITY PRESS

Oxford University Press, Walton Street, Oxford OX2 6DP

Oxford New York Toronto
Delhi Bombay Calcutta Madras Karachi
Kuala Lumpur Singapore Hong Kong Tokyo
Nairobi Dar es Salaam Cape Town
Melbourne Auckland Madrid

and associated companies in
Berlin Ibadan

Oxford is a trade mark of Oxford University Press

Each section was first published separately in the
Past Masters series as an Oxford University Press paperback and
simultaneously in a hardback edition
This edition first published 1992
First issued as an Oxford University Press paperback 1992

British Library Cataloguing in Publication Data
Data available
ISBN 0-19-283068-6

3 5 7 9 10 8 6 4 2

Printed in Great Britain by
Biddles Ltd
Guildford and King's Lynn

Foreword

THE three philosophers whose work is discussed in this book were men of great intellectual versatility whose investigations ranged over many different areas of life and thought. What unites them is that they all gave profound consideration to the nature of human understanding, its sources and its limitations. They examined the powers and principles of the human mind and they attempted to determine what forms of certain knowledge were possible.

This preoccupation with what is now called epistemology was characteristic of many thinkers who lived in the wake of the Scientific Revolution: that cluster of spectacular developments in astronomy, physics, mathematics and biology in the century and a half between Copernicus and Newton which dramatically re-drew the map of human knowledge. In particular, the contrast between science, which proceeded by experiment and deduction, and religion, which rested on faith and tradition, provoked an intense debate about the powers and limits of human reason.

Locke, Berkeley and Hume are normally regarded as the founders of British empiricism: that is to say they are held to have taught that human beings can have no knowledge of the world other than what they derive from experience. Locke rejected the doctrine of innate ideas and held that there was no room for *a priori* reasoning. For him, knowledge began in sensation, though it was developed by reflection. Hume reduced the person to a series of ideas and sensations, though he regarded some of the passions as inherent in human nature. Berkeley declared roundly in his notebooks: 'Foolish in men to despise the senses. If if were not for them the mind could have no knowledge, no thought at all.'

This empirical approach is often regarded as a characteristically British reaction to the more grandiose aspirations of Continental philosophers like Descartes or Leibniz, who erected large-scale rationalist philosophical systems by invoking reason rather than experience. In fact, 'empiricism' is a very loose term; and, as these three studies show, a general disposition to regard knowledge as deriving from experience can produce very different philosophical results.

John Locke, for example, followed the scientists of his time in assuming the real existence of the physical world, though drawing a distinction between the primary qualities of things, like solidity, extension or number, which, he held, were inseparable from them and secondary qualities, like colour, taste or smell, which were their powers to produce sensations in us. Although his defence of religious toleration and his case for responsible government have ensured Locke an enduring place in the history of political thought, what ultimately defeated him was the attempt to show that morality and religion are capable of demonstration, and that we can have certain knowledge of how we can live. For John Dunn this failure makes Locke a tragic thinker.

George Berkeley took the idea that knowledge arises from perception to the paradoxical extreme of arguing that there is no such thing as matter, since for a thing to exist it has either to be perceived or be the body that does the perceiving; and no one can perceive or imagine an inert material without colour, odour, tactile attributes or any other secondary qualities. This was the doctrine which Dr. Johnson ridiculed when he said to a gentleman who held it, 'Pray, Sir, don't leave us for we may perhaps forget to think of you, and then you will cease to exist.' J. O. Urmson argues that, far from being absurd, Berkeley's was 'one of the most elegant, clear and simple metaphysical systems ever devised'.

Berkeley was a bishop in whose philosophical scheme God played a central role. Locke had a Puritan upbringing, devoted much energy to biblical commentary and regarded atheists as a threat to civil society. But David Hume abandoned Christianity in his teens and made the discrediting of every form of religious belief one of his primary aims. In his hands, empiricism resulted in scepticism, not just about organised religion but even about the possibility of demonstrating the link in science between cause and effect. It is not surprising that the late A. J. Ayer found Hume a profoundly sympathetic figure and regarded him as 'the greatest of all British philosophers'. His study examines Hume's theories of perception and self-identity, his analysis of causality and his treatment of morals, politics and religion. He cites Adam Smith's judgment that Hume came 'as nearly to the idea of a perfectly wise and virtuous man, as perhaps the nature of human frailty will admit'.

The three self-contained essays reprinted in this volume were originally written for the Past Masters series, which sets out to expound the ideas of notable thinkers of the past in a lucid, accessible and authoritative manner. Because they are necessarily short, they do not attempt to discuss every aspect of their subjects' lives and work. There is only a little here, for example, about Locke's writings on education or Berkeley's contribution to economics or Hume's six-volume *History of England*. But readers will find admirably penetrating expositions of the main doctrines of three thinkers whose ideas will continue to be discussed and argued about so long as philosophy is studied.

Corpus Christi College
Oxford

KEITH THOMAS
General Editor
Past Masters

Contents

LOCKE

Preface

LOCKE addressed his intellectual life as a whole to two huge questions. How is it that human beings can know anything? And how should they try to live? He began his career as a university teacher and ended it as very much a man of the world. In its course he thought, and thought hard, about a bewildering range of issues, from the prospects for English foreign trade and the economic consequences of the state of the English coinage to the politics of revolution in the 1680s, the interpretation of St Paul's *Epistles* and the cultivation of fruit trees. Because his interests were so broad, and because he pursued them with such intelligence and energy, he left behind him a large and impressive body of writings. In a brief work it would be impossible to do justice to the range of his ideas, let alone to assess their originality and unravel their intricate contribution to the intellectual history of the next two centuries. Accordingly, I shall not attempt to assess in any detail the contribution which he made to the various branches of modern thought: economics, theology, political theory, scriptural interpretation, ethics, anthropology, the theory of knowledge, education and so on. (In particular, I shall not set out a systematic exposition and criticism of his theory of knowledge as a classical moment in the history of British empiricism. To do so would distort his own approach; and it would also, in my view, do little to illuminate questions of current interest.) Instead, I shall focus on the shape of Locke's intellectual life as a whole and attempt to explain how he saw the relation between the two huge and unwieldy questions which he addressed with such courage and tenacity over so many years.

During the last two decades of his life, from 1683 until his death in 1704, it was the question of how men can know to which he devoted his keenest intellectual energies. His answer to it, however poorly understood, marked the mind of Europe for generations. Philosophers today disagree sharply on the merits of this answer. Some see it as a more or less mistaken response to a legitimate and important question. Others regard the question itself as confused and the demand for a comprehensive explanation of the scope and limits of men's cognitive powers as both absurd and impossible to satisfy. Still others see Locke's approach as fundamentally correct, whatever errors he may have made in working it out. It would be presumptuous here to pretend to adjudicate this disagreement. But it is essential to try to show what made Locke himself so eager to construct a theory of knowledge.

It was the second question, the question of how men should try to live, from which his thinking began. By the end of his life he was confident that he had largely answered the question of how men can know—at least in so far as its answer lay within the reach of human powers. But he was far less confident of his ability, on the basis of human powers alone, to show men how they should try to live. Initially he had hoped that an explanation of men's power to know would show them *why* they should try to live as he supposed they should. But the theory of knowledge which he constructed proved to show nothing of the kind. In consequence his theory of practical reason (of what men have good reason to do) was from his own point of view a disastrous failure. Unlike his theory of knowledge, it offers scarcely even the core of a view which we might ourselves hold. Some philosophers today do not regard the question of how men should try to live as a philosophical question at all; and more would not regard it as very clearly expressed. For these or other reasons, Locke's enterprise may well have been doomed from the start; but it remains profoundly instructive. The greatness of a thinker is not always best measured by the confidence and clarity of his intellectual solutions. Sometimes it can be shown at least as dramatically by the resonance of his failures.

What Locke hoped to show men was that a rational understanding of man's place in nature required them to live like Christians. But what he in fact showed was that a rational understanding of their place in nature did not, and does not, *require* men to live in any particular fashion. Worse still, the close relation between conceptions of how to live and the history of particular languages and cultures places all men's lives at the mercy of history. Even if there were a God who had designed the order of nature as a whole for men to live well within it, they could not draw their conceptions of how to live directly from this order through the exercise of their reason alone. Instead they must fashion their values for themselves as best they can out of the more or less seductive or menacing suggestions of others and by their own powers of reflection.

Our views today about how we can know still owe something to Locke. It remains an open question whether they would benefit from, for example, owing more to a better understood Locke or from purging what they still owe to a not very well understood Locke. Our views today about how we should try to live owe little directly to Locke's own beliefs. But it may well be that we have still not taken the measure of his failure. On the whole, Locke is discussed by historians and philosophers today as an optimistic thinker whose optimism was founded on understanding not very well what we ourselves understand altogether better. The case which I wish to put in this book is very different. It is that we should see Locke instead as a tragic thinker, who understood in advance some of the deep contradictions in the modern conception of human reason, and so saw rather clearly some of the tragedy of our own lives which we still see very dimly indeed.

Contents

Acknowledgements

I AM DEEPLY grateful to Michael Ayers for his generosity in lending me in manuscript a large portion of his major forthcoming study of Locke's philosophy and for the pleasure and excitement which I have derived over the last few years from his remarkable knowledge and understanding of Locke's works. For Oxford University Press, Henry Hardy, Keith Thomas and Alan Ryan have given me extremely helpful advice in preparing the text and have shown me throughout far more patience than I deserved. I am greatly indebted, as so often before, to many friends who have at different stages and for different reasons read drafts of part or all of it. For their encouragement, help and criticism I should particularly like to thank Cynthia Farrar, Michael Ignatieff, Takashi Kato, Jonathan Lear and Quentin Skinner.

Note on abbreviations

The following abbreviations are used in references to Locke's works:

E   *An Essay concerning Human Understanding*, ed. Peter H. Nidditch (Clarendon Press, Oxford, 1975)

EA   *Draft A of Locke's Essay concerning Human Understanding*, ed. Peter H. Nidditch (Department of Philosophy, University of Sheffield, 1980)

G   *Two Tracts on Government*, ed. Philip Abrams (Cambridge University Press, 1967)

LC   *The Correspondence of John Locke*, ed. E. S. de Beer, 8 vols. (Clarendon Press, Oxford, 1976–)

LN   *Essays on the Law of Nature*, ed. W. von Leyden (Clarendon Press, Oxford, 1954)

LT   *Epistola de Tolerantia and A Letter on Toleration*, ed. R. Klibansky and J. W. Gough (Clarendon Press, Oxford, 1968)

M   *An Examination of P. Malebranche's Opinion of Seeing All Things in God, Works*, 7th edn., vol. IV

R   *The Reasonableness of Christianity as delivered in the Scriptures, Works*, 7th edn., vol. III

T   *Two Treatises of Government*, ed. Peter Laslett, 2nd edn. (Cambridge University Press, 1967)

V   *Venditio*, printed in J. Dunn, 'Justice and the Interpretation of Locke's Political Theory', *Political Studies*, XVI 1 (February 1968), 84–7

W   *The Works of John Locke*, 7th edn., 4 vols. (London, 1768)

Important manuscript texts by Locke are cited from:

D   John Dunn, *The Political Thought of John Locke* (Cambridge University Press, 1969)

FB   H. R. Fox Bourne, *The Life of John Locke*, 2 vols. (London, 1876)

1

Life

JOHN Locke was born in a Somerset village in the summer of 1632. He died in the country house of his friends the Mashams, at Oates in Essex, late in October 1704. Until his mid-thirties he lived what was, at least in its externals, a rather unexciting life. But for more than three decades—from the year 1667—he was closely involved with the vagaries of English national politics. In his late fifties, for the first time and quite suddenly, he became a very famous man. From then on almost any of his correspondents might have described him without irony, with Lady Mary Calverley, as simply 'the greatest man in the world' (LC IV 105). When at last it did come, fame came to him as a philosopher, from the publication of his writings and especially, in the year 1689, of the great *Essay concerning Human Understanding*. It is this fame which has persisted, without interruption, until today.

By the time that Locke was forty he had in most ways grown very far away from his Somerset origins; and the real social distance between him and the rest of his family must have widened fairly steadily for the rest of his life. But in some fundamental respects, what he owed (for better or worse) to his parental upbringing remained the centre of his feelings and attitudes until the day he died. It is unusual in the case of a man or woman of the seventeenth century to be able to assess continuities of this kind with any confidence. But one of the peculiarities of Locke's temperament was his extreme reluctance to throw away any papers on which he had written. Since, by great good fortune, most of those which remained at his death have come down to us, we do in fact know more about him than we do about all but a handful of his contemporaries or predecessors. What this mass of manuscripts makes clear is that throughout adulthood Locke sustained a deeply Puritan pattern of sentiment, a pattern which places a sense of duty at the centre of the individual life. He was not in any way a morose and joyless person. But he did impose very fierce demands, upon himself as much as on others; and he was extremely moralistic in his reactions when these demands were not met. There was nothing Puritan about most of the philosophical views which won him immortality; and many of them would have shocked any Puritan alive in 1632. But the personal identity which gave his thought as a whole its integrity and human depth was that of a deeply Puritan self.

Locke's father and mother each came from Puritan trading families, clothiers on the father's side and tanners on the mother's. His father earned a not very impressive living as an attorney and clerk to the Justices of the Peace in Somerset. In addition he owned some land; not enough in itself to enable either him or his son to live the life of a gentleman, but enough to lead the son in later years to style himself as such on the title page of his greatest work. In itself this background did not guarantee Locke much of a future. But if his immediate family was parochial in its interests and somewhat ineffectual in its worldly pursuits, it did have more powerful and successful acquaintances. The most important of these was Alexander Popham. Like Locke's father, Popham had fought as an officer in the Parliamentary cavalry in Somerset in the early stages of the Civil War; and he went on to be a West Country Member of Parliament and a prominent figure in national politics. In 1647, as Member of Parliament for Bath, he was in a position to offer his attorney and brother officer the opportunity to send the latter's elder son to Westminster school. In later years Locke's father continued to hope for patronage from his influential political allies. But except perhaps for his son's crucial passage from Westminster school to Christ Church, Oxford, where a powerful patron appears once again to have been indispensable, his hopes seem always to have been disappointed. But if he left little impact upon a wider world, it is clear enough that this austere and, in later life, somewhat embittered man left a deep impress upon his brilliant son: an independence of spirit and force of self-discipline which were to mould Locke's entire life.

It is easiest to see the shape of this life in terms of three large movements, each of which carried Locke further away from his Somerset origins. The first move, to Westminster and then to Christ Church, marked the furthest stretch of his family's own resources and reasonable expectations. It carried him within easy reach of a clerical career, either inside or outside the university, a career which, with only moderate fortune and prudence, might fully match his intellectual abilities. ('A man of parts,' wrote his cousin John Strachey, 'let him study but complyance, hee need want noe preferment' (LC I 215).) But even as a young man with very few prospects, Locke clearly did not find compliance agreeable; and he seems never to have been attracted by the idea of a clerical career. A second possibility, less conventional and narrower but also more congenial, was to become a doctor. This was a possibility which Locke in fact pursued with some vigour, studying medicine systematically over several decades and offering extensive medical advice to friends and acquaintances. He worked closely with one of the great physicians of the seventeenth century, Dr Thomas Sydenham, a pioneer in the treatment of infectious diseases. Sydenham's approach to the study of illness was unusually self-conscious and systematic, and Locke's own conception of how men come to know about the natural world may well have been influenced by this collaboration. Fittingly, also, it was his medical interests, not his expertise as a philosopher or theologian, which gave him the great opportunity of his life.

The second movement came in 1666. In that year, through another medical friend, David Thomas, Locke met for the first time Lord Ashley, later the first Earl of Shaftesbury, a leading political figure at the court of Charles II. The occasion for the meeting was casual enough—a visit by Ashley to Oxford to drink the spa waters of Astrop. But its consequences, for Locke at least, were momentous. Within a year of this first meeting he had joined Ashley's household in London. A year later, in 1668, his patron underwent under Locke's supervision a major operation, for a suppurating cyst on the liver; and against all the odds the operation proved successful. For the next fourteen years he 'studied complyance' with Shaftesbury's whims and shared his master's turbulent fortunes. The move from the placid, if sometimes ill-tempered, backwater of Restoration Oxford to the seething life of Shaftesbury's household was a drastic one. Not that Locke himself ever voluntarily abandoned his position at Oxford (he was in fact expelled from it on government instructions after fleeing into exile in 1683); but the weight of his energies and hopes and fears, for the remainder of his life, rested elsewhere. From this time on, his personal fortunes rose and fell with those of his master and, after Shaftesbury's death in 1683, with those of the broad political grouping he had led.

In the years between 1667 and 1683 Shaftesbury was at different stages the most powerful political figure at Charles II's court and the leader of a national political opposition to that court which in the end threatened and perhaps planned a revolution to overthrow it. Both his triumphs and his failures marked Locke's imagination deeply. It was Shaftesbury who taught him to understand the economic responsibilities of the English State in its domestic market and in foreign commerce, who taught him to see the conditions and possibilities for economic prosperity as a central preoccupation for statecraft and a fundamental consideration in assessing any society's merits. If Locke's intellectual energies were in the end harnessed to any great degree by the cruel but vigorous dynamism of the English economy of his day, it was Shaftesbury who caused them to be so. There is a direct line of continuity between Locke's service on the Council of Trade during Shaftesbury's Chancellorship in 1672 and his service on William's Board of Trade in the 1690s, and an equally direct line between the economic understanding set out in his first economic writing in 1668 and the major works on regulating the rate of interest and on restoring the coinage which he wrote to advise William's government. Equally direct in terms of content, though not perhaps of motivation, is the link between Shaftesbury's steady commitment to toleration for Dissenters in the face of Restoration Anglicanism and Locke's spirited public and private campaign for toleration and freedom of the Press in the last two decades of his life. Equally clear is the tie between Shaftesbury's somewhat belated insistence, in the course of the so-called Exclusion crisis (the struggle to exclude Charles II's Catholic brother, James Duke of York, from the succession to the throne), on the representative basis of political legitimacy and Locke's great defence, in the *Two Treatises of Government*, of the rights to be governed only with consent and to resist unjust power.

The extent of this impact was, no doubt, largely a consequence simply of the range of experience which Shaftesbury's service opened up to Locke, the quite new practical vision of the social and political world with which it presented him. But it is clear, too, that it was a deeply personal impact. In the course of his life Locke had many close friends and very many more friends who, if less close, were also men and women of great power or wealth or very high intelligence: political grandees like Pembroke and Somers, scientists like Robert Boyle and Isaac Newton, theologians like Limborch. However much he liked and respected Locke as a man, Shaftesbury was, of course, very much master as well as friend. But lop-sided though their friendship plainly was, it did not lack emotional energy; and over those sixteen years it is clear that his great patron made Locke into a very different man.

They make a strange pair, these two figures between whom Locke's adult life was moulded: the awkward, repressed failure of a father and the glittering, untrustworthy, endlessly fascinating courtier who at the close of his life failed far more spectacularly. Strange—but in some ways singularly propitious. For each served admirably to offset the deficiencies in imagination of the other: the worried, ineradicable scruple of the first and the force, recklessness and irresponsibility of the second. From the tension between the two—and after the deaths of each—came the extraordinary intellectual framework of Locke's philosophy.

This third movement, the commitment to philosophical understanding, was, of course, far less obvious to the outsider and more gradual than either the shift to Westminster and Oxford or the entry into Shaftesbury's service. Locke's concern with philosophical questions of political authority and toleration, of ethics and the theory of knowledge, went back at least to the late 1650s. Indeed there is no reason to suppose that he would not have thought and written at length about philosophy if he had in fact taken holy orders, had never encountered Shaftesbury and had remained an Oxford don for the rest of his life. Nor did he ever succeed, until he was a very old and sick man, in extricating himself from the political and public responsibilities in which Shaftesbury's service had initially involved him. But if philosophy and politics continued to compete for his energies and attention from 1667 until shortly before his death, the balance between the two was struck very differently at different stages of his life.

Up till the year 1667, during the fifteen years which he spent at Oxford as a Student at Christ Church, Locke's philosophical writing was confined essentially to two major pieces of work. The first of these was a pair of essays on the demerits of claims to religious toleration, one in English and one in Latin, written in 1660 and 1661 and unpublished until the present century, the *Two Tracts on Government*. The second was a set of Latin lectures on the law of nature, delivered by him in 1664 as Censor of Moral Philosophy at Christ Church and also unpublished until this century, the *Essays on the Law of Nature*. The questions of the scope and limits of religious liberty and of how men ought to live remained central to Locke's thinking in later decades. But these first two pieces of writing lacked the breadth and urgency of his mature works; and they showed a very different political attitude. The most important intellectual opportunity which Oxford offered him in these years was not the chance to begin to work out and express what we should now think of as philosophical opinions, but rather the chance to participate in the chemical and medical researches of Boyle, Hooke, Lower and Sydenham. From these men Locke learnt the value of sustained and disciplined observation, of humility, patience and diligence in man's attempt to grasp the secrets of nature. As Sydenham put it in 1669, in a manuscript written in Locke's own hand:

True knowledge grew first in the world by experience and rational observation, but proud man, not content with the knowledge he was capable of, and which was useful to him, would needs penetrate into the hidden causes of things, lay down principles, and establish maxims to himself about the operations of nature, and thus vainly expect that nature, or in truth God should proceed according to those laws which his maxims had prescribed to him.

It was this background of practical scientific enquiry which Locke brought to bear on his reading of the two great Continental philosophers of the early scientific revolution, René Descartes and Pierre Gassendi, whose views affected him deeply in the late 1660s. Of the two, Locke's mature views were in many ways considerably closer to those of Gassendi. But, as he told Lady Masham, it was those of Descartes which first strongly attracted him to philosophy, to the attempt to understand very precisely and systematically what knowledge man 'was capable of'. The *Essay concerning Human Understanding* itself was, as he said in his *Epistle to the Reader*, an attempt 'to examine our own abilities, and see what objects our understandings were or were not fitted to deal with'. Most of the *Essay* was not in fact written until the late 1680s. But there exist extended drafts of many of the main arguments which were written as early as the year 1671. Besides these first sketches of the *Essay*, Locke also wrote other important works in this period: in 1668 a lengthy manuscript on the futility of governmental efforts to regulate the rate of interest, and in 1667 an essay on toleration, fully in the spirit of Shaftesbury's policies on the subject and decisively reversing his own more authoritarian views of the early 1660s. On the whole, however, his time in these years was too taken up with administrative work in Shaftesbury's public or private concerns, as colonial proprietor, great landowner and Minister of the Crown, to leave him the leisure for sustained philosophical work. By 1675 Shaftesbury was firmly in opposition to the King's government under Danby, and Locke himself was in very poor health. For the next three and a half years, a time of considerable danger for Shaftesbury, Locke travelled in France, for much of it in the rather trying company of Caleb Banks, the son of one of Shaftesbury's richest political associates. In the course of his travels he met many French doctors, scientists and theologians and made close friends with several of them. He also translated some of the moral essays of the Jansenist Pierre Nicole. But he does not appear to have worked on any original writings of his own.

At the end of April 1679, however, he returned to London. The next four years, up to the late summer of 1683 when he fled to Rotterdam, are a time of some obscurity in his life. His patron Shaftesbury had already lost his political influence at court by the time of Locke's departure to France in 1675. Even at this point Locke's services to him 'in his library and closet' were no longer confined to the 'business of a Minister of State'. He may well, for example, have drafted the 1675 pamphlet, *A Letter from a Person of Quality to his Friend in the Country*, in which Shaftesbury's opposition programme was set out; a pamphlet which earned the distinction of being burnt by the public hangman. By 1679 Shaftesbury's opposition to the policies of Charles II's government had sharpened. In the course of the next four years, during the Exclusion crisis, he organised and led a national political movement against the Crown, aimed at strengthening the constitutional restraints on royal authority, protecting the rights of the elected House of Commons and excluding Charles II's

Catholic brother James from the succession to the throne. It was a bitter and dangerous struggle in which the line between exercising legally recognised political rights and committing high treason was always difficult to draw. But there was no doubt at all of Charles's eagerness to draw it at the earliest possible stage. By 1682, if not before, Shaftesbury himself and Locke, Algernon Sidney, Lord William Russell and the Earl of Essex were all gambling with their lives. In the event Shaftesbury, at least, contrived to escape to the Netherlands, where he promptly died. But in June 1683, after the failure of the Rye House Plot to kidnap Charles and James on their return from Newmarket races, Sidney, Russell and Essex were all arrested. Essex subsequently committed suicide in the Tower of London, while Russell and Sidney met their deaths on the scaffold. Amongst the charges against Sidney at his trial was the authorship of seditious manuscripts. The latter included a lengthy attack on Sir Robert Filmer's ultra-royalist tract *Patriarcha*, an attack which was published posthumously, following Sidney's execution, as his *Discourses on Government*. Locke too was certainly under close governmental observation during the late summer of 1683, though he was scarcely a figure of the political importance of Essex, Russell or even Sidney. But he too, it now seems clear, must have had in his possession at that time an extremely seditious manuscript, the *Two Treatises of Government*, which likewise attacked the political theories of Filmer and which roundly endorsed the people's right of revolution against even a legitimate monarch where that monarch had grossly abused his powers. As it turned out, Locke managed to slip away into exile in Holland by September 1683; and, although his Christ Church Studentship was withdrawn from him on royal command the next year and the British government made unsuccessful attempts in 1685 to have him extradited, along with other Whig exiles, he was in much less danger from then on.

Exactly when and why he settled down to write the *Two Treatises* is still unclear and it is likely to remain so. Sedition was a hazardous business in seventeenth-century England; and the *Two Treatises of Government*, written in the circumstances of the Exclusion crisis, was an intensely seditious work. At least from 1683 on Locke showed himself to be a markedly cautious and secretive person. But we do know one or two interesting details about what he was doing in these years. In 1680, for example, he spent a considerable amount of time at Oakley, the country house of his friend James Tyrrell, who himself in 1681 published an attack on the political theory of Filmer, *Patriarcha non Monarcha*. Between 1680 and perhaps 1682 Tyrrell and Locke worked together on a lengthy (and still unpublished) manuscript work, defending the principles of toleration against a leading Anglican apologist, Edward Stillingfleet. It was to Tyrrell, amongst others, as a government spy reported, that Locke entrusted 'several hand-baskets of papers' while preparing for his departure from Oxford in July 1683. For Shaftesbury's political followers in those years, the defence of the political and religious rights of the Dissenters and the criticism of the most vehement English theorist of royal absolutism were both tasks of great urgency.

When he went into exile late in the summer of 1683 Locke had already passed the age of fifty and had published nothing of his own which was of the least consequence. The only major work of his own which we may be certain had been written for publication, the *Two Treatises of Government*, was for the moment more a source of hazard than a ground for self-congratulation. On the other hand, exile, however disagreeable and even dangerous in some ways, did present certain opportunities. For one thing, Locke made many friends, some of them very close, amongst the English merchant community and Dutch theologians and, after the revocation of the Edict of Nantes in 1685, amongst French Protestant refugees. For another, he had the time to think and write systematically and at length, without the immediate distractions of politics. He might not be in good health and his worldly prospects might be unenticing; but at least he had the chance to muster his powers and leave something substantial to posterity. It was during these years that he wrote both the *Essay concerning Human Understanding* and the *Letter on Toleration*.

In 1688 his worldly prospects improved sharply, with the landing of the Protestant William of Orange in England and the flight of the Roman Catholic King James II. Early the next year Locke returned to England and in the course of it his three greatest works were printed. Two appeared anonymously, the *Letter on Toleration* first in Latin in Holland in April and then in English in London in October, and the *Two Treatises of Government* in

London at the end of the year. But one, the *Essay concerning Human Understanding*, was issued in mid-December in a fine folio volume and with his own name firmly on the title-page. It was a remarkable publishing début.

In the fifteen years which remained to him before his death in 1704 his commitments remained as diverse as ever. Some were political in the narrowest sense: the consolidation of William's constitutional and political position, the reorganisation of the English coinage, the establishment of an effective credit system for the English State through the new Bank of England, and the development of institutions through which the government could exercise more effectively its responsibilities for the prosperity of English foreign trade. In each of these Locke himself was actively engaged, in the last three as a trusted intellectual adviser to the country's leading statesmen and over foreign trade as a lavishly rewarded public official on the new Board of Trade. Each of these preoccupations represented, in some measure, a fulfilment of Shaftesbury's programme of the late 1660s and early 1670s, a programme of highly self-conscious commercial imperialism in a narrowly English interest. In the legal and political arrangements of the Revolution settlement Locke played a more discreet and a considerably less influential role. It seems likely, too, that on the central issue of constitutional reform and the increase in the political power of an elected legislature, the outcome was much further from his wishes that it was in the case of monetary, fiscal or economic policy. More importantly perhaps, it is also clear that the political character of the Revolution settlement engaged his feelings and beliefs far more deeply than the technical details of governmental economic policy, and that he saw the significance of the former in a much broader and less chauvinistic context.

In the course of the Exclusion controversy itself, and later in exile in Holland in the tolerant and sophisticated company of Dutch Arminian theologians and merchants and of some of the younger Huguenot refugees, he had come to see the interests of European Protestantism and those of political freedom as bound tightly together. The Catholic absolutism of Louis XIV, with its direct military menace to surviving Protestant States and its intractable commitment to religious uniformity, had come to symbolise politically all that Locke hated: the deep confusion between the arrogance, ambition and corruption of human beings and the purposes of God. As soon as Locke entered Shaftesbury's household his views on the toleration of Dissenters from the Established Church shifted to a more relaxed and pragmatic attitude. In subsequent years the detachment fell away and he came to see (and, more importantly, to feel) the issue of toleration less and less as an issue of State policy and more and more as one of individual human right. In exile, for nearly six years, he had watched with growing fear the political and cultural, perhaps even the religious, future of Europe hang in the balance as the English Crown passed to a Catholic monarch and as Louis XIV threatened to overrun the last major bastion of Continental Protestantism in the Netherlands, revoked the Edict of Nantes, and settled down to crush the Huguenot Church and literally to dragoon its hapless adherents into the Catholic faith. (This last episode was sufficiently dramatic to add a verb to the English language.) It was in response to these events, to counter a peril which was European and not merely English, that he wrote the *Letter on Toleration*, which, unlike any of the other books that he published in his own lifetime, was first printed in the Latin which still served as the international language of European intellectuals. By 1689 the 'Protestant wind' had carried William of Orange safely across the Channel and the balance had at last begun to dip in the direction which Locke desired. The *Letter* was translated into English by a Unitarian merchant, William Popple; and, as we have already seen, it was published in England later in the same year that it had first appeared in Holland. Its insistence that any human attempt to interfere with religious belief or worship was blasphemously presumptuous was far more extreme than the modest concessions to the Dissenters which William and his government thought it prudent to make. In April of the next year the *Letter* was attacked at length in print by an Oxford cleric, Jonas Proast, the first of Locke's works to receive this honour. In the next few years Locke published two lengthy replies to Proast, and the latter, in each case, replied once more himself.

Locke remained, however, not merely unwilling to disclose his authorship of the *Letter* and the *Two Treatises*, but more than a little hysterical when friends incautiously or inadvertently threatened to disclose it for him. Even Limborch, to whom he was genuinely devoted, was savaged for acknowledging Locke's authorship of the *Letter* to other mutual friends in Holland, while the unfortunate Tyrrell, with whom Locke's relationship had grown increasingly testy, was brutally reprimanded for ascribing the *Two Treatises* to him. As late as 1698 (though admittedly under highly embarrassing circumstances) Locke refused obdurately to admit in writing even to one of his closest and most trusted friends, William Molyneux, that he had indeed written the *Two Treatises*. There can be no doubt at all that by this time his authorship of these works was a matter of common knowledge, and it is clear, not merely from the terms of his will but from some remarkably coy instances of self-praise (W IV 602, 640), that he continued to his death to endorse at least the essentials of their arguments. In the case of the *Two Treatises*, moreover, he carefully supervised the printing of a second edition in the year 1694 and worked painstakingly over a further edition, incorporating some important additions, which did not appear until after his death.

In these years too he published a number of further works of some importance. Two of these, in 1691 and 1695, were concerned with the coinage. A third, *Some Thoughts concerning Education*, was issued in 1693 and went through three editions in the next few years. It had originated in a lengthy series of letters to a friend, the Somerset gentleman Edward Clarke, and to his wife Mary, advising them on the health and upbringing of their children. One of Locke's most accessible works, it shows a notably unsentimental view of a child's psychological development, both intellectually and morally. Besides the light it casts on Locke's conception of how a human being becomes fully human (principally by learning to control his or her less admirable desires), it seems also to have been of some historical importance in shaping English toilet-training practices, at least amongst the educated classes. In the case of these works Locke was decidedly less reluctant to acknowledge his authorship, though he did not in fact issue any of them initially under his own name. But in the case of his last unquestionably major work, *The Reasonableness of Christianity*, which appeared in 1695, he was once again determinedly secretive. As it turned out, he had good reason to be so, since the book proved extremely controversial, being attacked twice within two years by John Edwards for Socinianism, a recondite Continental heresy stressing the authority of reason and scripture which rejected the doctrine of the Trinity and which Edwards himself roundly equated with atheism. Locke replied to these attacks in two anonymous and somewhat disingenuous *Vindications* of his work. To make matters worse, in 1696 he was attacked once again on similar grounds by a far more formidable antagonist, none other than Edward Stillingfleet, the Anglican apologist for religious intolerance whom Locke and Tyrrell had worked together to refute during the Exclusion controversy, who now held the bishopric of Worcester.

The attack was especially damaging, not merely because the charge of Socinianism (unlike that of atheism) was an extremely plausible one to level at Locke's religious views, but also because Stillingfleet elected to press it not on the grounds of the *Reasonableness*, a text which Locke was by now most unlikely to acknowledge as his own, but rather on those of the *Essay*, a text which he could hardly in principle have repudiated since it was published under his own name, and which in any case he keenly desired to defend. He duly replied to Stillingfleet too, in three further works in 1697 and 1699. Apart from the amendments to the fourth edition of the *Essay* which appeared in 1700, these replies in effect constituted his last public intellectual appearance in his lifetime.

By this stage of his life Locke's concerns were beginning to narrow and it becomes possible to pick out more clearly the strategy and tactics of his own custody of his intellectual legacy. We must postpone until the next two chapters a detailed assessment of the scope and limits of his intellectual achievement. But it may be illuminating to consider here in outline some of the more public tensions within that legacy and the practical implications which followed from them.

At his death Locke at last assumed full responsibility for all his published works. But until then, as we have seen, he remained anxious to segregate the *Essay*, a work of philosophy which he had always acknowledged as his own, from his anonymous writings on politics and religion. We do not know very clearly why he was so anxious to keep these apart. Perhaps, indeed, he did not know especially clearly himself. But one likely reason is the simple recognition, strongly confirmed from 1690 onwards, that the difficulty of retaining control over opinions expressed in one work is greatly accentuated by juxtaposing them with related opinions on further topics, expressed in one or more other works. Defending or improving the *Essay* was an ample assignment in itself; and Locke was always, with good reason, confident that it was the *Essay* that was his great achievement.

The theory of knowledge set out in the *Essay* is in some ways extremely sceptical. Locke himself did not regard it as in any way impugning the truth of Christian belief. But most of his contemporaries were hardly in a position to share his confidence since, if the arguments of the *Essay* were true, the particular interpretations of Christianity which they happened themselves to believe were certainly false. By the same token, Locke's sceptical view of man's capacity to know and his vigorous emphasis on the duty to tolerate religious beliefs which one happens to disbelieve and dislike might be natural partners in someone whose own religious convictions are clear and strong. But in anyone whose own religious convictions were less substantial, their union might seem alarmingly arbitrary and unstable. If Locke's reasons for insisting on religious tolerance were distinctively religious reasons (and reasons which led him to withhold toleration both from Catholics and from atheists), the consequences of his insistence, together with the later influence of his conception of man's capacity to know, might readily be (and largely were) to weaken religious conviction in others. This danger, of course, was one on which his critics were from the beginning eager to insist—and not merely in the form of Edward's gutter polemics or Stillingfleet's ecclesiastical hauteur, but also of intellectual assessments of real weight such as that of the great German philosopher Leibniz. On the question of toleration in particular, Locke might well have seen by the date of his death the extreme political instability of his position between an authoritarian Anglicanism (such as Stillingfleet's), which was simply a pale shadow of the Sun King's absolutist pretensions, and the cheerily licentious deism of men like John Toland who claimed unabashedly to be pursuing the implications of Locke's theory of knowledge. As Locke advocated it, religious freedom was freedom to be religious in one's own way. It was emphatically not, as Toland gleefully took it to be, freedom to be utterly indifferent to religious considerations.

A comparable difficulty arose in the year 1698 over the conception of political duty set out in the *Two Treatises*. Locke's close friend William Molyneux was a Member of the Irish Parliament, which was at that time in conflict with the English House of Commons over the latter's entitlement to control the Irish economy and prevent its products from competing with those of England. Locke himself was closely concerned with the formulation of English State policy on the question through his membership of the Board of Trade. In 1698 Molyneux published a book on the issue, *The Case of Ireland*, which was to become one of the classic texts of Irish nationalism. In it he argued that for one country to legislate for another was incompatible with the theory of political rights set out in the *Two Treatises*. The work caused sufficient offence to be burnt by order of the House of Lords; and within months Molyneux came to England to meet for the first time, and to stay with, his friend. We do not, unfortunately, have any idea what they said to each other about the matter. But the meeting is dramatic enough even without such knowledge. For Molyneux's arguments about the implications of Locke's political theory paralleled very closely the arguments of the American colonists in the 1760s and 1770s; and whatever Locke did have to say in reply would apply directly enough to the use which American pamphleteers and spokesmen, from James Otis to Thomas Jefferson, were to make of his text. More interestingly still, as one of Molyneux's critics pointed out, in the case of Ireland, what Locke's theory implied (if it applied at all) was not that the resident English Protestant gentry in the Dublin Parliament had a right to control the economy of the country in which they lived, but rather that the native Catholic Irish had a right to do so. It is hard to think of a conclusion less likely to appeal to Locke, with his deep dislike of Catholicism and his nervous sense of the geopolitical vulnerability of European Protestantism. (The year 1698 was only eight years after the Battle of the Boyne, the most important military engagement which William III had had to face in consolidating his hold on the English Crown.) The political liberty that Locke had sought to vindicate in the *Two Treatises* was a liberty for Protestants within the British State. There is no reason to believe that he would have been reluctant to extend it to foreign Catholics in foreign Catholic States. What it emphatically was not intended to be was a liberty for Irish Catholics from the British Crown.

Some of the impact of Locke's writings was simply a product of the arguments which they contained; and if the impact they

made was not always an impact which he would have desired, all
complicated thought is potentially subject to this hazard. But
some—perhaps especially in the case of the *Essay*—was also a
product of the form in which his writings reached readers and of
the particular range of readers whom they reached. In England
the *Essay* made its own way and made it with some rapidity,
forcing itself upon the attention of even the universities (which
were generally hostile to novel ideas, particularly those which they
took to be theologically subversive) in the course of the author's
lifetime. But the channels through which it reached a European
public were rather narrower and more distinct. The first appearance of any part of the *Essay* in print was a French abridgement,
issued in Amsterdam as a separate pamphlet in February 1688
but originally prepared for, and also included within, a leading
intellectual journal, the *Bibliothèque Universelle*. Most of Locke's
subsequent works were also reviewed at length in one or other of
the variety of intellectual periodicals which were published in the
Netherlands over the next few decades and edited in their earlier
years for the most part by French Protestant refugees like Pierre
Bayle and Jean Le Clerc. Since the diffusion of several of these
journals was remarkably broad, Locke's works reached a wide
intellectual public, particularly in France, comparatively quickly.
A second important channel of diffusion, also a consequence of
Locke's relations with French Protestantism, was more accidental
and personal. Jean Barbeyrac, a French Protestant refugee, had
exchanged letters with him in the last few years of his life. Early
in the eighteenth century Barbeyrac began his great series of
translations and critical editions of Grotius, Pufendorf and other
leading European texts on the Law of Nature. In these, for the
first time, he offered a full and very carefully judged summary of
the implications of Locke's philosophy and political writings for
the central issues of ethics and politics. For several decades these
texts were probably read more widely in many European countries
than any other modern writings on ethics and politics; and they
were at the centre of a major branch of law teaching in a wide
array of British and European universities. Just as Locke's own
most important philosophical thinking was first prompted by Descartes and Gassendi, the scope of his European experiences and
friendships guaranteed that its intellectual impact was in no
danger of being confined to the British Isles.

In the last decade and a half of his life, as an old, sick and immensely distinguished man, he was at last in a position to see more clearly the shape of his life as a whole and to sense the scale and meaning of his achievement. At the centre of this achievement lay the experience and the labours of his exile. At Shaftesbury's right hand Locke had been competing for public office and political power in his own country, living what even Machiavelli would have seen as a life of political virtue. When he returned from exile in 1689 he continued to discharge his political responsibilities. But in exile, for the first time in his life, he had acquired other and more pressing responsibilities. They had come essentially from his change of mind on the question of toleration. If freedom or restriction of religious practice was simply a matter of State policy, like foreign trade or defence, religious policy and civic virtue could not be seriously at odds. But if the right to worship God in one's own way was an individual right against any possible State power, the limits of religious policy were too important and too puzzling to be left to the crude judgement of civic virtue. With the massive intellectual labours of his exile, the *Letter* and the *Essay*, Locke had come to put his trust, not in English nationalism and the political fortunes of the English State, but in working through, and making more accessible to other human beings, a culture of shared religious good intentions. He continued, certainly, to do his best, despite exhaustion and illness, to make the world in general and England in particular a safer setting for this culture. But his main energies were devoted to the construction and fuller understanding of the culture itself, to exploring how exactly human capabilities could enable men to live in tune with God's world and to know that they were doing so. In this effort he depended very heavily on the emotional support of his friends Limborch and William Molyneux, and on younger men such as the deist Anthony Collins and the future Lord Chancellor Peter King. Shared religious good intentions were easier to trust than purely private hopes. But he also depended, and needed to depend, on at least one purely private hope, the hope that the better this culture was understood the easier it would be to believe in it and to live it. His hope remained very much a faith in a human future, not the future of a particular political unit but that of a potential civilisation of indefinite geographical scope and historical duration.

Great historical movements are never the product of a single person's achievements. But there is a real justice in seeing the European Enlightenment as Locke's legacy: both his triumph and his tragedy. As it turned out, the culture which he wished to fashion did not become easier to believe in and to live the better it was understood. Instead it fragmented alarmingly. Shared religious good intentions gave way to shared secular good intentions; and the latter, too, gave way to violent and acrimonious wranglings over which secular intentions truly are good. The clearer his view of what men can know became, the less convincing became his view of how they have good reason to live their lives. If the Enlightenment was genuinely his legacy, it was scarcely the legacy which he wished to leave.

We are all of us the children of his failure.

2

The politics of trust

IN THE year 1660 Locke composed his first two major writings (now commonly known as the *Two Tracts on Government*),
a tract in English, *Question: Whether the Civill Magistrate may
lawfully impose and determine the use of indifferent things in reference
to Religious Worship*, and a briefer but more systematic Latin work
on the same theme.

It was also in 1660 that Charles II was at last restored to the
English throne, eleven years after his father's trial and death on
the scaffold, when he returned to England from exile, determined
never to go on his travels again. In the preceding twenty years a
succession of English governments had sought to impose a wide
variety of religious practices upon their recalcitrant subjects,
always offending many and usually giving pleasure to remarkably
few. Political disorder and religious dispute had been inextricably
linked, leaving the great majority of the nation weary of the
incessant wranglings and eager for peace and settlement. Locke's
Tracts certainly echo the mood of this year, and they confront an
issue which had been central to religious and political controversy in the turbulent decades which led up to it. The detail of their
arguments is of little significance. But it is important to understand the main outline of the issue which they treated and to
identify the difficulties which this issue presented to the young
Locke.

The issue itself was eminently practical. In a society in which
virtually everyone believed in the truth of the Christian religion
but in which there were profound differences of opinion about
how to practise it, who should decide which religious practices
were to be permitted and which were to be prohibited? Should
there, for example, be a single Christian Church, sponsored by
the political authorities, to which every subject would be compelled to belong and within which he would be forced to worship
in the forms which it prescribed? Or should religious worship,

since it was properly the expression of sincere religious belief, be a matter purely for the conscience of each individual, a private transaction between him and his God, to be shaped as each believer felt appropriate? It is difficult for any Christian wholly to deny the force of either of these conceptions, and each receives some textual support from the New Testament. Locke himself at this time clearly felt the force of both, of authenticity as well as order and decency. But he had no difficulty in deciding the priority between the two.

If only religion in practice could safely be left to private choice, 'if men would suffer one another to go to heaven every one his own way, and not out of a fond conceit of themselves pretend to greater knowledge and care of one another's soul and eternal concernments than he himself,' this might indeed 'promote a quiet in the world, and at last bring those glorious days that men have a great while sought after the wrong way' (G 161). But twenty years of religious wranglings had shown the peril of such tolerance. Almost 'all those tragical revolutions which have exercised Christendom these many years have turned upon this hinge, that there hath been no design so wicked which hath not worn the vizor of religion, nor rebellion which hath not been so kind to itself as to assume the specious name of reformation . . . none ever went about to ruin the *state* but with pretence to build the temple' (160). It was the confusion of 'ambition and revenge' with 'the cause of God' that had devastated England (161). To set the claims of authenticity above those of decency was to foment political disorder. And in 1660, like most of his fellow-countrymen, Locke was deeply afraid of political disorder.

It was not only on the national political stage, moreover, that the claims of decency and authenticity clashed. The immediate stimulus for Locke's English tract was a work by his fellow Student of Christ Church, Edward Bagshaw, *The Great Question Concerning Things Indifferent in Religious Worship*, published in September of 1660. Bagshaw was a vehement exponent of the claims of authenticity at a time when the College's religious practices were being drastically restored to an Anglican orthodoxy of which he strongly disapproved. Surplices and the organ were reintroduced into Christ Church in November, while in January of the following year Bagshaw's supporters in the College stole as many of the surplices as they could get their hands on

and deposited them in the College sewers. Both locally and nation-
ally Locke espoused the claims of authority, stressing the gross
untrustworthiness of the majority of mankind, at worst a real threat
of anarchy and at best a formidable impediment to decency. The
political views which he advanced were crude and evasive. What is
interesting about them is their firm subordination of religious sentiment to the demands of politics. Whatever its origins, political
authority, to be adequate to its tasks, must be total. God made the
world and men in such a way that this is so; and, hence, it must be
his will that political authority be unrestricted by anything but his
express commands. 'Things indifferent' are all matters about which
God has not naturally or by revelation made known his will. (The
desirability or otherwise of wearing surplices, for example, was a
matter about which few even amongst Anglicans supposed that God
had made known his will.) No Christian political theorist could deny
to an individual the right to believe his own beliefs. Religious ceremonies are in themselves not matters of belief but simply of practice.
Good Christians should do what the magistrate tells them, and
believe what they themselves believe. The problem, plainly, came
when they happened to believe that they ought not at any price to
do as the magistrate had commanded them. In the case of religious
ceremonies it was a problem which came with some frequency. The
conception of 'indifferent things' could not in principle settle it and
Locke's tracts accordingly also failed to resolve it. It was also a
problem which the Anglican Church at the Restoration singularly
failed to solve in practice.

At this point Locke himself had dealt with the issue largely by
ignoring it. Religious ceremonies simply were 'indifferent', a matter
for human discretion. Anything that was simply a matter for human
discretion could be decided authoritatively by the civil magistrate,
because the purpose of having a magistrate at all was precisely to
override the wilful partiality of each man's personal judgement.
Peace required civil authority, and civil authority, in order to secure
peace, could do anything whatever which God himself had not
expressly prohibited. None of this, plainly, cast much light on what,
specifically, the civil authority ought to do.

The Essay on Toleration

Seven years later, having escaped from the musty world of the
Oxford don into the glamour and excitement of Shaftesbury's

service, Locke considered these questions a second time from a very different angle and came to markedly different conclusions. These can be found in the *Essay on Toleration*, which, unlike the famous *Letter on Toleration*, was never published by Locke himself. The practical verdict which he reached in this *Essay* was very much that of Shaftesbury: toleration promotes civil order and harmony by 'making the terms of church communion as large as may be' (FB I 194). It is still the responsibility of the sovereign magistrate to regulate religious practice for the peace, safety and security of his people. But although the magistrate remains firmly the judge of what will promote these ends, his judgement is no longer expected to be any more trustworthy in practice than that of any other believer. He 'ought still to have a great care that no such laws be made, no such restraints established, for any other reason but because the necessity of the state and the welfare of the people called for them, and perhaps it will not be sufficient that he barely thinks such impositions and such rigour necessary or convenient unless he hath seriously and impartially considered and debated whether they be so or no; and his opinion (if he mistake) will no more justify him in the making of such laws than the conscience or opinion of the subject will excuse him if he disobey them, if consideration and inquiry could have better informed either of them' (I 180).

The range over which the magistrate has discretion remains as broad as the whole field of 'indifferent things'; but his exercise of this discretion is governed rigorously by the end which he exists to serve. If he acts, as best he can, to carry out the duties which follow from this end he will not even 'be accountable in the other world for what he does directly in order to the preservation and peace of his people, according to the best of his knowledge' (I 185). But if he attempts to meddle with the religious convictions as such of his subjects (as the Anglican authorities were certainly attempting to interfere with those of the Dissenters), his actions will be as unjust as they are absurd. Each individual is responsible for his own salvation; and no one could have good reason to entrust his salvation to the necessarily incompetent discretion of another human being (I 176–7). In any case and more decisively, even if he wished to do so, it is quite simply the case that no one can do so. No 'man can give another man power . . . over that over which he has no power himself.

Now that a man cannot command his own understanding or positively determine today what opinion he will be of tomorrow, is evident from experience and the nature of the understanding, which cannot more apprehend things otherwise than they appear to it, than the eye see other colours in the rainbow than it doth, whether these colours be really there or no' (I 176).

The *Essay on Toleration* is an argument addressed to a sovereign on how he should employ his discretion. It carefully avoids the least hint that subjects have any right to a discretion of their own in the face of the sovereign's commands. The duty of subjects is to obey passively. But already, within the field of indifferent things, Locke has marked out a zone in which passive obedience is simply impossible. Still more decisively, he has made it clear that this zone crosses the borders of the field of indifferent things. Human belief cannot submit to the claims of authority; and it cannot be true for any human being that he has good reason to abandon his own beliefs about what God requires of him at the command of another human being. It is as holders of beliefs, and most decisively as holders of religious beliefs, that human beings are equal with one another: both 'the multitude that are as impatient of restraint as the sea . . . whom knowing men have always found and therefore called beasts' (G 158), and the rulers whom they so urgently need to restrain their fraud and violence towards one another (FB I 174). Each is fully responsible for his own beliefs and will have to answer for them to God at the Last Judgement. But, in the meantime, it is the business of the magistrate to attend rigorously to the necessity of preserving civil order, not to try to stand in, unavailingly and impertinently, for the Deity. It is no longer difficult to see how, in the very different circumstances of the Exclusion controversy and faced by a hostile and vindictive ruler, the duty of passive obedience would come to seem to Locke a vicious absurdity.

The Two Treatises of Government

We do not know when exactly Locke wrote the *Two Treatises of Government*. We do not even know for certain how much of it he wrote for the first time (or rewrote extensively) shortly before he published it in 1689. Indeed we do not really possess decisive proof that he wrote any of it in the course of the Exclusion controversy. But the most imaginative and scholarly writers to

consider the question in recent decades have agreed on at least
two points. Firstly, Locke had written the great bulk of the text
which he published in 1689 by the time that he left the country
for Holland late in the summer of 1683. Secondly, he had written
different passages in the book (as this stood in 1683) over a
number of years previously, and the text accordingly reflects a
number of the changing positions which Shaftesbury's party had
adopted in the course of this dispute.

As we have it today, the *Two Treatises* is a work principally
designed to assert a right of resistance to unjust authority, a right,
in the last resort, of revolution. (There are, of course, on any
reading many other major themes of the book: an account of
what makes governments legitimate in the first place (the theory
of consent) and of how subjects and rulers ought to interpret
their relations with each other (the theory of trust); an account
of how human beings can become entitled to own economic
goods and of the extent and limits of their title to do so (the
theory of property); an account of the similarities and differences
between different types of human authority, and above all of the
differences between authority in a family and authority in a State.
All of these questions, too, are considered in the context of
English politics at the time and of English constitutional doctrine.) It is clear enough that even from the first the *Two Treatises*
attacked the pretensions of absolute monarchy and that it drew
firm conclusions from this attack about the constitutional limits
on the prerogative powers of the King of England. But it is
certainly not clear that when Locke began to write it his intention
was to defend a right of active disobedience on the part of the
elected House of Commons, let alone the possession and use of
such a right by individual aggrieved subjects with no formal
position of authority in their society.

The *Two Treatises* is a long and complex work which contains
a great many arguments. Most of these, naturally, were arguments which Locke had not previously advanced elsewhere. But
only in the case of the right of resistance did he explicitly and
decisively reverse a theoretical view which he had defended at
length in earlier works. Both in the *Tracts* of 1660 and in the
Essay on Toleration of 1667 the duty of a subject in the face of
the unjust commands of his sovereign was clearly asserted to be
to obey these commands passively: not of course in any sense to

endorse their justice, but at least to recognise the authority from which they issued and certainly not at any price to obstruct them forcibly, let alone to attack their author. As recently as 1676 he had argued once more that although human political authorities are designated by human laws, the duty of political obedience is laid down by the law of God 'which forbids disturbance or dissolution of governments', and that every human being is obliged in good conscience to obey the government under which he or she lives (D 49 n.).

The impetus behind this change of mind plainly followed directly from Locke's own political involvement in the years of the book's composition. It was a fundamental shift in intellectual judgement as well as in political commitment; and Locke set himself to think through its implications with great thoroughness. He did not, of course, consider systematically the implications of all the views which he asserted in his book. In particular he chose not to discuss at all the question of how men can naturally know the law of nature, the binding law of God, on which, according to the argument of the book, all human rights rested and from which the great bulk of human duties more or less directly derived. The omission has attracted much intellectual criticism from later writers on political theory. It has also earned, both at the time of publication and more recently, some suspicion that the pious tone of its discussion of the law of nature might have been evasive or insincere. What is certain is that already in his 1664 lectures on the law of nature at Christ Church he had identified some of the main difficulties in the traditional Christian conception of natural law, and that he had, if anything, sharpened his understanding of these difficulties in the course of his preliminary work, recorded in the drafts of 1671, for the *Essay concerning Human Understanding*. By 1680, for example, he was certainly aware that the question of how men can *know* the content of the law of nature was deeply problematic. Yet in the *Two Treatises* he writes as though, however complete their freedom to choose whether or not to obey, *knowledge* of the law of nature was virtually compulsive for all men: 'so plain was it writ in the hearts of all mankind'.

On the whole these suspicions are beside the point. There is no doubt at all that Locke's attempt to explain how men can know the law of nature was in the end a failure even in his own eyes. But there is strong evidence that he persisted in this attempt for several years after the publication of the first edition of the *Essay* in 1689, and it is absurd to doubt that he did so because he continued to hope that the attempt might succeed. It is clear, too, that he did not, at this or any other period of his life, find at all attractive the uncompromisingly secular conception of natural law as a theory of purely human convenience adopted, for example, by Thomas Hobbes. A more attractive possibility, which he explored later in *The Reasonableness of Christianity,* would have been to rest human duties and rights directly on the revealed doctrines of Christianity. But even if he had supposed it possible, with the great French theologian Bossuet, to draw the principles of politics directly from the very words of the holy scriptures, it could scarcely have served Shaftesbury's political purposes in the struggle against Charles II to attempt anything of the kind. From the point of view of a modern unbeliever there is every reason to doubt the cogency of the political theory which Locke advances in the *Two Treatises,* because of its abject dependence on a view of man's place in nature as one in which each man is fully instructed by the Deity on how he ought to live. For most people today (including a great many devout Christians) such a view is barely intelligible. But there is no historical reason whatever to doubt that it was Locke's view.

For him, political rights follow from political duties and both derive from God's will. As he asked rhetorically in 1678: 'If he finds that God has made him and other men in a state wherein they cannot subsist without society, can he but conclude that he is obliged and that God requires him to follow those rules which conduce to the preserving of society?' (D 49 n.). The pivotal change in his political views, from a commitment to passive obedience to a vindication of the right of resistance to unjust political authority, was a change in his conception of how men could and should judge what is capable of preserving their society. Instead of leaving this judgement entirely to the ruler and retaining for the rest of the population merely the right to believe their own religious beliefs (a right which in any case he supposed that they had no power to abandon), Locke in the *Two Treatises* returned the right and duty of judging how to preserve society to every adult human being. It was in no sense an unprecedented conclusion. But for Locke himself it was certainly a very drastic change of mind.

How exactly should we see his reasons for this change? The most immediate pressure, clearly, was the directly political experience of the Exclusion controversy. There is no reason to believe that Locke would have written a work of political theory that at all resembled the *Two Treatises*, had it not been for Shaftesbury's role in this political struggle. Both the occasion of and the motive for its composition make the *Two Treatises* an Exclusion tract. But in a number of ways it was poorly designed as such—and not merely because of its original length, more than twice that of the published text, as the Preface to the Reader tells us. Even on constitutional questions which were of immediate importance at the time, Locke's arguments and Shaftesbury's tactics sometimes diverged widely. But quite apart from such details of practical political judgement, the character of the book as a whole makes it clear that Locke was thinking through the implications of his own change of mind, not simply writing up an extended brief for his factious master. It was Locke's own political experience at the time which altered the way in which he saw politics. Above all, it altered how he saw the relation between politics and the rest of human life. And it was the vigour with which he attempted to understand the implications of his own change of mind which made the *Two Treatises* a great work of political theory.

No doubt, more or less chance political experiences of just such a kind stand behind most of the great works of political theory. It is natural enough for the stimulus to think even very deeply about politics to be crudely political. But in the case of the *Two Treatises* the chance circumstances of its composition intrude further and more puzzlingly into the text of the work itself. The *First Treatise* is a lengthy criticism of the political writings of an earlier political writer, the Kentish squire Sir Robert Filmer, a royalist writer of the Civil-War period. Filmer was a thinker of some critical ability. As we have already seen, two other Exclusion tracts, by James Tyrrell and Algernon Sidney, had taken the form of attacks on Filmer's works. There was, therefore, nothing eccentric about Locke's choice of a target. Filmer stood out from other royalist ideologues, dead and living, by the uncompromising character of his theory of political authority, devout enough in tone and premises to reassure any Anglican, but also sufficiently absolute in its claims to match the practical appeals of the distressingly less devout theory of Thomas Hobbes. It is not altogether clear whether the choice of Filmer as an enemy in the early 1680s was a tribute to his popularity amongst supporters of Charles II or whether it was more a reflection of his attractions as an intellectual target. But here too what mattered for the quality and content of the book which Locke wrote was not the original motive which led him to undertake it, but the intellectual effect of organising his thinking to such a large degree, in the *Second Treatise* as well as in the *First*, around an attack on Filmer.

The most important direct consequence of this focus was on his treatment of property, an achievement of which he was clearly extremely proud (W IV 640). But perhaps even more important was the imaginative impact upon his book as a whole of confronting such a vivid rendering of the view of politics which Locke himself had come to reject so very recently. In the political context of the Exclusion controversy and the social context of late seventeenth-century England before and afterwards, it is clear that Locke's political views were not unusually radical. He neither expected, nor, as far as we know, would he even have desired, a realisation in his day of the radical programmes for extending the right to vote put forward by the Levellers in the English Civil War or by the Chartist movement a century and a half after him. But the theory which he set out in the *Two Treatises* was a very radical theory, a theory of political equality and responsibility, resting on the judgement of each individual adult; and, at intervals throughout the book, Locke himself expressed the theory as though he meant it to be taken literally. For the audience which he supposed himself to be addressing, there was little danger of his being so taken. (Most English adults at the time could scarcely have read and understood the *Two Treatises*.) Indeed it was for some time subsequently only his conservative critics who pretended to believe that he meant or deserved to be taken literally. But in due course the theory and even some of the slogans set out in the book were to reach a much wider audience in England and in America. When they did so, its radicalism became extremely hard to deny. The clarity and force with which that radicalism was set out in the *Two Treatises* was largely a product of Locke's own imaginative response to the challenge of Filmer.

That challenge was at its most intellectually effective in its criticism of political theories which sought to derive political authority and rights of ownership from the free choices of human beings. Despite its ideological resonance, it was distinctly less impressive as a theory of legitimate authority in its own right. The essence of Filmer's view was bizarrely simple; and even to some of his contemporaries it plainly appeared more than a little quaint. All authority amongst human beings, he believed, was essentially of the same kind, the authority of a father in his family and the authority of a monarch in his kingdom. All authority of one human being over another was given directly by God. Since no human being had a right over his own life and since all human rulers had a right to take the lives of their own subjects or of foreign enemies when these in their judgement had sufficiently damaged the public good, it must follow that rulers derived this right not from their subjects but from God himself. The Christian prohibition on suicide and the rights of a sovereign could be compatible with each other only on the assumption that the rights of the sovereign were given to him by the Deity. The Christian scriptures (or, to be more accurate, the Old Testament) record the precise occasion of this gift. God gave the whole earth to the first man, Adam, and all political authority and all rights of ownership are a historical and legal consequence of that gift. Adam's dominion was a fact of history which only the impious (or those unfortunate enough never to have encountered the Christian revelation) could have any occasion to deny. From the time of this first disposition of the world, Adam's dominion, a form of ownership of things as well as a form of rule over men, had become much subdivided by the course of human history. But every subdivision had been a direct expression of God's providence and must be recognised as representing his will. The political responsibilities of any man (and still more so, those of any woman) who did not happen to be a ruler were simply to do what he was told, to recognise the providence of God in the political authority to which he found himself subject, and to honour and obey this authority accordingly. Filmer's statement of this view was neither clear nor economical. It seems most unlikely that many who did not already feel obliged to obey their ruler were convinced by reading it that they were obliged in conscience to do so.

But if his own theory lacked cogency, Filmer did raise a number of embarrassing problems for anyone who believed that the practical sources of political authority were purely human. Perhaps equally importantly, the form which his theory took presented the claims of absolute political authority in a memorably disagreeable light. Locke, as we have seen, had no difficulty in regarding political obedience as a very simple and fundamental duty for most men (and almost all women) at most times, a consequence of that law of God 'which forbids disturbance or dissolution of governments'. In the circumstances of the Exclusion controversy, of course, he had strong motives for reconsidering the scope and comprehensiveness of the duty and for questioning his earlier presumptions about what made it truly a duty. Filmer's writings simplified the issue for him obligingly, offering a precise doctrine which he found it extremely easy to reject. For Filmer the rights of rulers are a personal gift from God. They are to be understood essentially as rights of ownership, over human beings as well as over land and material goods. Subjects belong to their ruler and owe obedience to him because God has, through the workings of his providence, given them to him. In reply Locke sought to distinguish sharply between the duties of subjects to obey and the rights of rulers to command. Most of the time in societies most men would have a duty to obey because civil peace and order are preconditions for the living of a decent human life. But rulers, by contrast, would have a right to command only where their exercise of power and the commands which they issued deserved obedience. If rulers themselves threatened civil peace and order, their subjects would have every right to judge the degree and immediacy of the threat and, if this seemed sufficiently serious, to resist it as best they could. Filmer, then, gave Locke just what he wished to deny: a clear practical equation of the all too human incumbents of political authority with the will of God himself. But he also set Locke several difficult intellectual problems. Two of these stood out with particular starkness: that of reconciling a purely human origin for political authority with the right to take human life and with the record of secular and sacred history; and that of explaining how human beings could come to have an individual property in any part of God's earth or its produce.

The problem of the right to property

The question of property was especially challenging. Filmer's own criticisms had been directed against the most influential seventeenth-century theory of property right, that advanced by the great Dutch natural-law writer Hugo Grotius. Filmer saw Grotius as proclaiming two inconsistent ideas, the view that non-human nature belonged to all human beings in common and the view that individual men or women could come by agreement privately to own parts of it. What made the two ideas plainly inconsistent, in his eyes, was the discontinuity which they implied in God's laws for men in the two contrasting situations, in one of which he had apparently 'ordained community' and in the other of which he had prescribed private ownership. For anyone with a more sophisticated sense of the historical development of human society this objection was unimpressive. But on the basis of it Filmer advanced two further lines of criticism which were less easy to shrug off. Firstly, he probed at some length the historical plausibility of the sequence envisaged by Grotius in which the human species as a whole (or some portion of it in a particular locality) must have come together and agreed unanimously to divide up ownership over all that they collectively possessed. If property is a matter of right and if all men originally owned everything together, then no man could lose his right to everything (or anything) without consciously choosing to abandon it. Secondly, he questioned whether even the unanimous consent of all living human beings at a particular time could bind any subsequent human beings who had not themselves been a party to the agreement, or whether, indeed, even such unanimous consent would necessarily bind any of the original contractors who subsequently changed his mind about its merits. For Filmer, property could only be practically secure and legally valid, if, like political authority itself, it were the direct expression of the will of God. Once it was seen as resting on human decision and commitment any right was open to indefinite revision. On this point at least, Locke was largely in agreement with him. It was the question of how existing rights to property could be guaranteed under a government chosen by the people as a whole on which the Leveller campaign in the Civil War had foundered. As Henry Ireton brutally demanded of the Leveller leaders at Putney in October 1647: 'I would very fain know what you gentlemen, or any other, do account the right you have to anything in England.' If political authority did not derive directly from God but instead rested on human choice, the idea of a right to property might seem alarmingly flimsy.

   Locke's response to this threat is extremely subtle. He takes it as a truth both of human reason and of revelation that the earth, like its human inhabitants (T II 6), belongs to its Creator and that God has given it to these human inhabitants in common (II 25) and given it to them to enjoy (II 31). He dismisses the idea that there could be any right of private property at all on Filmer's presumption that God had given the whole earth to 'Adam and his Heirs in Succession, exclusive of the rest of his Posterity' (II 25). But he sets himself to answer fully the main critical thrust of Filmer's attack on Grotius, the question of how men can come to have a private *right* to any part of this common heritage. It is his answer to this question which is famous and which has given his theory of property its immense and bewilderingly varied historical influence. Labour is what distinguishes what is privately owned from what is held in common; the labour of a man's body and the work of his hands. Labour is the unquestionable property of the labourer; and by mixing his labour with material objects— hunting (II 30), gathering (II 28), but also cultivating the ground (II 32–4)—a man acquires the right to what he has worked on and to what he has made of this material. The 'Condition of Humane Life, which requires Labour and Materials to work on, necessarily introduces private *Possessions*' (II 35). God gave the world to men 'for their benefit, and the greatest Conveniencies of Life they were capable to draw from it'. But he gave it to them to use well by their exertions—'to the use of the Industrious and Rational' and 'not to the Fancy or Covetousness of the Quarrelsom and Contentious' (II 34). The industrious and rational are *obliged* to make good use of it. It is not simply theirs, to do with precisely as they fancy. They are its stewards and must display their stewardship in their industry as well as in their rationality. They may appropriate and consume nature. (That is literally what nature is for.) But they have no right whatever to waste any of it. 'Nothing was made by God for Man to spoil or destroy' (II 31). In exercising their stewardship the industrious change the world which God originally gave to mankind, in a number of drastic ways. Labour is a creative activity. It '*puts the difference of value* on every thing' (II 40) and '*makes far the greatest part of the value* of things, we enjoy in this World' (II 42–3). Where labour has not been exerted effectively, as in an area like America, rich in land and furnished as liberally by nature 'with the materials of Plenty', the country will not have a hundredth part of the 'Conveniencies' enjoyed in seventeenth-century England. 'And a King of a large and fruitful Territory there feeds, lodges, and is clad worse than a day labourer in *England*' (II 41). Labour is a natural power of man and its exercise is commanded by God and encouraged by a rational understanding of man's place in nature. Its effects are almost wholly beneficial. It is as old as the Fall of Man. In 'the beginning all the World was America' (II 49); but by the seventeenth century much of it had been vastly improved by human labour. If labour is indeed the origin of property, then—at least at its origin, if not necessarily after the operation of inheritance—entitlement and merit are fused together; and the consequences for mankind as a whole can leave little ground for anxiety. At least initially, those who possess more will be those who deserve to do so and they will have nothing to apologise for to those who deserve and possess less.

But most of the world is America no longer—not simply because human labour has vastly increased its productivity, but also because human beings have discovered how to make possible a very different scale of economic inequality from that which the order of nature itself makes directly possible. Labour first begins '*a title of Property* in the common things of Nature' (II 51), a title bounded by use. In doing so it resolves the problem which Filmer set to Grotius. At this initial stage of human history property right was a simple and uncontentious matter. There 'could then be no reason of quarrelling about Title, nor any doubt about the largeness of Possession it gave. Right and conveniency went together; for as a Man had a Right to all he could imploy his Labour upon, so he had no temptation to labour for more than he could make use of' (II 51). The device which has made it possible for men to escape from this condition is the invention of money, a permanent store of value which 'being little useful to the Life of Man in proportion to Food, Rayment, and Carriage, has its value only from the consent of Men' (II 50). The invention of money greatly amplifies the inequality of possessions made possible by the 'dif-

ferent degrees of Industry' which men display (II 48). It makes
it possible, in Locke's judgement, for a man *fairly* to 'possess
more than he can use the product of', since he can hoard up,
without injury to anyone, the value of the surplus which his
property produces, in the form of gold and silver. Monetary
exchange does not depend upon political authority; and economic inequality, which is a consequence of monetary exchange,
does not depend for its legitimacy upon the civil law of a particular society (II 50).

Here Locke is pressing a very delicate case. In any political
society, as he fully admits, property rights are regulated by the
law (II 50). But it was essential for his purposes that such regulation could not justly be arbitrary, that it should instead be
guided by the purposes for which governments properly exist and
by the ends which give human beings rights over the material
world at all. Property rights founded directly upon labour, in his
eyes, neither required regulation by governments nor permitted
much just modification by governments. But labour had done
mankind nothing but good. The role of money was altogether
more ambiguous. Money had introduced in full measure reasons
for quarrelling about title, and doubts about largeness of possession. It was money which meant that right and conveniency no
longer went together. The entire social and economic order of
seventeenth-century England rested upon a human institution
about whose moral status Locke felt deeply ambivalent. At this
point in his theory, and without anachronism, we can see the
moral fragility of commercial capitalism come briefly but sharply
into focus. But we can see it so clearly, not because of our own
superior insight or the advantages of hindsight, but because
Locke himself felt so little inclination to deny it. What Locke's
theory of property was for was not to put a good face on the
social and economic order of the England of his day.

But what sort of right of property did he in fact wish to defend?
It is easier to be certain—and may perhaps have been clearer to
Locke himself—what sort of property he wished to deny.
'Property' in his vocabulary was the main term for expressing
human entitlements. If there were no human entitlements there
could be no injustice. To do injustice to a person is to take away
from him something to which he has a right: for example, his life,
his liberty or his material possessions. To protect human entitle-

ments is the purpose of government. Government, then, exists to secure to all human beings their lives, their liberties and their material possessions. Every human being is certainly entitled to his own life and his own liberty, unless he forfeits these by violent assaults upon the lives and liberties of others. Entitlement to material possessions, however, was a more delicate matter. Material possessions which were a direct product of a man's labour were truly his; and there is no evidence that Locke felt the least qualm at the prospect of their being given to others in their owner's lifetime or passing to his heirs after his death (I 42). But where the scale of economic inequality depended solely upon a human convention, doubts about largeness of possession were harder to avoid. We do not really know with any precision what Locke did think about this question. But there are several points about which we can be confident.

The first is that the main stimulus which led him in chapter V of the *Second Treatise* to discuss property in our sense, entitlement to material possessions, was the wish to deny a right on the part of a reigning monarch to do as he chose with the material possessions of his subjects, without their express consent. The claim to exercise such a right, for the public good, by King Charles I had been one of the main precipitants of the English Civil War; and the possibility of its revival by his son was an important political threat to the Whigs in the Exclusion controversy. It was, furthermore, a right which Filmer had trenchantly defended. The initial appeal for Locke of founding entitlement to property upon labour was the directness with which it met this challenge. It was God, not human convention, that had given men a title to the fruits of their labour. Indeed it was only human convention that gave a monarch such authority as he held over his subjects. Instead of possessing a royal dominion over subjects and territory inherited directly from God's gift of the world to Adam, Locke's ruler had in the first instance simply the duty to use such power as was available to him to protect the rights which God himself had given directly to his subjects. Locke was, of course, well aware, as his phrasing makes plain, that an immediate and transparent moral authority of possessions founded on physical effort did not (and could not be expected to) extend to the range of economic inequality produced by the operation of monetary exchange through a lengthy period of time. But what he needed, to refute royal claims to dispose of their subjects' possessions as they thought best, was not a theory of why every subject was fully and unequivocally entitled to everything which he legally owned, but simply an explanation of why private property could be (and often was) a right against even a legitimate political authority. Even on Locke's own account, to take away the fruits of a man's labour is a very different degree of injustice from taking away the profits of speculation, or taxing an aristocratic rent-roll which had reached its present owner by past brigandage or royal favouritism to a distant ancestor. But from Locke's own political point of view, of course, the latter possibilities were distinctly more urgent threats at the time; and there is no reason to believe that he would have *felt* any less disapproval in their case than in the former.

What is harder to assess is how exactly the theory of property which he had constructed appeared to him in retrospect, and particularly in the last few years of his life. We know, as already mentioned, that he felt some pride in it. But we do not know just which aspects of the theory gave him such satisfaction. The boldest answer to this question, advanced most strikingly by C. B. Macpherson, is that Locke intended his theory as an explanation of the moral legitimacy of capitalist production. There is little case for taking this seriously as an assessment of Locke's intentions in building his theory. But it is a more interesting question how far this suggestion may capture, if in mildly anachronistic terms, Locke's sense of his own achievement in having constructed his theory. In its strongest form the suggestion remains wholly unconvincing. Locke, like Thomas Aquinas, believed that all men had a right to physical subsistence which overrode the property rights of other humans. He believed that, even if the just price is the market price (V), to insist on selling only at the market price to a man in mortal need and to cause his death by doing so was to be guilty of murder. He believed that those who had worked hard all their lives had a right in their old age not merely to subsistence but to a decent standard of living. All of these were rights which rested directly upon God's gift of the world to men in common; and the idea that subsequent human conventions (like monetary exchange) might be entitled to entrench on them is fundamentally at odds with Locke's conception of property. He does, it is true, recognise that the paid labour of a servant can be owned by his master. But this comparatively casual acknowledgement of what was, after all, a fairly central feature of English economic relations in his day can hardly establish an enthusiasm for the central role of wage labour in capitalist production. In particular Locke denies explicitly that a man who has been deprived of the means of production (given by God to all men) can be forced into subjection through control over these means (T I 41–2).

Charity gives every Man a Title to so much out of another's Plenty, as will keep him from Extream want, where he has no means to subsist otherwise; and a Man can no more justly make use of another's necessity, to force him to become his Vassal, by withholding that Relief, God requires him to afford to the wants of his Brother, than he that has more strength can seize upon a weaker, master him to his Obedience, and with a Dagger at his Throat offer him Death or Slavery. (I 42)

On the whole there is good reason to believe that Locke felt his account of property to be a major advance on the leading theorists of property rights, Grotius and Pufendorf, in explaining the system of rights on which a commercial society rested. But there is no reason to believe that he viewed this system of rights with undiscriminating enthusiasm. The productivity of human labour had transformed the world for man's enjoyment, as God had intended it to do. Monetary exchange, a purely human device, had in many ways assisted this transformation; but it had also clouded the moral transparency of human ownership beyond recall. Where entitlements that flow directly from labour clash with entitlements that rest solely on complex monetary exchanges, Locke himself would be ill placed to endorse the latter. The tangled history of the labour theory of value ever since, in the justification and rejection of capitalist production, was already foreshadowed in the ambiguities of the theory which he fashioned.

The nature of political authority

The second major challenge which Filmer's writings posed for Locke was in some ways easier to meet, and it certainly elicited from him a less original response. But since the question directly at issue in this case was the right of resistance to unjust political authority, Locke addressed it at much greater length and with far more rhetorical energy than he devoted to the topic of property rights. Filmer, as we have seen, believed that all subjects owed obedience to their ruler because God had quite literally given them, along with the territories in which they lived, to this ruler. The relation in which their ruler stood towards them was that of an owner. Locke himself in earlier years had taken a very favourable view of the claims of political authority. But there is no reason to believe that he would ever have found the uncompromising Filmerian doctrine at all attractive. He accepted the force of Filmer's emphasis on the centrality of the Christian prohibition on suicide in political theory. But he used it to attack Filmer's ideas at their core. Since men belong in the last instance not to themselves but to the God who made them, any human right to take away the life of any man (oneself included) must rest directly on God's purposes for men in general. The idea of one man owning another, let alone millions of others, by inheritance has no plausible link whatever with God's purposes for men. Filmer's arguments made all political subjects into slaves. Slavery was a condition into which extreme wickedness could justly cause a man to fall. But it was the opposite of a truly human life and it could not under any circumstances justly follow from the wicked actions of another person. (This proviso should have been extremely embarrassing for Locke himself in his capacity as stockholder of the slave-trading Royal Africa Company, since it clearly implied that the status of a slave could not legitimately be inherited from one generation to another. All legitimate servitude was intrinsically penal and the crimes of the father or mother could not descend to their children.) For Locke slavery was the precise opposite of legitimate political authority. What made political authority legitimate, what gave legitimate rulers the right to command, was the practical services which they could and did provide for their subjects. So far from being the owner of those whom they ruled, a legitimate monarch was essentially their servant.

For Filmer (as indeed for the young Locke) men were too stubborn, selfish and quarrelsome to be left unaided to work out their own practical salvation. God's providence watched over them and it did so above all by subjecting them permanently to a grid of effective authority. Throughout his intellectual life Locke accepted this assessment of what men are like and of how they can be expected to behave. But with the *Two Treatises* he extended it confidently to rulers as much as to subjects, and drew from it implications very different from those which had occurred to Filmer. In his first writings there was a wide gulf between the godlike ruler and the multitude 'whom knowing men have always found and therefore called beasts' (G 158). But in the *Two Treatises* this gulf has disappeared and the ruler is seen as being just as likely as his subjects to enter upon 'force, the way of Beasts' (T II 181).

The opposite of force is reason. It is reason that distinguishes man from beast, and the way of reason is the way that God wills men to follow. It is through the exercise of their reason that men can and should know what God wills them to do; and it is their reason that enables them to judge what it would be best to do where God's will does not enter directly into the matter. All human adults who are not simply deranged have reason. All men are born free and rational, though these are potentialities which they must, through time, learn to exercise, not powers which they fully possess at their birth. As rational creatures of God, living within a world created by God, all men are equal with one another, equal in their fundamental entitlements and equal too in the duties which they owe.

In this equality of right and duty, and independently of the actual histories of all times and places, human beings confront each other in what Locke calls the state of nature. This is probably the most misunderstood of all his ideas. Principally it has been misunderstood because of the role of a partially similar idea in the writings of Thomas Hobbes. Hobbes describes the natural condition of mankind as a state of violent conflict produced by passion and animosity from which man's reason alone has the power to rescue him. Fear of mortal danger is the only motive strong enough to overcome man's deeply antisocial qualities. Locke takes a less excitable view of the practical peril which men present to each other and recognises social as well as antisocial features in human nature. But on the whole he does not differ widely from Hobbes (or indeed from Filmer) in his judgement of what men are like and how they can be expected to behave. But whereas in Hobbes the state of nature can in part be understood as a picture of how men would behave if they were not subjected to political authority, in Locke the phrase simply does

not refer to human dispositions and attitudes at all. What the
state of nature is for him is the condition in which God himself
places all men in the world, prior to the lives which they live and
the societies which are fashioned by the living of these lives. What
it is designed to show is not what men are like but rather what
rights and duties they have as the creatures of God.

Their most fundamental right and duty is to judge how the
God who has created them requires them to live in the world
which he has also created. His requirement for all men in the
state of nature is that they live according to the law of nature.
Through the exercise of his reason every man has the ability to
grasp the content of this law. But although Locke was deeply
convinced that human beings have the duty to understand this
law and both the duty and the capacity to observe its requirements, he was by the early 1680s far from confident of how
exactly they held and ought to exercise the capacity to understand it. As we shall see, the question of how men could distinguish the dictates of the law of nature from the prejudices
prevailing in their own society preoccupied him throughout his
intellectual life. In the *Two Treatises*, however, the question of
how men could know the content of the law of nature was one
which he could safely ignore. What mattered, simply, was their
duty and capacity to observe it and their capacity, as free agents,
to choose to break it. None of those against whom Locke was
intending to argue at the time would have dissented from this
judgement; and to have attempted to establish it in the course of
his argument would have been as uneconomical and as intellectually taxing as, for example, attempting to prove the existence
of a divine Creator in the same work.

In the state of nature the duties of each man under the law of
nature are matched by the rights which he possesses under this
law. The most important of these rights is the right to hold other
men responsible for their breaches of this law and to punish them
accordingly: the executive power of the law of nature which alone
makes this law operative amongst human beings on earth. No
man has a right to kill himself, because all men belong to God
(a clear limit to the sense in which men have a property in their
own bodies). But any man has a right to inflict penalties, up to
and including the death penalty, on any other man who has
violated nature's law drastically enough, and in particular on any

other man who has without justification threatened the life of any human being. To spoil and waste any of God's gifts was an offence against nature's law. But to spoil or waste any human being was a crime of especial horror. The state of nature was a condition of equality and one in which, even in the civilised world of Locke's day, it was still on occasion possible for human beings to encounter one another. Wherever men met outside the framework of a common legitimate political authority, they too met, in this sense, as equals: a Swiss and an Indian in the woods of America, or a King of England and a King of France settling the fates of their countries on a field of cloth of gold. For Filmer, as indeed for many eighteenth-century critics of theories of natural rights, the state of nature was a fraudulent allegation about the human past, an apocryphal amendment to the scriptural record or a piece of wholly fictitious profane history. But for Locke, of course, it was not a piece of history at all, being as much present in the world of his day as a thousand years earlier and shadowing every human political community throughout any possible future. What it showed men was not how the past once was, but merely what human political authority could amount to.

What such authority could amount to was simple enough: the joining together of the powers of individual human beings to enforce the law of nature and the consequent abandonment of these powers for most purposes by ordinary members of political society. The advantages of this fusion were the greater chance of impartiality in judging and implementing rules of common life, and the improved prospects for peace which such impartiality offers. The hazard of this fusion, a hazard at the forefront of Locke's mind as he wrote, was the huge increase in coercive power that it gave to a political sovereign and the ever present danger that this power too would be abused. Human partiality is central to the human condition. Greater power makes partiality more dangerous; and where greater power is corrupted by flattery and obsequiousness the dangers of partiality in practice become overwhelming. Locke recognised the practical value of great power for human purposes; but he feared it deeply and he thought, as we have every reason still to do, that it can only be trusted when those who hold it see themselves as responsible to (and can be held responsible to) those over whom they exercise it.

Many States of his day, as Locke well knew, were formed by violent conquest. Their political authority, therefore, in no sense rested on the joining together of the powers of their subjects to execute the law of nature. For Locke such States possessed no legitimate political authority. They were structures of force, not of right: not civil societies at all. The relation of a conqueror to the conquered, even after centuries, was a relation not of political authority but of concealed war (T II 192).

In civil societies political authority rests in the last instance on agreement, on consent. Absolute monarchy, by contrast, was inconsistent with civil society (II 90). On any given occasion in an absolute monarchy most of its inhabitants may well have a duty to obey the holder of political power, if what he commands is at the time beneficial or if disobeying him will cause pain and danger to others; but the holder of political power has no right to command his subjects. Only the agreement of adult human beings can give another human being political authority over them. This is a drastic claim; and it raised two principal difficulties for Locke. The first, important in relation to Filmer, was the need to show that such agreements had ever in fact taken place, and, more particularly, that they had done so in England. The second, more striking in the light of modern anarchist criticism of the concept of political authority itself, was to show how every adult member of a legitimate political society could reasonably be supposed to have consented to its political sovereign. In neither case was Locke's answer impressive. The historical challenge to provide instances of such agreement and to indicate when in English history these had occurred, he met simply by evasion. Since all parties to the Exclusion dispute agreed that England was a legitimate State and all paid at least lip-service to the role of English representative institutions in giving their consent to legislation, this was not a costly tactic. The second challenge, to show how each adult in a legitimate State could and did incur clear political duties towards that State, he met more elaborately by distinguishing two kinds of consent: express (overt) and tacit. Express consent made a man a full member of his society for life, with all the rights and duties which followed from such membership. Tacit consent, less intimidatingly, made a man subject to the laws of the country as long as he remained within it, but did not give him either membership of the society or the rights (above all, rights of political choice) which followed from such membership. Express consent explained why members of a legitimate polity had the appropriate range of rights and duties. But it did so by blandly ignoring the fact that virtually no Englishman at the time had voluntarily assumed any such responsibilities at adulthood. Tacit consent reassuringly guaranteed that everyone in England had a duty to obey the law. But it cast very little light on just who amongst his adult male contemporaries Locke considered to be a full member of his society.

In the time of the Exclusion controversy, however, the scope of membership in the political community was not actively at issue, as it had been in the Putney debates within the Parliamentary armies between the Leveller leaders and their generals Cromwell and Henry Ireton in the winter of 1647. Locke's treatment of consent is designed to handle a less ambitious range of questions. Principally it is intended to explain why there can be a fundamental distinction between legitimate and illegitimate political societies, a possibility denied both by Filmer and by Hobbes. Legitimate political societies are societies in which the government has a right to be obeyed. The duties which men owe one another under the law of nature, even in the state of nature, explain quite sufficiently why in a settled political society most men most of the time have a duty to obey their rulers. Locke's theory of consent is not a theory of the political obligations of subjects, of how subjects can have political duties. More particularly it is not a more or less forlorn attempt to prove to the socially disaffected the solid stake which they possess in the preservation of social order. Rather, it is an attempt to explain how rulers (the rulers of civil societies, though not of absolute monarchies) can have rights to political authority.

Locke certainly wrote to proclaim a right of revolution; but he was not in any sense an enemy of political authority. Within its due constitutional limits political authority was an immense human good. Even beyond the legalistic definition of these limits, the royal prerogative could and should be exercised for the public good, despite the letter of the law. If exerted with responsibility and good will, political authority could expect in practice to receive the trust that it deserved. If a narrow constitutionalism is above all an attempt to secure a government of laws, not men, Locke in the last resort set human good intentions above constitutional rigour. In the end all human governments were governments of men (D 122 n. 2). Much of the *Second Treatise* is taken up with constitutional issues, particularly with the connections between private property, popular consent, representative institutions and the power to make law. It was the vigour of its insistence on the illegitimacy of taxation without representation that nearly a century later so endeared it to the American colonists. But in its central commitments the *Two Treatises*, however skilful its handling of constitutional issues, was not a constitutionalist tract. Instead it proclaimed two intractable rights: the right of a ruler within a legitimate political society to use political power against the law for the public good; and the right of all men to resist the ruler even of a legitimate political society where he grossly abuses his power.

The centrality of trust

At the centre of Locke's conception of government—and catching the ambivalence of this vision—was the idea of trust. Government was a relation between men, between creatures all of whom were capable of deserving trust and any of whom could and sometimes would betray it. Trust was one of the oldest terms in Locke's thinking. The indispensability and the peril of trust were fundamental to human existence. Men, as he wrote in 1659, 'live upon trust'. A few years later, in his lectures, his sharpest criticism of the view that individual interest could be the foundation of the law of nature was that this would not only make such a law self-contradictory, but also make impossible society itself and the trust that was the bond (*vinculum*) of society (LN 213–14). The plainest embodiments of this human need were the actions of swearing and promising. Promises and oaths bound God himself (T I 6). Language might be 'the great Instrument, and common Tye of Society' (E 402): but what enabled it to tie men together in practice was its capacity to express their commitments to one another, the solemn promises, oaths and undertakings on which their trust in one another necessarily rested and which constituted the bonds (*vincula*) of their common life (LT 134). The menace of atheism (134) was that it removed all force from these undertakings, reducing the law of nature to the contradictory interests of individuals and dissolving the grounds for human trust. Bereft of a concerned Creator and left on their own, men could have no good reason to trust one another and hence no capacity to live in society together. If it were not for human degeneracy (the Fall of Man), men would still belong to a single community (T II 128). To lose sight of their dependence on their Creator would be the final degeneration, disintegrating the many 'smaller and divided associations' of Locke's day into the lonely and distrustful individuals of whom they were composed. In so far as human beings can deserve each other's trust, they help to hold together the community which God intended for them. In so far as they betray each other's trust, they help to promote its disintegration. Holders of political authority, of course, possess this power to sustain or thwart God's purposes in a far more drastic form. Because men are so aware of their need to trust one another and because they sense the aid which this concentrated power to execute the law of nature can offer to their lives, they will on the whole trust their rulers far beyond the latters' deserts. And because peace is so essential to 'the Safety, Ease and Plenty' (II 101) of their lives, it is on balance desirable that they should do so.

Locke does not, like a modern anarchist, distrust political power itself, though he is keenly aware of the dangers which it presents. What he distrusts, rather, is human beings left to their own devices, human beings who no longer grasp their dependence on their divine Creator. For human beings who are still aware of this dependence, the attempt to trust in one another, in rulers as much as in fellow subjects, is a duty under the law of nature. But it is a duty to seek peace, not a duty to deny the lessons of experience. The duty to trust is not a duty to be credulous, perhaps not even a right to be credulous. Even an absolute monarch, in a state of nature with his subjects, is not beyond the reach of human trust. Civil sovereigns are entitled to an ampler trust; and if they deserve it they may be confident of receiving it. But any man, even the sovereign of the most civil of societies, can betray trust. That is just what human life is like. We must try to trust one another, personally as well as politically; but we must all judge, too, when and how far our trust has been betrayed.

Trust may seem a feeble and clumsy concept to put at the centre of an understanding of politics. The connections between Locke's religious views and his sense of the scope of human trustworthiness will not (and should not) endear his estimate of the latter to many today. But, as it worked in his own imagination, the vision of politics and of human life more generally as resting ultimately upon trust was not a superficial view. Its imprecision was a necessary imprecision; and the impossibility of escaping from this imprecision was its central point. Politics is still like this.

The reverse of trust deserved was trust betrayed; and the remedy for the betrayal of trust was the right of revolution. An impartial authority to appeal to on earth was the major benefit that a legitimate political society offered its members. Where it existed, it excluded the state of war between men and removed the need to appeal directly to God's judgement which was intrinsic to this state (T II 21). But impartiality was a human achievement, not a fact of constitutional law. Rulers are real men and women. They hold their authority under law; and entitlement to the obedience of their subjects derives from the impartial administration of this law. Where they act against or outside this law to the harm of their subjects, they become tyrants. Wherever law ends, tyranny begins (II 202). For a ruler in authority to use force against the interests of his subjects and outside the law is to destroy his own authority. He puts himself into a state of war with his injured subjects, and each of these has the same right to resist him as they would have to resist any other unjust aggressor (II 202, 232).

In the England of Locke's day this was a very extreme doctrine; and he went to some pains to play down its practical implications. No ruler who truly means the good of his people will fail to make them feel this (II 209), and no such ruler need fear resistance from his people. Stray acts of tyranny will pass unchallenged, since their victims cannot in practice expect the support of their fellow subjects and cannot hope to challenge the tyrant on their own (II 208, 223, 225). Only a clear threat, actual or potential, to the estates, liberties and lives (and perhaps also the religion) of the majority (II 209), 'a long train of Actings' (II 210), will bring resistance. But if resistance does come, there is no ambiguity as to who is responsible for its occurrence. To disturb government is a breach of the law of nature; and to rebel without just cause against a legitimate government is to initiate a state of war. (To initiate a state of war is always an unjust act. The only

just wars are wars of self-defence.) But when the oppressed
people resist tyranny it is not they who disturb government or
bring back the state of war. Rebellion is an 'Opposition, not to
Persons, but Authority' (II 226). A tyrant has no authority. It is
tyrants who are the true rebels. Like any other man who has used
the force of war to enforce his ends unjustly upon another, a
tyrant has revolted from his own kind 'to that of Beasts by making
Force which is theirs, to be his rule of right'. In doing so he has
rendered himself 'liable to be destroied by the injur'd person and
the rest of mankind, that will joyn with him in the execution of
Justice, as any other wild beast, or noxious brute with whom
Mankind can have neither Society nor Security' (II 172).

The right to destroy noxious brutes is a right of every human
being. But in a legitimate political society even the worst of
tyrants cannot be seen simply as vermin. Besides the right to
revenge individual injuries, there is also the duty to preserve civil
society. Revolution for Locke is not an act of revenge; it is an act
of restoration, of the re-creation of a violated political order. In
the course of the Exclusion controversy and again in the reign of
James II, the King, in Locke's eyes, had become a tyrant and had
abused the licence given by his prerogative powers (II 242).
Within the English constitution, because the King held part of
the power of lawmaking, there was no superior to whom he was
obliged to answer. But behind the formalities of the constitution
there lay the reality of English society, the 'Body of the People'
(II 242, 243). Where a controversy arose between the ruler and
a section of his subjects and where the ruler refused to accept
the verdict of the representative institutions which expressed the
will of his subjects, the proper umpire must be the Body of the
People who had first placed their trust in him. The Body of the
People can and must judge in their own conscience whether or
not they have just cause to appeal to Heaven, to resist their ruler
by force (II 163, 243, 21). They have the right and duty to do
so because they alone can fuse the right of individual revenge
and the responsibility for re-creating political order, the right to
destroy those who have betrayed their trust and the duty to
restore the trust without which no truly human life is practically
possible.

The *Two Treatises* are addressed to the political needs of England, a country in which, through lengthy historical experience,

the inhabitants have shown that they form a single Body and possess the political capacity to act as such. In England there is an ancient constitution to restore (II Preface). We have no means of knowing how far Locke regarded the inhabitants of countries with less fortunate historical experiences as enjoying the same practical political capacity. Certainly their inhabitants, too, possessed the right individually and collectively to resist unjust force and to avenge the harm which it had inflicted upon them. But where there has never been a legitimate political order to restore, the prospects for uniting revenge and reconstruction are less inviting. Despite its economic, social and political complexity, an absolute monarchy (and we should remember that Locke had lived for years in France before the time when he was writing) was not a civil society at all. When, in the next century, David Hume set himself to criticise Locke's political theory, no element of it more offended him than this complacent and parochial contrast between England and the absolute monarchies of the Continent. Hume was in some ways an unsympathetic and inaccurate critic of Locke's arguments; and by the end of the eighteenth century the trajectory of the French Revolution had made it evident that, even on this question, there was more substance to Locke's conceptions than Hume had allowed. But he did see very clearly how closely Locke's view of politics in the *Two Treatises* depended upon a particular political experience and the culture which this experience had fostered, a community in which a wide range of ordinary citizens held and expected to exercise the right to act politically for themselves. The core of Locke's own understanding of the right to revolution was the right and capacity of such a community to act to preserve itself as a community. He never supposed that a just revenge by itself would suffice to create from nothing a new civil society.

The Letter on Toleration

The last major work of political theory which he wrote, in the mid-1680s in Holland, was less narrowly directed. The *Letter on Toleration* is a simpler as well as a more universal work than the *Two Treatises*. Its arguments do, it is true, depend upon accepting the truth of the Christian religion (or at least of some monotheistic religion in which authentic belief is a precondition for valid religious worship and religious worship is the central duty for

man). But within European Christendom the arguments hold, if
they hold at all, for every denomination or country. Because the
key duty of every man's life is to seek his own salvation (LT 124,
128), and because religious belief and practice are the means by
which he must do so, the power of human political authority
cannot rightfully extend over either of them. It is the responsibility of political authority to protect civil goods, more particularly the fruits of men's industry and the liberty and bodily
strength that are their means of acquiring these (124, 146). The
magistrate can have no authority in the care of men's souls. If he
judges his actions to be for the public good and his subjects judge
the contrary, there can be no judge on earth between them (128)
and the verdict must in practice be left to God. Where violent
persecution on religious grounds menaces men's properties and
lives, the persecuted have every right to repel force with force
(146); and they can and will exercise this right. Two main groups
are excluded from a right of religious toleration: those whose
religious beliefs are directly opposed to the legitimate authority
of the magistrate, and those who do not believe in God. The right
to save one's own soul is not a right to attempt to impose a
personal political judgement against the civil power. There is no
right, as Locke had already insisted in his *Essay* of 1667, to
disbelieve in the existence of God, since belief in a God is 'the
foundation of all morality' and a man who lacks it is a noxious
beast incapable of all society. The use of force against speculative
opinions or religious beliefs is unnecessary, since the truth can
look after itself and seldom receives much aid from the mighty
(122). It is also ineffective since no man can directly choose what
he believes or feels. But atheism is not simply a speculative
opinion. It is also a ground for limitlessly amoral action. Because
the right to toleration depends upon the right and duty of each
man to seek his own salvation, it is not a right which any atheist
can consistently claim.

The conviction that the truth can look after itself was certainly
optimistic. But it was not the foundation of Locke's commitment
to toleration. The existence of a God, startlingly, was not a truth
that could be left to look after itself. The denial of toleration to
atheists, accordingly, however affronting it may be to us today,
was fully consistent with Locke's argument. To take away God,
even in thought alone, dissolves everything (134). Locke had

written the *Letter* late in the winter of 1685, following protracted discussions with his friend Limborch and in the face of Louis XIV's mounting persecution of the Huguenots. He wrote it not for England alone but for a European audience; and it was perhaps to a European audience that it carried most effectively. For Voltaire in the next century the *Letter* was the essence of Locke's politics, a politics wholly in harmony with the message of the great *Essay* and unmistakably relevant to civilised life everywhere on earth. But if its political message was as cosmopolitan as it was clear, it also rested ultimately on a single conviction, the conviction that men have religious duties and can know what these are. It was Locke's struggle to justify this conviction that led to his greatest intellectual achievement. But the struggle itself ended not in triumph but in something very close to surrender.

Knowledge, belief and faith

A S FAR as we know, there was no point in Locke's life at which he doubted, simply as a truth of experience, that some men did know their duty to God. But there was also no point in his intellectual life at which he supposed the grounds for this conviction to be clear and easy to explain. As early as 1659, before any of his formal writings, he had set out with vigour and imagination a picture of the relation between men's beliefs and their desires in which reason was seen unblinkingly as the slave of the passions. Instead of austerely controlling men's actions it served merely as a device for finding grounds for what they already wished to do. Worse still, its failure was not just a failure of control, a moral defect. For the moral failure in its turn both contaminated the entire range of their understanding, and imperilled any solid sense that each man possesses an individual identity of his own (LC I 122–4). These three themes recur throughout his intellectual life, sometimes with more assurance and sometimes with greater pain. The view that many human beliefs deserve blame, that men are in large measure *responsible* for their beliefs, was one of Locke's deepest convictions, but also one which he found acute difficulty in justifying. To be coherent at all, it required a clear conception of how in principle men can remove the contaminations of passion from the operation of their understanding, how they can perceive and comprehend God's world and themselves as these truly are and not as they would prefer them to be. As well as this, it also required a clear conception of each individual man as a being capable of taking responsibility for his own actions. The conceptions of moral agency and of the scope and limits of human understanding were closely linked in Locke's thinking. Where the tension between them became acute, as it did in the years following the publication of the *Essay*, it was the implications of the conception of moral agency that he chose to follow. But of the two, of course,

it was the picture of the scope and limits of human understanding, set out in the *Essay*, that Locke himself recognised as
his masterpiece; and it has been this that has marked the imagination of posterity.

The first work in which he attempted to explore these themes
was a set of lectures at Christ Church, the *Essays on the Law of
Nature*. Natural law is decreed by God's will and it can and
should be grasped by the light of nature, through the exercise of
human reason. Within the order of nature, it shows men what
they should and should not do: what this order requires of them
as rational agents (LN 110). In the central controversy in Christian ethical theory since the Middle Ages, the dispute between
those who saw human obligations as resting fundamentally on
the will of God and those who saw them as resting solely on the
requirements of reason and the real features of the natural world,
Locke's position was equivocal. Clearly he felt (and indeed continued to feel throughout his life) the force of each of these views.
But wherever he was compelled to choose between the two (and
most conspicuously where he felt that human compliance with
the law of nature was importantly in doubt), it was the will of
God in which he trusted. In the *Essays* he made little attempt to
explore, still less to resolve, the apparent tensions between these
views. Nor did he spend much energy in defending the existence,
and the binding force, of a law of nature against sceptical objections. (It is instructive, however, that his final response to such
doubts was the charge that the absence of a law of nature would
make each man the utterly free and supreme arbiter of his own
actions (118)—an objection which falls very strangely on the
modern ear.)

Instead he concentrated his attention on the question of how
exactly men could know what the law was. Four possible ways
of knowing are outlined: inscription, tradition, sense-experience
and supernatural, or divine, revelation. The last is discarded
(122), not because there is any reason to doubt its occurrence,
but because it is clearly not something that men can know merely
through their own minds, reason or sense-experience. (It is,
however, to this possibility that Locke returns more than thirty
years later in *The Reasonableness of Christianity*.) Inscription is
rejected as simply false. If it were true that the law of nature was
written in the hearts of all men (140, 144), all would agree both

in the moral and in the speculative principles which they believed; and the young, the uneducated and the barbarous would have an especially clear grasp of these principles (138, 140). Tradition is rejected because the moral convictions of different societies differ so drastically. One society's property is another society's theft. One people's lechery is another people's good fellowship or religious worship. In certain circumstances and in some countries, even murder and suicide can be applauded (166–76). Only the rational interpretation of the experience of the senses survives unscathed. Locke says rather little about how he sees its operation (146–58). But he emphasises strongly that the main lessons which it offers concern the power and will of God (152–6). He also makes it very clear why he believes that it alone can serve as a foundation for the law of nature. Only a law grounded in the clear working of the human understanding and taking accurate account of the real features of the natural world could have rational authority for human beings as natural creatures. As they actually exist, men's beliefs, as he repeatedly insists, come to them largely from the speech of other men (128, 130, 140–2). The speech of other men is marked by the corruption of human sin. It is only when his beliefs depend upon the workings of his own mind and the lessons of his own experience that a man has good reason to place his trust in them.

The Essay concerning Human Understanding

In the *Essay* itself, and more practically in *Some Thoughts concerning Education* and *The Conduct of the Understanding*, Locke attempted to show how men can use their minds to know what they need to know and to believe only what they ought to believe. Because human beings are free, they must think and judge for themselves (E 100, 264). Reason must be their last judge and guide in everything (704). Where reason does not guide their formation, men's opinions are 'but the effects of Chance and Hazard, of a Mind floating at all Adventures, without choice, and without direction' (669). Although it has its own pleasures (6, 43, 233, 259), 'all Reasoning is search, and casting about, and requires Pains and Application' (52). Because it is so easy for men to judge wrongly, and because there is much more falsehood and error amongst men than truth and knowledge (657), all human beings have good reason to 'spend the days of this our

Pilgrimage with Industry and Care' (652) in the search for truth.
What the *Essay* attempts to offer is practical aid in this search. It
does so in two rather different ways. The first is to show how the
human understanding works successfully: how it is capable of
knowledge and of rational belief, what human beings can know and
what they cannot. The second is to explain why on the whole in
practice it works so badly. Both these preoccupations were essential
to Locke. If human beings could not in principle know what they
needed to know, their predicament would place in doubt either the
good will or the power of a divine Creator. But if they could not
help acting as they did, not only would they be unfree, and hence
not responsible for their apparent actions; but God himself would
be the cause of all that Locke most loathed in human beings.

Both preoccupations are clearly present in the earliest draft of the
Essay (EA 142–56). The published text of the first edition devotes
much fuller attention to the former. But the balance is partially
redressed in Locke's lifetime by a series of amendments, to the
second (1694) and fourth editions (1700); in particular by his major
change of mind on the nature of free agency, and by the new
chapters on enthusiasm and on the association of ideas. (This last
chapter was of enormous importance in the history of psychology
as a would-be science throughout the eighteenth and nineteenth
centuries, as well as in the development of utilitarian ethics.) But
even after these amendments, the *Essay* very much retained the
shape and character of its first published edition; and in this form,
the picture of human knowledge and belief that it presents is on the
whole an optimistic one. It is optimistic not because it makes
extravagant promises of the degree to which human nature can be
changed by political design, nor because it exaggerates the extent
of human knowledge or minimises the difficulties which men face
in regulating their beliefs in a rational manner, but because it considers the workings of men's minds in such simple, sober and
unpretentious terms. The optimism is more a matter of tone than
of content; but as a tone, it proved exceptionally beguiling.

What underlies it, above all, is a remarkable assurance about the
scope of possible agreement in human thought.

I am apt to think, that Men, when they come to examine them, find
their simple *Ideas* all generally to agree, though in discourse with one
another, they perhaps confound one another with different Names. I

imagine, that *Men* who abstract their Thoughts, and do well examine the *Ideas* of their own Minds, cannot much differ in thinking. (E 180: and see LC IV 609).

If men will only use their minds and their senses—the 'inlets' of knowledge—carefully and sincerely, they will find themselves *compelled* to know and believe what they should and thus compelled to agree with those of their fellows who make an equally sober and honest use of their faculties. A key element in achieving and sustaining such agreement is a recognition of the limitations, what Locke himself calls the 'mediocrity', of human understanding. As elsewhere, at the centre of his thinking there lay a fine balance between scepticism and faith.

The salience of the faith is hardest to miss when he itemises what men do in fact know, or sketches how they have good reason to live their lives. The most important single item of possible knowledge is the existence of God: 'we more certainly know that there is a GOD, than that there is any thing else without us' (E 621; and see 619, 628–31, 638). What makes it so important is its immediate and overwhelming implications for how men should live (542, 570, 651). Man's very power to know anything is not something that simply appears from nothing in the course of the history of the world—so that there 'was a time then, when there was no knowing Being, and when Knowledge began to be' (620). Rather, it was a direct gift from an all-knowing God who has existed for all eternity (625). The true ground of morality is 'the Will and Law of a God, who sees men in the dark, has in his Hand Rewards and Punishments, and Power enough to call to account the Proudest Offender' (69).

The nature of moral belief

Locke's view that morality was a science as much open to demonstration as mathematics, forcefully expressed in the *Essay*, caused him much subsequent distress as one friend or enemy after another enquired insistently about his progress towards carrying out the demonstration. There were several reasons for his confidence in the project. Moral ideas were inventions of the human mind, not copies of bits of nature. This contrast has fundamental implications for the character of moral ideas and for how, if at all, these can be known to be valid. It is the foundation in modern philosophical thinking of the presumption of a stark gap between facts about the world (which can potentially be known) and values for human beings (which can merely be embraced or rejected). The distinction between fact and value is both a product of Locke's conception of human knowing and the subversion of his beliefs about human values. Because moral ideas were inventions of the human mind, and because they were marked by words which were also inventions of the human mind, a man could, if only he took the trouble, grasp them perfectly himself and discuss them with other men in a manner which secured an equally perfect understanding on their part.

Much more importantly, human mental invention in the field of morality is not an arbitrary matter. What prevents it from being so, in Locke's view, is the fact that all men can secure, if they will only take the trouble to consider the question, a demonstrative knowledge of the existence of an omnipotent God who prescribes a law to human actions and punishes those which violate it. In the course of their history human communities have invented a wide variety of moral conceptions and adopted extremely diverse moral values. They have also succeeded in some measure in enforcing these values, both through direct coercion and through the subtler pressures of mutual approval or disapproval, the 'law of reputation'. Moral consciousness is not innate in human beings. Indeed, it takes very different forms in different countries. But for Locke, there is a single form which it should take everywhere and always: the form indicated in the Christian revelation and required by the law of nature, a law which men are just as capable of understanding, both extensively and precisely, as they are the truths of mathematics. There is no reason to believe that he ever abandoned this view. But what he clearly did abandon, after a series of abortive attempts to construct a demonstrative scheme of this kind, was the hope that such attempts stood the least chance of affecting how most men chose in practice to behave.

It seems clear from what we know about the *Essay*'s composition that this abandonment represented a major change in intellectual judgement. Indeed there is some reason to believe that it reflected the surrender of one of Locke's two main ambitions in writing the work, and even the disappointment of the initial hope and purpose which first led him to undertake it at all (E 7, 11,

46–7: EA 35–41, 80). But however unwelcome an outcome it may have been, it was not a surprising conclusion to draw from the arguments of the *Essay* as a whole. Both knowledge and rational belief are on Locke's account in the last instance compulsive. Faced with the clearly perceived relation between ideas, the direct evidence of their senses, or the plainly apparent balance of probabilities, men cannot but know, sense, or judge as these dictate. Demonstrative ethics would consist of a sequence of relations between ideas which, if considered with care and in good faith, a man or woman could not but see as they are and hence could not deny. In the same way, a man cannot but in the end do what appears to him most desirable, though he certainly can, and often should, check his impulses and force himself to consider carefully and conscientiously whether what he feels immediately drawn to do will in fact be the best action from all points of view. (It is particularly important for him to do this, since absent goods do not catch the attention as insistently as present pains and hence have less purchase on human desires (E 260–1).) In itself human understanding for the most part, and in the most important respects—'those which concern our Conduct' (46)—works just as it should. But it can do so only if men use it with energy, care and good intentions. In the case of the practical knowledge of nature, the abuse of the human mind is hardly likely to be deliberate. A careful consideration of the ways in which the mind works when it works successfully can therefore be expected to assist men in future to use their minds more effectively: in scientific and practical enquiry into the character of the natural world, and in pursuit of the conveniences of life. But when it comes to deciding how to live, all men have strong and insistent motives to think less and to do so altogether more evasively. Not only do they have such motives; but, as Locke was at pains to insist, most men in fact succumb to them with rather little resistance. Instead of living their lives in the light of divine threats of infinite and eternal pain (74–5, 255, 273–4, 277, 281–2), many even in civilised countries live as though they were atheists (88). All men are 'liable to Errour, and most Men are in many points, by Passion or Interest, under Temptation to it' (718). To improve men's moral conduct, what is most urgently required is not greater intellectual clarity but more effective imaginative aid in resistance to temptation. (Hence Locke's decision within a few years of the *Essay*'s first publication to supplement it with a further work, *The Reasonableness of Christianity*, which set out what he took to be a particularly clear, simple and directive version of Christian belief.)

This shift of attention, followed as it was by the meticulous paraphrasing of St Paul's *Epistles* (on which Locke laboured almost till his death), is profoundly revealing. What it underlines is the close dependence of his conception of the good life for man on the presumption of a God who sees men in the dark, cares how they choose to act, and punishes them after death for acting against his law. Two of the most important and impressive additions to the *Essay*, the altered treatment of free agency and the wholly new chapter on identity, are centrally concerned with the question of how divine punishment can make sense and be just (E 270–1, 340–6; and 717). At no point was Locke prepared to contemplate a conscious preference of faith to the conclusions of reason (667–8, 687–96, 698, 705). Even after writing the *Reasonableness*, he remained confident that the existence of a deity of the required kind could be demonstrated and that it therefore could and should be regarded as a conclusion of reason (LC VI 243–5, 386–91, 596, 630, 788–91). It is easy to see why this judgement was so crucial if we consider in its absence the implications of some of the *Essay*'s other main lines of thought.

The natural condition of man is not a placid one.

We are seldom at our ease, and free enough from the sollicitation of our natural or adopted desires, but a constant succession of *uneasinesses* out of that stock, which natural wants, or acquired habits have heaped up, take the *will* in their turns; and no sooner is one action dispatch'd, which by such a determination of the *will* we are set upon, but another *uneasiness* is ready to set us on work. (E 262).

In the world, men are 'beset with sundry *uneasinesses*' and 'distracted with different *desires*' (257). Pain and pleasure, good and evil, move men's desires and do so by entering into their conception of happiness (258–9). All men constantly pursue happiness and desire anything which they see as making part of it. This is not a matter of choice. They cannot choose not to pursue happiness. But this does not in any way diminish their responsibility for what they choose to do. God himself 'is under the necessity of being Happy'; and it is the point of human liberty that men should have the power and responsibility to judge for themselves what really is good (264–5). Just as men's tastes in food differ— some loving lobster and cheese but others loathing them—so do their tastes in those broader and more diverse conceptions of pleasure which depend on the mind. Some value riches; others bodily delights; others virtue; and others contemplation. Since pleasure is a matter of taste, it is absurd to deny that men's happiness in this world will take very different forms.

If therefore Men in this Life only have hope; if in this Life they can only enjoy, 'tis not strange, nor unreasonable, that they should seek their Happiness by avoiding all things, that disease them here, and by pursuing all that delight them . . . For if there be no Prospect beyond the Grave, the inference is certainly right, *Let us eat and drink*, let us enjoy what we delight in, *for tomorrow we shall die* . . . Men may chuse different things, and yet all chuse right, supposing them only like a Company of poor insects, whereof some are Bees, delighted with Flowers, and their sweetness; others, Beetles, delighted with other kind of Viands; which having enjoyed for a season, they should cease to be, and exist no more for ever. (E 269–70)

Occasionally Locke does attempt to argue that even in this life the rewards of virtue exceed those of vice (281–2). But the main weight of his judgement clearly falls against this view (W III 93). If happiness depends solely upon individual taste and taste itself is beyond criticism, human appetites can be restrained only by human threats—psychological, moral and physical. Even within this world, the restraint of men's appetites will be indispensable if society is to remain possible. 'Principles of Actions indeed there are lodged in Men's Appetites, but these are so far from being innate Moral Principles, that if they were left to their full swing, they would carry Men to the over-turning of all Morality' (E 75). If men's nature compelled them to see their moral predicaments as Locke saw these—'a Pleasure tempting, and the Hand of the Almighty visibly held up, and prepared to take Vengeance' (74)—most of them would certainly alter their habitual choices. But if men's reason came to question and reject the reality of this threat, their habitual choices might prove quite well considered, indeed might compare favourably with those of Locke himself. The key judgement for Locke is that a man can deserve punishment for an evil action because this action demonstrates that he has 'vitiated his own Palate' (271). It depends for its coherence, as well as its force, on there being a valid standard for human conduct independent of what men happen to find attractive.

The nature of knowledge

Most of the *Essay* is not directly concerned with moral questions. But even in the parts of the book which set out his theory of how men can know about nature, Locke's conception of the relations between God and man often plays an important role. It does so, not by qualifying the conclusions of the ambitious and impressively systematic theory which he developed, still less by questioning the value of any such theory, but rather by setting it in a congenial imaginative frame. In some respects he sees the scope of human knowledge as sharply restricted. But within this scope, he has no doubt whatever of its reality as knowledge. Although he explicitly denies that knowledge enters history along with the human race, he thinks of knowledge as something of which we may be quite certain that men are naturally capable. God—and even angels and other spirits—may know vastly more and know it more directly (M 52). All men may be mistaken in many of their beliefs (though he doubted in fact if the beliefs which they actually possess are often as absurd as much of what they are induced to say that they believe (E 719)). But any human being whose wits are sufficiently in order to consider the question may be perfectly confident, may *know*, that he or she *can* know.

Locke's theory covers many of the great issues of philosophy: the relation of human thought and experience to their objects, how words get and retain their meanings, how men perceive, how human knowing and understanding operate. It is, as he makes very clear, not intended as a scientific theory: a theory, for example, about how exactly in human sight material objects can exercise the power to modify men's minds (M 10), or of why exactly parts of nature act upon other parts just as we observe them to do. On these questions Locke was highly sceptical whether men's natural faculties equipped them to understand very profoundly and precisely: sometimes too sceptical, as it has turned out. But by contrast with these piously affirmed limitations, he believed firmly that men can understand clearly how to distinguish what they can hope to know from what they cannot. More importantly still, he was equally sure that if they applied this understanding in actually using their minds in real life, they could be confident not merely of learning much practically useful information and of greatly extending their scientific under-standing of nature, but also of seeing more clearly how they ought to conduct themselves as moral agents. Instead of letting loose their thoughts 'into the vast Ocean of *Being*' (E 47), men would be better advised to consider soberly the capacities of their own understanding and to direct their thought and action accordingly (46).

The *Essay* itself promises to 'consider the discerning Faculties of a Man, as they are employ'd about the Objects, which they have to do with'. Through 'this Historical, plain Method' it aspires to give an 'Account of the Ways, whereby our Under-standings come to attain those Notions of Things we have' (44). Its first book attacks the doctrine of innate ideas, ideas with which human beings are born. The view that men do have innate moral and religious ideas Locke had already rejected, as we have seen, in his *Essays on the Law of Nature*. Given the variety of moral values and religious beliefs in different societies of which he was aware, he had no difficulty in making this view appear extremely foolish. This mockery caused grave offence amongst the Anglican clergy of the day and was an important source of Locke's reputation as a propagator of irreligious opinions. More important for the *Essay* as a whole was his rejection of the view, held for example by Descartes, that man's capacity to understand nature also rested upon the innate knowledge of a number of maxims of reason, such as 'What is, is' (48–65). Since most men (and virtually all small children) are quite unaware of any such maxims, it is absurd to attribute knowledge of these to them. The way in which men come to understand the truth of such maxims is through experiencing particular objects. While it is true that they depend for this understanding on the exercise of their ra-tional faculties, this in no sense makes knowledge of the maxims themselves innate.

The remaining three books of the *Essay* set out Locke's own positive theory of how men can know and of how they can form beliefs which it is rational for them to believe. The first develops his account of the nature of ideas, the sole immediate objects of human thought and therefore the only objects about which human knowledge is 'conversant' (525). (By an 'idea' Locke

meant merely (47) 'whatsoever is the Object of the Understanding when a Man thinks'.) The second considers the nature
of words, and of language in general, while the third summarises
the implications of the first two in a bold discussion of the nature
of human knowledge. Knowledge itself is a form of perception:
the perception of the '*connexion and agreement, or disagreement and
repugnancy of any of our Ideas*' (525). What men immediately
perceive, and even what they immediately reason about, is always
particular ideas existing in their own minds. Any true general
conclusions at which they arrive apply only in so far as other
particular relations in nature, or in the thought of other men,
correspond to them (680–1). Ideas themselves are all either
simple or complex. If simple, they derive directly from the senses
(310–12), the inlets of knowledge. If complex, they are formed
by the voluntary mental union (163) of simple ideas. All human
knowledge is founded in and ultimately derived from experience;
either from the observation of perceivable objects in the world,
or from the inspection and assessment of the workings of men's
own minds (106). Men can think, know and judge for themselves, and must do so since they cannot in the end trust others
to do so for them (100–1, 7, 264). The minds of children at birth
are like white paper (81, 104). Although at first they are marked
plainly by the purely natural impact of particular ideas through
the senses, they are also speedily defaced by the often superstitious and irrational teaching of adults (81–4, 394–401). Once so
defaced, since custom is a greater power than nature (82), only
a lifetime's unrelenting effort, fired by a genuine love for truth
itself (697), can do much to repair the damage.

One of the main ways in which human understanding under-
goes this corruption is through the words in which men express
their thoughts. The systematic discussion of language in the third
book came, as Locke himself acknowledges (401, 437, 488), as
something of an afterthought. But he had no doubts as to its
practical importance: 'The greatest part of the Questions and
Controversies that perplex Mankind depending on the doubtful
and uncertain use of Words' (13). Since most men most of the
time think in words, and since general truths are almost always
expressed in words (579), confusion or unnecessary vagueness in
the use of words can do immense harm (488–9). Because words
'interpose themselves so much between our Understandings, and

the Truth', their obscurity and disorder can 'cast a mist before our Eyes' (488). This effect is particularly disastrous in law, divinity and moral argument (433, 480, 492, 496).

This insistence on the significance of verbal clarity, the emphasis which he lays on the predominant role of the senses in furnishing men with knowledge of nature, and his conception of the infant mind as blank paper on which experience writes are perhaps the most optimistic of Locke's themes in the *Essay*. The first two still meet with some modern philosophical approval; and all three were important in shaping Locke's image as provider of the philosophical basis for Enlightenment optimism. By contrast, his stress on the power of custom, on the elaborate and treacherous processes through which men form, modify and protect their beliefs, and on the unedifying character of most men's worldly desires (67, 662) suggests decidedly more pessimistic conclusions. Certainly, it offers no encouragement whatsoever for the more extreme Enlightenment hopes of reforming human nature *en masse* through political control of the environment in which individuals develop. This is especially important because of the close links which Locke himself saw between men's grounds for trusting their senses and the force of their worldly desires. In the last resort he rejected sceptical doubts as to whether our senses really do deliver us any knowledge at all, on two very different grounds. His own conception of how they do so can be considered shortly. But the grounds for rejecting scepticism must first be underlined.

One ground, a partial echo of Descartes, is simple, devout and unlikely to impress a secular audience: that a good Creator would not have endowed men with senses which systematically deceive them (E 375, 302, 624–5, 631, M 10). But the second is far more complicated and requires no devotion whatsoever. Not only does the evidence of each sense support its own veracity through time. It also supports that of the others. Trust in the senses is so indispensable for practical life and so directly linked to the overwhelmingly powerful stimuli of pleasure and pain—'the hinges on which our Passions turn' (E 229, 128–30, 254–80, 631, 633–4)—that Locke cannot believe that any human being could sincerely doubt the validity of sense-experience, let alone live as though he supposed it illusory. Whatever the force of particular arguments in its favour, sceptical doubt in practice can only be trivial because the senses play such a central role in how men adapt themselves to and control nature. Because he held such a vivid conception of the demands of virtue (LC I 123) and the seductions of vice, and because belief in God was so essential to sustaining this conception, Locke himself drew no strong implications from this relation between sense and desire. For him, as for Nietzsche nearly two centuries later, if God did not exist, man 'could have no law but his own will, no end but himself. He would be a god to himself, and the satisfaction of his own will the sole measure and end of all his actions' (D 1). The fundamental choice for man would be the choice of what sort of creature to become. But for those (like Jeremy Bentham) whose imaginations were less captivated by virtue, honour and their repressive demands, the myriad links between sense and desire would in due course suggest a more comfortable and worldly style of life. Locke himself was a utilitarian only in the light of a world to come. But it is easy to see how less devout minds could base an entirely secular utilitarianism on his conception of the human understanding. Whatever his own philosophical judgement of how men who had lost a faith in God would have good reason to live, it is also easy to see how, under these circumstances, Locke would expect them in practice to choose to live. Given the history of religious belief in Western Europe since his death, it is hard to imagine that the corresponding history of moral belief and sentiment would have come to him as much of a surprise.

The varieties of knowledge

In the *Epistle to the Reader* which prefaces the *Essay*, Locke expresses the ambition to serve the master builders of seventeenth-century natural science—Boyle, Huygens and Newton—as a mere under-labourer 'removing some of the Rubbish, that lies in the way to Knowledge' (E 9–10). The rubbish is to be removed in two main ways, one negative and the other positive. In the understanding of nature the inventive powers of reason must be restrained sharply in favour of a trust in the less fanciful testimony of the senses. Men cannot hope to understand the workings of nature with the clarity with which they understand, for example, algebra. But by understanding how their minds operate in the acquisition of knowledge, by careful observation of nature and equally careful expression of the results of such observation (476–7, 484, 501), they can hope to extend their understanding greatly. The natural tendency of the human mind is towards knowledge (385). One reason why a comprehensive scepticism is so absurd is that the contrast between truth and illusion which it draws depends upon the very capacity to distinguish which it denies: 'we cannot act any thing, but by our Faculties; nor talk of Knowledge it self, but by the help of those Faculties, which are fitted to apprehend even what Knowledge is' (631).

Men have three principal types of knowledge: intuitive, demonstrative and sensitive. (The status of memory is a little unclear.) Of these, intuition is the most certain because it is the least avoidable. God's knowledge is intuitive. He sees everything at once and hence has no need, as men do, to reason (M 52). The main truth which men know intuitively is their own existence: this they cannot doubt. Valid demonstration is just as definitely knowledge as is intuition. But, since it necessarily involves relations between several different ideas, it is 'painful, uncertain and limited' (52) in comparison with intuition; and men can be, and often are, mistaken in supposing themselves to have achieved it. Mathematical knowledge is demonstrative. But the most important truth which men can know demonstratively is the existence of God. Sensitive knowledge is caused by the action of objects in the world upon human senses (E 630–8). We do not know exactly how it is caused (M 10). But this ignorance does not make it any less certain (E 630). Seeing white paper as one writes on it, it is as impossible to doubt the colour seen or the real existence of the paper as it is to doubt the act of writing or the movement of one's hand: 'a Certainty as great, as humane Nature is capable of, concerning the Existence of any thing, but a Man's self alone, and of GOD' (631). Sensitive knowledge fully '*deserves the name of Knowledge*' (631). It extends '*as far as the present Testimony of our Senses*, employ'd about particular Objects, that do then affect them, *and no farther*' (635); with the crucial exception that our memories, when accurate, give us knowledge of the past existence of some things of which our senses once assured us (636).

Memory is an important supplement to demonstrative as well as to sensitive knowledge. Without it, no general truths in mathematics could be known; nor could we possess even 'habitual' knowledge of the truth of any demonstrations we had completed in the past unless we saw perfectly in the present just how to repeat them; nor could Newton, for example, be said to know what he had demonstrated in his *Principia* except when he held its full chain of reasoning 'in actual view' (528–30).

This conception of knowledge has been criticised from many angles. Few modern philosophers would accept Locke's demonstration of God's existence. But much the most important and widespread attack has been levelled at his analysis of sensitive knowledge. A succession of able critics of widely varying views, from Berkeley, Thomas Reid and Kant to the present day, have questioned the compatibility of the two main components of his view: that the senses give men knowledge of the external world, and that all knowledge consists of mental acquaintance with ideas. Locke's doctrine is in fact a complicated and subtle one; and many of the objections which have been raised against it certainly miss the mark. He definitely does hold that simple ideas of natural objects correspond in some strong fashion to the way natural objects actually are: namely, by giving men knowledge of their qualities. In doing so, such ideas differ radically from, for instance, moral conceptions, which do not involve the attempt to match some pre-existing 'archetype' outside the human mind. He also definitely holds an essentially causal theory of perception: that the way in which the senses furnish us with knowledge of nature is by the qualities of objects causing ideas in our minds. He also plainly imagines the causal mechanisms in question very much in the seventeenth-century scientific idiom of matter and motion (M 10): it is plain that 'Motion has to do in the producing of them: And Motion so modified is appointed to be the cause of our having them.' But he did not suppose for a moment that human beings in his day possessed any clear understanding of how exactly this causality works, and he plainly doubted that their senses were acute enough to equip them to understand it even in principle. Yet, although his theory was in this way more elaborate and sceptical than is sometimes recognised, it does have important weaknesses. It is reasonable to insist that all knowing involves mental action and some element of consciousness. It remains a plausible claim, at least in relation to the external world, that 'since the Things, the Mind contemplates, are none of them, besides it self, present to the Understanding, 'tis necessary that something else, as a Sign or Representation of the thing it considers, should be present to it: And these are *Ideas*' (720–1). But the view that the whole of man's capacity to know can be adequately explained as the acquisition and recombination of simple ideas, furnished by the individual senses or by reflection, remains unconvincing.

On this basis, nevertheless, Locke was able to erect an impressive analysis of natural philosophy: 'The Knowledge of Things, as they are in their own proper Beings, their Constitutions, Properties, and Operations' (720). It was an account which recognised the potential deceptions of the senses and of memory, without succumbing to a comprehensive scepticism. It distinguished firmly, if not always very clearly, between those 'primary' qualities of nature (such as shape) which exist in bodies quite independently of human or other observers and the 'secondary' qualities (like colour) which depend in part upon the perceptual powers of an observer. Men perceive a solid cube as such because, whether they inspect it or not, that is simply the way it is. But they perceive a rose as red because when they see it in daylight its physical properties happen to cause them so to perceive it. All simple ideas are caused by the 'qualities' of objects by means which we do not and probably cannot understand. But unlike secondary qualities, primary qualities in no sense depend upon the relation between human beings and external objects. It is natural for men to think of both sorts of qualities as simply existing in external objects. But only in the case of primary qualities is this natural belief wholly valid.

Knowledge of nature is confined to simple ideas of sensation, perceived in the present or recalled to the mind by memory. But, of course, men's belief about nature extends vastly beyond this. It is founded principally on judgements of probability, based on elaborate comparisons between, and combinations of, simple ideas. Accordingly, it is not a form of knowing about nature, but a form of more or less well-considered guessing about this. Over most of the more important issues in their lives men cannot truly know what to do or what is the case. All they can do is to judge these as prudently as possible. But this they certainly must do. To insist on knowledge in practical questions where it cannot be had would be self-destructive. It would incapacitate men from taking any action at all and bring their lives to a nervous halt.

No general truths about nature can be known; and therefore there can in the strict sense be no *science* of nature. Men are entirely correct to believe that they know their simple ideas of sensation and reflection to match reality, the way the world is and the way they are themselves. But when they attempt to understand themselves and nature, the complex ideas which they fashion in their minds out of these simple materials cannot be known to match reality. Instead, what human beings are compelled to do is to judge whether reality matches their own complex ideas. If they judge attentively and prudently this will serve very adequately for all practical purposes. What God requires of them they cannot afford not to know. But to deal effectively with nature does not demand knowledge. It merely demands skilful guessing.

To possess a true science of external nature, men would need to have sensitive knowledge of general truths about its workings. They would need to be able literally to see how all natural effects are caused. God himself certainly possesses this power of direct vision. It is even possible that angels too, if to a lesser degree, may be able to perceive some of nature's workings directly. But human beings, because of the limitations of their senses, must depend for their understanding of nature quite largely on the self-conscious control of their own conceptions and classifications. If they cannot know general truths about nature, they have the most practical of motives for attempting to form valid general beliefs about its workings. To increase the probability of success in this venture, they must attend particularly to the ways in which they form their own complex ideas and in which they employ the words with which they name these ideas. Simple ideas are natural signs of qualities of natural objects; and words are human signs for ideas in the mind. Simple ideas are entirely involuntary, words wholly voluntary. Standing between these two, complex ideas can be subjected to deliberate regulation by the mind but depend for their materials wholly upon the involuntary deliverance of the senses. Extreme mental and verbal self-consciousness is required for men to secure the fullest control of the conduct of their own understandings. Systematic scientific research and philosophical discourse are the public and practical expressions of a form of mental care and responsibility that all men, within the limits of their social opportunities, have the duty to undertake.

Scientific research does not in Locke's view yield knowledge; and hence for him does not deserve the name of science. But it certainly does enable men to improve their understanding of nature. In the work of his admired contemporaries Boyle, Newton and other leading lights of the Royal Society, scientific research had recently made great strides. It is not clear how far Locke himself expected this specialised, systematic and highly theoretical enquiry into the natural world by itself to increase man's control over nature or to enhance his enjoyment of life in the world. (In the field of medicine, of course, he hoped for some immediate worldly benefits; but he clearly did not anticipate a transformation of man's capacity to control disease or alleviate pain.) Yet, whatever its distinct contribution proved to be, he clearly did see scientific research as a natural extension of the active and practical effort to understand and control nature which distinguished 'polished' from 'rude' nations and made life in the former, in his view, so much more enjoyable than it was in the latter (646–7).

Perhaps the most impressive feature of this understanding of natural science was its explanation of the limits of men's natural knowledge. In some ways, to be sure, Locke plainly misjudged these limits, seeing a larger gap between human classification and the workings of nature than the subsequent history of chemistry, or even biology, has proved to justify. But the balance between confidence in the explanatory power of the mechanical model and conviction that men cannot directly know the workings of nature still seems well judged. Modern philosophers of natural science have very different sciences to consider, some with awesome practical effects. They share few of Locke's assumptions, or even interests. Unlike Locke, also, they do not think of knowledge as a form of vision and do not contrast the limitations of man's knowledge of nature with the supposedly perfect vision of an omniscient God. But they too, for the most part, for all their disagreements, put such confidence as they can muster largely in the direct deliverances of the senses and in the explanatory power of models; and they too would deny that human beings can know just why nature works as it does. Natural science, accordingly, is not so much a form of knowledge (as Locke understood this) but, rather, a peculiarly complicated and cunning form of belief—a matter of judgement (or guessing), not of direct vision.

Locke does not doubt that something causes nature to work in every detail just as it does. Objects have qualities and human beings know of their existence because these qualities affect their senses in particular ways. But, unlike Aristotle, he doubted whether nature itself was divided up into distinct kinds of things, with clear boundaries between them; he was confident that human beings could not know exactly how it is divided; and he was quite certain that human beings cannot know about it by knowing precisely how it is divided. However nature itself is divided up—whether it forms a blurred continuum or is made up of a multiplicity of entirely distinct kinds of things—it causes men to see it just as they do; and God can see clearly how and why it does so. But all that men can do is to assemble together their own simple ideas with care and accuracy and to use the verbal signs which refer to these assemblages with equal care and accuracy. What men can know about nature (apart from the simple ideas of sensation and reflection) is how exactly they themselves conceive it. They cannot know in general what they are thinking or talking about. They cannot, except at a particular moment, know how it truly is.

With ideas that shape action—and especially with moral ideas—the position is very different. Here there is no gap between what men think about and what really is the case. It is easy to be confused about moral issues since there is no palpable external standard, given by the senses, which men must seek to match and with which their ideas can readily be compared. But the moral ideas which men consider simply *are* the realities about which they are attempting to think. Because there is no gap in this sense between what Locke calls their 'nominal essence' and their 'real essence', ideas about morality can be understood with a clarity which ideas about nature necessarily lack. This is why Locke supposed that morality could be demonstrated, and continued to suppose so long after he had abandoned the attempt to demonstrate it himself.

What made moral conceptions potentially so clear (and moral misunderstanding so likely in practice) was the absence of a given world for them to match. Unsurprisingly, however, this very absence made them vulnerable in quite another way. All men, as we have seen, have powerful internal principles of action which impel them to act in a manner wholly contrary to Locke's own moral beliefs. Human societies are possible because they restrain these motives by the contrary pressure of approval and disapproval and by effective threats of legal punishment. Both of these are simply practical obstacles to an individual's pursuit of pleasure. In themselves they can give no man a reason for wishing to act morally, or for choosing to do so where he is confident of avoiding in practice the threats which they level at him. Hence the decisive importance for Locke's conception of morality of a threat which no one can rationally hope to avoid, the punishments of a God 'who sees Men in the dark'. This dependence is set out with particular clarity in an uncompleted manuscript, 'Of Ethics in General', perhaps intended as the final chapter of the *Essay* (LN 11). In face of this dependence, the *Essay* as a whole shows one glaring defect. The demonstrative argument for God's existence which it offers goes no distance at all towards establishing the reality of a God concerned to punish or save human beings. The unmistakably Christian conception of a God on which Locke's moral convictions rested could be vindicated only by an appeal to revelation. (Fortunately, God's law of nature and his revealed will were necessarily identical and offered 'the only true touch-stone of *moral Rectitude*' (E 352).)

Faith

In his last major work, accordingly, Locke turned firmly to revelation. He did so in part to proclaim, as its title declares, *The Reasonableness of Christianity as delivered in the Scriptures*. (It is reason which must judge whether a particular message is or is not a revelation from God and which must interpret precisely what it means.) But he did so more urgently because it was only by means of the Christian revelation that he retained the confidence that men's moral duties were effectively 'made known to all mankind'. Natural law in its full extent had never been demonstrated by anyone (R 89), and by 1694 Locke had abandoned hope of demonstrating it himself (LC IV 768, 786). But God had shown all men how he wished them to live by proclaiming to them the law of faith through the Messiah Jesus. The close correspondence between the Messianic prophecies of the Old Testament and the events of the life of Jesus, together with the miracles which he performed, gave to his disciples a revealed knowledge that he was the Messiah. Jesus himself proclaimed the

law of faith, demanding obedience and promising salvation in
return (R 71–5, W III 466).

Nearly seventeen centuries later, men cannot expect the same
direct compulsion to believe that the disciples enjoyed, since
traditional revelation depends on historical reasoning and not on
direct experience (E 664, 690–1). But if they consider the evidence and open their hearts, faith will not be denied to them.
The faith that Jesus was the Messiah, and a genuine effort to
obey his law, will together be sufficient to save them. Faith is a
form of trust, not against reason, but beyond reason. It demands
effort (which is why infidelity can be a sin). But it makes truly
open to every man the opportunity to live a good life.

This is not an inspiring conclusion to a philosophical quest that
had covered three and a half decades. There is no reason to
believe that Locke himself regarded it with enthusiasm; and he
would scarcely have been happy to espouse it from the outset. It
had, moreover, a number of distressing implications. It meant,
for example, that men, by Locke's own criterion and because of
the limitations of their own natural abilities, cannot, and do not
have the opportunity to, *know* how to live. Judgement and faith
may be sufficient for salvation. But what they offer does not
amount to a form of knowledge. Moreover, the fate of all those
human beings who had not been fortunate enough to receive the
good news of the Christian revelation was hard, on this view, to
reconcile both with Locke's conception of man's place in nature
and with his understanding of the power and benevolence of
God.

But, however discouraging an outcome this must have been for
Locke himself, it does serve to illuminate some of the key con-
straints on his imagination. Judgement and faith together could
give men sufficient reason to live as he supposed that they ought.
In the last instance, it was more important to him that they
should have sufficient reason to live in this way than that they
should possess the power to know how to live. Genuine knowledge of morality, accordingly, turns out in practice to be as much
beyond men's own reach as a true science of nature. What re-
places it in the real lives of men, as Locke imagined these, is a
combination of judgement with trust in divine benevolence. His
picture of men's powers to know about nature—as modest natural abilities—is contrasted with a picture of God's power to know

about nature. In the face of these modest natural abilities, sceptical doubt appears strained and silly because, unlike them, it can
play no part in meeting the practical demands of day-to-day life.
In a sense (and here Locke's profound engagement with the
philosophy of Descartes gave him some real insight), the force of
scepticism comes largely from an implicit contrast between the
modest ability to understand nature which men palpably do
possess and a form of understanding—clear, distinct, unchallen-
geable and final—which they might in faith be led to attribute to
God, but which they themselves certainly cannot attain. From
Locke's point of view, that is to say, it comes from the presumptuous demand that men should be able to understand nature as
clearly as God does.

With the faltering of trust in the existence of a God, both
natural knowledge and morality inevitably look very different
from the way that Locke saw them. In a godless world the limits
of scepticism were certain to prove (and have proven) far harder
to draw.

Conclusion

IN JANUARY 1698, in a letter to his friend William Molyneux, Locke summed up the convictions of a lifetime.

If I could think that discourses and arguments to the understanding
were like the several sorts of cates [sc. foodstuffs] to different palates
and stomachs, some nauseous and destructive to one, which are pleas-
ant and restorative to another; I should no more think of books and
study, and should think my time better imploy'd at push-pin than in
reading or writing. But I am convinc'd of the contrary: I know there is
truth opposite to falsehood, that it may be found if people will, and is
worth the seeking, and is not only the most valuable, but the pleasantest
thing in the world. (LC VI 294–5)

That the truth is independent of human desires and tastes, and
that at least part of it lies within the reach of human understanding, is a simple and widespread conviction. But it is not an
easy conviction to explain and justify in any great depth. For
Locke, the task of a philosopher was to provide just such an
explanation and defence. Many modern philosophers doubt
whether any such defence can be constructed. Even amongst
those who believe that it might, few see Locke's own attempt as
especially successful.

There is no reason to quarrel with this verdict. What distinguishes Locke from the great majority of philosophers is not the
cogency today of his arguments as a whole. Rather, it is the
profundity with which he understood the bearing of philosophy
on how men have good reason to live their lives. If truth does in
the end depend upon human desire, and if men have no end but
their own wills, then the life which Locke himself lived was a
ludicrous exercise in self-denial. Nearly three centuries later, the
same is still likely to be true of many aspects of our own lives.
The idea that whether or not our lives make sense might depend
upon the deliberations of university departments of philosophy
is at first sight mildly comic. But in the last instance the joke, as
Locke saw, is on us. Once we have lost the religious guarantee
that reason, 'the candle of the Lord', shines bright enough for all

our purposes, we have no conclusive reason to expect it to shine bright enough for any. And once we can no longer see our purposes as authoritatively assigned to us from outside our selves, it becomes very hard to judge just which purposes we have good reason to consider as (or to make) our own.

In the face of these two hazards, the instability of human belief in its entirety and the obscurity of how we do have good reason to live our lives, Locke's philosophy offers us more illumination on the first than on the second. This is certainly not what he would have wished: but it is easy enough to explain. Many philosophers today, unsurprisingly, share his belief that truths about nature and about complex inventions of the human mind, like mathematics and logic, are independent of human desire. But for Locke the central truths about how men have good reason to live are just as independent of what at a particular time they happen consciously to desire. Few today share this belief with any confidence; and perhaps no one today has much idea of how to defend it. But some still live (and many more attempt intermittently to live) as though it were in fact true. As Coleridge, a savage critic of Locke's ethics, put it a century and three-quarters ago: 'Almost all men nowadays act and feel more nobly than they think.'

The view that the game of push-pin, if men happen to enjoy it as much, is just as good as poetry, is a slogan of the most influential modern theory of human good, the utilitarianism of Jeremy Bentham. What led Locke to reject it is not the equally utilitarian (and singularly unconvincing) claim that truth is the pleasantest thing in the world, but the more fundamental conviction that truth is different from falsehood, that it can be found and is worth the seeking, and that when it is found it will tell man clearly how to live. It was in this conviction that he placed his trust and lived his life. Because of it, he still offers to us across the centuries the example of a lifetime of intellectual courage. It may well be that he was wrong to trust it. And if he was, we can hardly rely on his thinking to steady our own nerves. But what is certain is that we too shall need such intellectual courage every bit as urgently as he did.

Note on sources

THE manuscript by Sydenham quoted on p. 16 is from Kenneth Dewhurst, *John Locke, Physician and Philosopher* : *A Medical Biography* (Wellcome Historical Medical Library, London, 1963). Henry Ireton's question to the Leveller leaders in the Putney debates quoted on p. 42 is taken from A. S. P. Woodhouse (ed.), *Puritanism and Liberty* (J. M. Dent & Son, London, 1938). Coleridge's comment cited on p. 85 comes from Kathleen Coburn (ed.), *The Notebooks of Samuel Taylor Coleridge*, vol. 2, 1804–1808 (New York, 1961), entry 2627.

Further reading

FULL bibliographical details of the editions of Locke's works that have been used in references are given in the list of abbreviations at the beginning of the book.

The Clarendon Press is at present engaged in publishing an edition of all Locke's published writings and many of his unpublished manuscripts. So far the *Essay concerning Human Understanding* and eight volumes of his *Correspondence* have appeared, superlatively edited by Peter Nidditch and E. S. de Beer respectively, followed by *A Paraphrase and Notes on the Epistles of St Paul* (ed. Arthur Wainwright), the first volume of the *Drafts for the Essay* (ed. Peter Nidditch and G. A. J. Rogers, *Some Thoughts concerning Education* (ed. John and Jean Yolton), and Locke's *Writings on Money* (ed. Patrick Kelly). There are also excellent modern editions of the *Two Treatises of Government* (ed. Laslett), *Two Tracts on Government* (ed. Abrams), *Essays on the Law of Nature* (ed. von Leyden), *Educational Writings* (ed. James Axtell, Cambridge University Press, 1968) and of Drafts A and B of the *Essay* (ed. Nidditch, 1980 and 1982), and a somewhat less satisfactory edition of the *Letter on Toleration* (ed. Klibansky and Gough). There is as yet no adequate modern edition of *The Reasonableness of Christianity*. Other published works of Locke are most conveniently consulted in the eighteenth- or nineteenth-century editions of his *Collected Works*.

Maurice Cranston's *John Locke: A Biography* (Longman, London, 1957) is informative but less vivid than Laslett's Introduction to the *Two Treatises*. There is a major modern biography of Shaftesbury by K. H. D. Haley, *The First Earl of Shaftesbury* (Clarendon Press, Oxford, 1968). The Introductions by von Leyden and Abrams are particularly illuminating on the development of Locke's understanding of morality. The best systematic treatment of this is now provided by John Colman, *John Locke's Moral Philosophy* (Edinburgh University Press, 1983). Locke's religious views are clearly (and on the whole approvingly) presented in M. S. Johnson, *Locke on Freedom* (Best Printing Co., Austin, Tex., 1978). There is as yet no really satisfactory analysis of his philosophy as a whole, though this gap will be filled in the near future with the publication of Michael Ayers's major study. Amongst the more helpful works, written from a wide variety of perspectives, are John W. Yolton, *Locke and the Compass of Human Understanding* (Cambridge University Press, 1970); Roger Woolhouse, *Locke's Philosophy of Science and Knowledge* (Basil Blackwell, Oxford, 1971); Richard I. Aaron, *John Locke*, 3rd edn., (Clarendon Press, Oxford, 1971); James Gibson, *Locke's Theory of Knowledge and its Historical Relations* (Cambridge University Press, 1917); Kathleen Squadrito, *Locke's Theory of Sensitive Knowledge* (University Press of America, Washington, DC, 1978); J. L. Mackie, *Problems from Locke* (Clarendon Press, Oxford, 1976); Jonathan Bennett, *Locke, Berkeley, Hume: Central Themes* (Clarendon Press, Oxford, 1971); Peter A. Schouls, *The Imposition of Method* (Clarendon Press, Oxford, 1980); and the essays collected in I. C. Tipton (ed.), *Locke on Human Understanding* (Clarendon Press, Oxford, 1977). There are a number of important articles by Michael Ayers (see particularly 'Locke versus Aristotle on Natural Kinds', *Journal of Philosophy*, May 1981; 'Mechanism, Superaddition and the Proof of God's Existence in Locke's *Essay*', *Philosophical Review*, April 1981; 'The Ideas of Power and Substance in Locke's Philosophy', *Philosophical Quarterly*, January 1975). The central importance for Locke of men's responsibility for their own beliefs is brought out very elegantly in John Passmore, 'Locke and the Ethics of Belief', *Proceedings of the British Academy*, 1978. On Locke's conceptions of persons and their identity, see Ruth Mattern, 'Moral Science and the Concept of Persons in Locke', *Philosophical Review*, January 1980, and David Wiggins, 'Locke, Butler and the Stream of Consciousness and Men as a Natural Kind', in A. O. Rorty (ed.), *The Identities of Persons* (University of California Press, Berkeley, 1976). For the formation of Locke's own identity, see J. Dunn, 'Individuality and Clientage in the Formation of Locke's Social Imagination', in Reinhard Brandt (ed.), *John Locke* (W. de Gruyter, Berlin and New York, 1981). The originality and influence of Locke's conception of language is discussed magisterially in Hans Aarsleff, *From Locke to Saussure* (Athlone Press, London, 1982).

The best introduction to Locke's political thought is now Geraint Parry, *Locke* (George Allen & Unwin, London, 1978). The *Two Treatises* itself is discussed in J. Dunn, *The Political Thought of John Locke* (Cambridge University Press, 1969). Its analysis of property is best treated in James Tully, *A Discourse of Property* (Cambridge University Press, 1980); but compare C. B. Macpherson, *The Politi-*

cal Theory of Possessive Individualism (Clarendon Press, Oxford, 1962); Jeremy Waldron, *The Right to Private Property* (Clarendon Press, Oxford 1988), and the Introduction to Istvan Hont and Michael Ignatieff (eds.), *Wealth and Virtue* (Cambridge University Press, 1983). Political obligation is discussed by W. von Leyden, *Hobbes and Locke* (Macmillan, London, 1981); compare J. Dunn, *Political Obligation in its Historical Context* (Cambridge University Press, 1980), chapter 3. There are several helpful articles in J. W. Yolton, *John Locke: Problems and Perspectives* (Cambridge University Press, 1969): see especially Aarsleff and Ashcraft. The most penetrating discussion of the evolution of Locke's own political commitments is to be found in Richard Ashcraft, *Revolutionary Politics and Locke's Two Treatises of Government* (Princeton University Press, Princeton 1986), and in his contribution to J. G. A. Pocock and R. Ashcraft, *John Locke* (William Andrews Clark Memorial Library, Los Angeles, 1980); in Mark Goldie, 'John Locke and Anglican Royalism', *Political Studies*, March 1983, and in the Introduction to Laslett's edition of the *Two Treatises*. Amongst more recent articles see especially James Tully, 'Governing Conduct', in Edmund Leites (ed.), *Conscience and Casuistry in Early Modern Europe* (Cambridge University Press, Cambridge, 1988), 'Trust and Political Agency' in Dunn, *Interpreting Political Responsibility* (Polity Press, Cambridge, 1990), and Dunn, 'Freedom of Conscience: Freedom of Speech, Freedom of Thought, Freedom of Worship?' in O. P. Grell, J. Israel, and N. Tyacke (eds.), *From Persecution to Toleration* (Clarendon Press, Oxford 1991).

The writings of the main target of the *Two Treatises*, Sir Robert Filmer, are available in a convenient modern edition by Peter Laslett (Basil Blackwell, Oxford, 1949). The distinctiveness of Filmer's views is best brought out in James Daly, *Sir Robert Filmer and English Political Thought* (University of Toronto Press, 1979). The background to his thinking can be approached through Gordon J. Schochet, *Patriarchalism in Political Thought* (Basil Blackwell, Oxford, 1975). The relations between the political theory of Locke and his eighteenth-century successors are discussed in J. Dunn, 'The Politics of Locke in England and America in the Eighteenth Century' *(Political Obligation*, chapter 4), and 'From Applied Theology to Social Analysis; the break between John Locke and the Scottish Enlightenment' (in Hont and Ignatieff (eds.), *Wealth and Virtue).* There are important modern studies on Locke's political theory in French, German and, particularly, Italian. An annual periodical,

The Locke Newsletter (published by Roland Hall, Department of Philosophy, University of York), provides regular information on current research into Locke's life and thought. Its first issue was an invaluable bibliography, now republished in a fuller form as Roland Hall and Roger Woolhouse, *Eighty Years of Locke Scholarship: A Bibliographical Guide* (Edinburgh University Press, 1983).

Five works which illuminate the background to important aspects of Locke's writings are Michael Hunter, *Science and Society in Restoration England* (Cambridge University Press, 1981); Quentin Skinner, *The Foundations of Modern Political Thought* (2 vols., Cambridge University Press, 1978); Richard Tuck, *Natural Rights Theories: Their Origins and Development* (Cambridge University Press, 1979); John W. Yolton, *John Locke and the Way of Ideas* (Clarendon Press, Oxford, 1956); Richard H. Popkin, *The History of Scepticism from Erasmus to Spinoza* (University of California Press, Berkeley, 1979).

BERKELEY

Contents

Note on abbreviations

The following abbreviations are used in references to Berkeley's works:

A   *Alciphron*

C   *Philosophical Commentaries*

L   *The Works of George Berkeley*, ed. Luce and Jessup (see p. 178)

M   *De motu*

O   *Passive Obedience*

P   *Principles of Human Knowledge*

S   *Siris*

V   *A New Theory of Vision*

References to L are by volume and page, references to A, M, O, P, S and V by paragraph. References to C follow the numbering (not Berkeley's) adopted in L i.

1

The corpuscularian philosophy

AT SOME time not precisely known, but certainly when he was in his very early twenties, if not earlier, George Berkeley, newly graduated B.A. of Trinity College, Dublin, had a metaphysical inspiration. It was one which seemed to him, on reflection, to be blindingly obvious; it served as a basis for answers to at least most of the outstanding problems of metaphysics; it removed the temptation to scepticism and atheism presented by current philosophical orthodoxy; it preserved, perhaps in a more sophisticated form, everything that either common sense or the revelations of the Christian religion maintained. This new insight was that there was no such thing as matter, that the concept of matter was totally superfluous and even unintelligible.

So stated, baldly, out of context and without explanation, this alleged insight will presumably appear utterly ridiculous to the reader not already acquainted with Berkeley's thought. It appeared utterly ridiculous to, for example, Dr Johnson, who believed, ignorantly but not unnaturally, that he could refute it by kicking a stone. One of the principal aims of this book will be to show the reader how, in the context of the philosophical and scientific beliefs of his time, Berkeley's thesis was a very rational one to adopt, and to show how ingeniously Berkeley developed it within the bounds of one of the most elegant, clear and simple metaphysical systems ever devised. The reader will not be asked to accept the doctrine, though some philosophers do accept it; but he should come to see that it is the work of one of the world's great philosophical geniuses and worthy of admiring study.

To understand how Berkeley came to propound this, at first sight, absurd and irresponsible thesis we must first have some acquaintance with the philosophical and scientific outlook of the vast majority of seventeenth-century thinkers against which Berkeley was revolting.

The seventeenth century, towards the close of which Berkeley was born, saw the birth of modern experimental science. Broadly speaking, for the historian of science will easily cite counter-examples to the generalization, scientific investigation had ceased during the dark and middle ages. Already during the Renaissance it was beginning to revive. But it was at the beginning of the seventeenth-century that Galileo set out to establish the main principles of statics and made a beginning in dynamics, the two main branches of the great science of mechanics which had been largely neglected since Archimedes and which Newton was by the century's end to bring to a perfection which for two further centuries seemed to be final. Galileo also developed the microscope and the telescope, the indispensable tools for the investigation of the minute and the distant. Between him and Newton came Harvey, the Dutch mathematician Snell, Descartes, the Italian physicist Torricelli, Pascal, Sydenham, Boyle, Huygens, Hooke; great academies of science, including the Royal Society of London, were instituted; kings and nobility, including Charles II, had their own experimental laboratories; to many it seemed that all the secrets of nature would before long be revealed, though by the end of the century this optimism had waned.

Underlying and partly determining this burst of scientific activity was a new philosophical outlook which had replaced the scholasticism of the past few centuries. It was called sometimes the modern philosophy and sometimes the corpuscularian philosophy. Largely through the agency of the Frenchman Peter Gassendi (1592–1655), classical scholar, astronomer and general intellectual factotum, a knowledge of the ancient atomic hypothesis of Democritus and Epicurus was revived, and this ontology of atoms and the void quickly won acceptance. Enthusiasm for it broke through even in a report to the puritan government of the Protectorate on the state of the English Universities; in his *Examination of Academies* John Webster wrote in 1654: 'What shall I say of the Epicurean philosophy, brought to light, illustrated and completed by the labour of that general scholar Petrus Gassendus? Surely if it be rightly examined it will prove a more perfect and sound piece than any the Schools ever had or followed.' Though Descartes and his followers could not accept the void they enthusiastically subscribed to the ideal of mechanistic explanation, and a Catholic eclectic like Sir Kenelm Digby could write that all could be explained by particles 'working by local motion'.

This 'modern philosophy' became the theoretical foundation of science in England. The truly magnificent title of a book by Henry Power, Dr of Physick, published in 1664, *Experimental Philosophy in Three Books, containing New Experiments Microscopical, Mercurial, Magnetical with some deductions and probable Hypotheses raised from them in avouchment and illustration of the now famous Atomical Hypothesis*, well illustrates the mood of the times.

What, then, was this modern philosophy, the corpuscularian philosophy, which Dr Power called the atomical hypothesis? Since we are constantly informed by ignorant persons that the ancient Greeks had a merely speculative atomic fantasy whereas the modern atomic theory was founded on solid experimental observation, any resemblance being coincidental, it would be as well to say again that the corpuscularian philosophy simply is the ancient Greek theory revived and is clearly stated to be so by its main proponents. Since it was to be the main target of Berkeley's criticism, a theory which he regarded as the fountain of all error, we had better become quite closely acquainted with it. Berkeley had studied it carefully.

The corpuscularian philosophy held that the world consisted of atoms in motion in an infinite void; in the ancient version the atoms so moved in infinite time, but the Christian philosophers of the seventeenth-century accepted, on the authority of the Bible, that they were created and set in motion by God. Thus Newton, in Query 30 to his *Optics*, said: 'It seems probable to me that God in the beginning formed matter in solid, massy, hard, impenetrable, movable particles, of such sizes and figures, and with such other properties and in such proportion to space as most conduced to the end for which he formed them.' These atoms were considered to be of many different shapes and sizes, solid, indestructible and in motion.

But if we ask with what other properties God endowed the atoms, the answer will be: 'None.' 'Hot and cold are appearance, sweet and bitter are appearance, colour is appearance; in reality there are the atoms and the void' said Democritus in one of the few surviving fragments of his scientific writings, and with this the seventeenth-century scientists entirely agreed. The corpuscularian philosophy is a theory of pure mechanism.

Everything is to be explained in terms of the shape, size, mass and motion of the particles and their impact on each other; in other words, mechanical explanation is the only acceptable form of scientific explanation. Impact was the only way in which anything could be conceived to act on anything else. This was agreed on all hands; thus Locke, in Book II of his *An Essay concerning Human Understanding*, spoke of 'impulse, the only way which we can conceive bodies operate in', and even the arch-rationalist Leibniz (1646–1716), commenting on this passage of Locke, says: 'I also am of the opinion that bodies act only by impulse.' So what was explicable was ultimately to be explained mechanically; what could not be so explained was not scientifically explicable at all and had to be referred to the direct decrees of God.

This insistence on mechanical explanation cannot be overemphasised. It can be illustrated by reference to the theory of gravitation. Newton had discovered the famous law that bodies tend to move towards each other with an acceleration proportional to the product of the masses and inversely proportional to the square of the distance between them. It might seem that here is an example of a force of attraction, of action on each other of bodies at a distance and not by impact. Whatever later followers of Newton may subsequently have said, this view was sternly rejected by Newton himself. By gravitation, he insisted, he meant nothing beyond the observed phenomenon, of which he offered no explanation: 'Hypotheses non fingo.' In a letter to Bentley, the Master of his College, who had been incautiously referring to a force of gravitation, Newton wrote: 'That gravity should be innate, inherent, and essential to matter, so that one body may act upon another at a distance through a *vacuum*, without the mediation of anything else, by and through which their action and force may be conveyed from one to another, is to me so great an absurdity that I believe no man who has in philosophical matters a competent faculty of thinking can ever fall into it.' A force of gravitation as an explanation of motion would, for Newton, have been just another of those occult qualities which the seventeenth-century so derided, an explanation on a par with the 'dormitive power' which Molière's medical student offered as an explanation why opium sends us to sleep. As Leibniz remarked of such alleged attractions in the Preface to *New Essay on the Human Understanding*, 'it is impossible to conceive how this takes place, i.e., to explain it mechanically'. It was acknowledged that magnetism, gravitation and the like were difficult to explain mechanically; but to explain them in terms of magnetic or gravitational forces would have been regarded as a merely verbal subterfuge.

So it was plain orthodoxy to ascribe to bodies, to atoms, those properties which mechanical science imputed to them. It was an equally unquestioned orthodoxy to deny to them all those other qualities, such as colour, taste and smell, that the common man uncritically ascribed to them. Thus Galileo, echoing the fragment of Democritus already quoted, said in *The Assayer* that 'tastes, odours, colours, and so on are no more than mere names so far as the object in which we place them is concerned, and reside only in the consciousness. Hence, if the living creature were removed, all these qualities would be wiped away and annihilated.' Bodies, Galileo claimed, cause such sensations in us by motion and impact, just as a hand may produce in us the sensation of a tickle by motion and impact; it is as absurd to locate the colour in the body as to locate the tickle in the hand that causes it. Newton expressed the same view in his magnificent prose:

If at any time I speak of light and rays as coloured or endued with colours, I would be understood to speak, not philosophically and properly, but grossly and accordingly to such conceptions as vulgar people in seeing all these experiments would be apt to frame. For the rays, to speak properly, are not coloured. In them there is nothing else than a certain power and disposition to stir up a sensation of this or that colour. For as sound in a bell or musical string, or other sounding body, is nothing but a trembling motion, and in the air nothing but that motion propagated from the object, and in the sensorium it is a sense of that motion under the form of sound, so colours in the object are nothing but a disposition to reflect this or that sort of rays more copiously than the rest; in the rays they are nothing but their dispositions to propagate this or that motion into the sensorium, and in the sensorium they are sensations of those motions under the forms of colours.

We have seen that we can find the mechanistic corpuscularian philosophy in many of the great scientists and philosophers of the seventeenth-century. But perhaps the best and clearest statement of this fundamental theory is to be found in the works of Robert Boyle, the traditional 'father of chemistry'; since it is vital

for us to be well acquainted with it if we are to understand
Berkeley's philosophy more than superficially, we can with advantage read Boyle's statement of it. He gives it in a monograph
entitled *The Origin of Forms and Qualities* (1666), with the aim
of explaining the corpuscularian philosophy to the amateur.
'Among those', he says, 'that are inclined to that philosophy,
which I find I have been much imitated in calling corpuscularian,
there are many ingenious persons, especially among the nobility
and gentry, who . . . delight to make or see variety of experiments, without having ever had the opportunity to be instructed
in the rudiments or fundamental notions of that philosophy.' So,
he hopes, 'this tract may in some sort exhibit a scheme or serve
for an introduction into the elements of the corpuscularian philosophy'.

Here, then, are these elements, in Boyle's own words so far as
is convenient:

1 'I agree with our Epicureans in thinking that the world is
made up of an innumerable multitude of singly insensible corpuscles endowed with their own sizes, shapes and motions.'

2 'If we should conceive that the rest of the universe were
annihilated, except any of these entire and undivided corpuscles,
it is hard to say what could be attributed to it, besides matter,
motion (or rest), bulk and shape.'

3 God, Boyle holds, created the world: 'but the world being
once framed, and the course of nature established, the naturalist
(except in some few cases where God or incorporeal agents
interpose) has recourse to the first cause but for its general
support and influence, whereby it preserves matter and motion
from annihilation and destruction; and in explicating particular
phenomena considers only the size, shape, motion (or want of
it), texture and the resulting qualities and attributes of the small
particles of matter'.

4 As for other apparent qualities of bodies, 'I have already
taught that there are simpler and more primitive affections of
matter, from which these secondary qualities, if I may so call
them, do depend.'

5 Corpuscles strike on the sense organs and cause motions
which are transmitted to the brain. 'Sensation', Boyle says, 'is
properly and ultimately made in, or by, the mind or discerning

faculty; which, from the differing motions of the internal parts of the brain, is excited and determined to differing perceptions to some of which men have given the name of heat, cold or other qualities.'

6 'I do not deny but that bodies may be said, in a very favourable sense, to have those qualities we call sensible, though there were no animals in the world: for a body in that case may differ from other bodies which now are quite devoid of quality in its having such a disposition of its constituent corpuscles that in case it were duly applied to the sensory of an animal, it would produce such a sensible quality which a body of another texture would not.'

The reader now has before him a sketch of the corpuscularian philosophy. He will have noticed that it was accepted by a number of eminent philosophers and scientists before the publication of John Locke's *Essay Concerning Human Understanding*, which did not appear until 1689. It is therefore rather strange that this theory is traditionally known as Locke's theory of primary and secondary qualities. Locke was, indeed, an enthusiastic disciple of Robert Boyle, whose laboratory in Oxford he visited from time to time as a young man; he was also an admiring friend of Sir Isaac Newton, and described himself as an under-labourer in the same field as those two eminent men. He gives a version, by no means original, of the corpuscularian philosophy in Book II, Chapter VIII of his *Essay*, and, since Berkeley studied this version carefully and followed its terminology, we must take notice of it, the more carefully since Locke's ambiguous language seems to have misled Berkeley into some misunderstanding of the theory. The extent to which Locke was reproducing generally accepted doctrine is well illustrated by a remark of the Rev. Henry Lee in his *Anti-Scepticism or Notes upon each Chapter of Mr Locke's Essay Concerning Human Understanding*, published in 1702. Of Locke's account of this topic he says: "tis common to all that pretend to the Mechanical Philosophy' and that 'all this is so very clear, now so universally own'd, that this Author might have spared many of his Arguments to prove it'.

Locke lists the qualities that are 'utterly inseparable from the body' as being solidity, extension, figure, motion or rest, and number. His notion of solidity is unclear, but the most favourable interpretation of it is as the exclusive occupation of a given portion of space. These he calls primary qualities. Colour, heat, cold, taste etc. he, like the other philosophers whose views we have quoted, did not regard as being true qualities of bodies but as sensations produced in us by bodies. So he defines secondary qualities as being 'such qualities, which in truth are nothing in the objects themselves, but powers to produce various sensations in us by their primary qualities, i.e., by the bulk, figure, texture, and motion of their insensible parts, as colours, sounds, tastes, etc.'. Locke thus clearly defines secondary qualities as powers to produce sensations in us, not as being the sensations thus produced; but Locke himself occasionally, and Berkeley together with most subsequent commentators regularly, depart from this terminology and call the colours, tastes, smells etc. themselves secondary qualities.

In saying that primary qualities are utterly inseparable from bodies Locke seems to mean two things. First, these qualities are defining properties of body—whatever lacks these would not count as a body. Perhaps some bodies actually are colourless, or tasteless, or soundless, and it is at least conceivable that some are; but an unextended body, a body that was neither in motion nor at rest, a body with no shape, however irregular, would be a contradiction in terms. Secondly, nothing which has these properties can ever cease to have them, whatever be done to it, whereas a body may be deprived of its smell, its taste or its colour. So primary qualities are inseparable from bodies, while secondary qualities are not; there may be bodies which lack the power to cause our sensations of colour, smell, taste etc.

Locke, like other upholders of the corpuscularian philosophy, holds that all our sensations, whether of primary or of secondary qualities, are caused by the impact of insensible atoms on our sense organs, the motions thus generated being then transmitted by the nerves to the brain; these sensations he calls ideas. Using this terminology he claims that the ideas of primary qualities (shape, bulk, motion etc.) resemble these qualities themselves, whereas the ideas of secondary qualities do not resemble anything in the body or the powers which are the secondary qualities. Since, as I believe, Berkeley misunderstood this claim, it would be well to state it in Locke's own words: 'Ideas of primary qualities of bodies are resemblances of them, and their patterns do really exist in the bodies themselves; but the ideas produced in us by these secondary qualities have no resemblance of them at all. There is nothing like our ideas existing in the bodies themselves.'

Now when Locke says that ideas of colour and other secondary qualities do not resemble anything in the body, he does not mean that bodies are always of a colour different from that of the ideas that they produce in us; for bodies have no colour at all according to the corpuscular philosophy. He means that bodies are coloured only in the sense that they have the power to produce ideas of colour. Consistency requires that when he says that ideas of shape and of other primary qualities are resemblances of those qualities in bodies he cannot mean that bodies are always of exactly the same shape as the ideas they produce in us, that is, look to be the shape that they really are, which, in any case, is obviously false. He must mean that when we ascribe shape to bodies we do so in the same sense of 'shape' as when we ascribe it to ideas; thus 'square' when applied to either an idea or a body will have the same geometrically definable meaning. To put the point in technical jargon, ideas of primary qualities and bodies instantiate the same determinable properties—shape, size, motion etc.—but not necessarily the same determinates of those determinables on each occasion. We shall find that Berkeley attributes to Locke that interpretation of the doctrine which I have rejected; Locke does once or twice say things which give some justification for so doing; but so interpreted the doctrine is pointless and no part of the corpuscularian philosophy.

We have begun to use the terminology of ideas which was standard in the seventeenth and eighteenth centuries, and something should be said about it to conclude this introductory chapter. Descartes was the first important philosopher to use it; Locke followed him in this use and Berkeley followed Locke. So we must try to understand it now in a preliminary way, though we shall be continually faced with problems about it.

In colloquial English in the seventeenth century the word 'idea' was a synonym of 'picture', as was the word 'idée' in French. Thus Shakespeare, in *Richard III*, has Buckingham tell Gloucester that he is the 'right idea', that is, the very picture, of his father. Descartes himself said that ideas are, properly speaking, like pictures of things. The word apparently got into philosophical use in connection with a very simple theory of visual perception in which the soul sees pictures of the outside world projected on the surface of the brain, a version of the doctrine of representative perception. The term was retained even as this theory became modified or abandoned, and was also extended to cover all objects of consciousness—all sensations of all senses, the objects of memory, the objects of imagination, the objects of thought (which was often regarded as being primarily the framing of mental images), and all emotions. This widely extended use of the term 'idea' by Locke was felt to be strange and even indefensible at the time. In criticism of him Stillingfleet, then Bishop of Worcester, fulminated against 'the new way of ideas' as even dangerous to Christianity; Henry Lee, in *Anti-Scepticism*, protests that 'that only can be call'd an Idea, which is a visible Representation or Resemblance of the Object'; even well into the eighteenth-century Boswell reports Johnson as chastising current usage and pronouncing that 'it is clear that idea can only signify something of which an image can be formed in the mind'. It is indeed very hard to doubt that their liberal use of the word 'idea' did involve the philosophers who employed it in ambiguity and obscurity, as we shall find in our study of Berkeley's philosophy.

The philosophers of this period, like many philosophers at all other times, were quite convinced that in perception what they were aware of was an idea, an image, a sensation, caused by inherently imperceptible matter. The reader may well wonder why they were so sure that such a causal theory was true and that the 'vulgar' notion that we are immediately aware of physical objects was not worthy of serious philosophical debate. They were moved by two basic considerations. The first was that an accurate account of what we perceive, that is, of how things look to us, will be different from an accurate account of how the world is, even as it is popularly conceived to be. Thus the stick in the water is straight, but the 'stick' we perceive is bent and has no physical reality; the railway lines are parallel, but we see two lines converging in the distance; the medium dry table wine will taste sweet after we have drunk very dry sherry and dry after we have drunk a cream sherry. If the descriptions of the world and of what we perceive are thus different, what we perceive cannot be the world.

A second consideration weighed just as heavily. If the scientific account of physical reality and of the complex physical and physiological processes involved in perception is even approximately true, it is impossible to claim that we perceive such a world immediately and directly; if, for example, sound is physical vibrations in the atmosphere and is transmitted to us via motions in the ear, the nerves and the brain, then what we hear will not be physical sound, for what we hear is not a motion nor anything else mentioned in a physical account of sound.

Whether these arguments are satisfactory we must inquire later on, but not yet. But they certainly convinced the philosophers whom we have been discussing, and though Berkeley could not make use of the second of the two arguments just presented, he certainly accepted without any serious debate the conclusion that what we are aware of is ideas.

2

The attack on matter

GEORGE Berkeley was born on 12 March 1685, near Kilkenny in Ireland. His ancestry was English, but his grandfather, a royalist, moved to Ireland at the time of the restoration. Berkeley considered himself to be an Irishman; he referred to Newton as 'a philosopher of a neighbouring nation' (P 110) and, commenting sarcastically in his private notebook on what he regarded as a philosophical absurdity, he wrote: 'We Irishmen cannot attain to these truths' (C 392). He was sent to Kilkenny College, which Congreve and Swift had recently attended, and then, aged only fifteen, to Trinity College, Dublin, in 1700. There he studied mathematics, languages, including Latin, Greek, French and Hebrew, logic and philosophy; the philosophy course was up to date and included the study of Locke, the French philosopher-theologian Malebranche, and other very recent and contemporary thinkers. He graduated B.A. in 1704 at the age of nineteen and then remained at Trinity College studying privately until he was elected to a fellowship in 1707. He was ordained deacon in 1709 and priest in 1710; he continued to hold his fellowship until 1724, when he resigned to become Dean of Derry, though extended leaves of absence took him first to London and then to Italy.

Though he continued to write for many years after leaving Trinity College, Dublin, it was during the tenure of his fellowship that he wrote the works for which he is now famous. His first work, *An Essay towards a New Theory of Vision*, appeared in 1709, when he was twenty-four; it is a work as much of experimental psychology as of philosophy, and in it he principally discusses how we perceive by sight the distance, size and position of objects. The next year, in 1710, he published *A Treatise concerning the Principles of Human Knowledge*, usually known simply as *The Principles*; this is the most important of all Berkeley's writings and contains the most complete account we have of the philosophical position which he was never to abandon. In 1713 he published the *Three Dialogues between Hylas and Philonous*, a more popular exposition of his view in which Philonous (whose name means 'lover of mind') vanquishes in argument and converts to his view Hylas ('matter'), the materialist. In 1712 he published his Latin essay *De motu* [*On Motion*] which contains by far the fullest account we have of Berkeley's view of the nature of the natural sciences.

Those are the main works published by Berkeley from which we may learn his basic metaphysical and epistemological doctrines, bearing witness to a youth of extraordinary intellectual activity. But, in addition to his published writings, we also have available to us a unique and most interesting document. In 1705, soon after graduating, Berkeley started to write a series of notes on philosophical topics in which he worked out the basis of his new and revolutionary views and made strategic plans for their publication. These notes contain ideas which he immediately rejects and theories which are silently abandoned in his published works, as well as the essential of his position; one cannot therefore safely attribute to him views found only there and not in the published work. But these notes are most valuable as an aid to the correct understanding of the published works and shed fascinating light on the creative processes of a philosopher of genius. They were written in a quarto notebook which was unknown until it was discovered by A. C. Fraser and published by him in 1871 under the title *Commonplace Book*; later editors disliked this name and the notes are now generally called *The Philosophical Commentaries*.

Berkeley's main targets for attack were to be John Locke and Sir Isaac Newton; he was well acquainted with the works of both and admired both of them greatly. Of Newton he wrote: 'I have taken as much pains as (I sincerely believe) any man living to understand that great author, and to make sense of his principles . . . So that, if I do not understand him, it is not my fault but my misfortune' (L iv 116). He also referred to Newton as 'a philosopher of a neighbouring nation whom all the world admire' (P 110), and as 'an extraordinary mathematician, a profound naturalist, a person of the greatest abilities and erudition' (L iv 114). Of Locke he wrote in his notebook: 'Wonderful in Locke that he could, when advanced in years, see at all thro' a mist; it had been so long agathering and was consequently thick. This more to be admired than that he did not see farther' (C 567). He is, of course, using the word 'admire' in its usual sense at that time of 'wonder at'.

But this respect was not extended to all those whom Berkeley called the mathematicians; in his private notebook he wrote: 'I see no wit in any of them but Newton. The rest are mere triflers, mere Nihilarians' (C 372). But these words were for his eyes only; he realised that in a publication, as a young man attacking the establishment, he must exhibit a more conciliatory attitude. So in the same notebook he wrote: 'Mem. Upon all occasions to use the utmost modesty—to confute the mathematicians with the utmost civility and respect, not to style them Nihilarians, etc. N.B. To rein in ye satirical nature' (C 633–4). There are many self-addressed memoranda in the notebooks, often significant, often amusing, and only rarely opaque like: 'Mem. Story of Mr. Deering's aunt' (C 201).

So the principal objects of attack were Newton and Locke. But there was only one main element in their views that he repudiated, that being the doctrine of matter. Berkeley shared their view that ideas are the sole object of the human mind, for example. It is most vital to remember the historical context in which he was writing; often the modern reader finds Berkeley assuming, without more than perfunctory argument at most, things which to him are obscure and doubtful; these are generally things that at the time were accepted by most men and certainly by his opponents, who would have found it tedious and uncalled-for if he had argued them at length. It is also important to be aware that Berkeley never questioned the value of Newton's scientific work, which he believed to be independent of the doctrine of matter. But this doctrine he regarded as an unintelligible and totally superfluous element in his views and one that could be excised without damage to what was left. He attacked it because he believed that it was false, and he attacked it with passion because he believed that it had evil practical consequences. The full title of the *Principles*, the work in which he first attacked the doctrine of matter, is significant: *A Treatise concerning the Principles of Human Knowledge wherein the chief causes of error and difficulty in the sciences, with the grounds of scepticism, atheism, and irreligion, are inquired into.*

So there are at present four main tasks before us: first, to understand why Berkeley thought matter unintelligible; second, to understand why he thought matter superfluous; thirdly, to discover why he thought belief in it dangerous; fourth, to see what account of the world Berkeley was able to give without incorporating matter into it.

The unintelligibility of matter

To understand why Berkeley thought that matter was unintelligible, that the word 'matter' was without meaning in the way it was used by Newton and Locke, we must first realise that he was in a certain respect an extreme empiricist. The concept of empiricism is itself vague, and different philosophers have understood it differently; but luckily we need not go into this problem, for the way in which Berkeley was an empiricist becomes clear from the very first sentence of the *Principles of Human Knowledge*. This sentence reads as follows:

It is evident to any one who takes a survey of the *objects of human knowledge*, that they are either *ideas* actually imprinted on the senses; or else such as are perceived by attending to the passions and operations of the mind; or lastly, *ideas* formed by help of memory and imagination—either compounding, dividing, or barely representing those originally perceived in the aforesaid ways.

By ideas imprinted on the senses he means visual images, heat, smells, tastes and all what Locke would have called ideas of primary and secondary qualities; ideas obtained by attending to the passions include introspective awareness of love, hatred, joy, grief and the like—we can think of these passions because we have experienced them. By attending to the operations of the mind we acquire the ideas of thought itself, of memory, of imagination, and so forth. The ideas gained in these various ways can be recalled in the memory, and in the imagination we can compound and divide to produce what are in some sense new ideas—we can imagine a dragon or a mermaid. But this *is* composition and division; we divide our ideas of the human body and the body of a fish, and by compounding the top end of a human body and the lower end of a fishy body we make the idea or mental picture of a mermaid. So all the materials of thought are such as are supplied by experience, and we cannot think about or have knowledge about what is not the kind of thing we have experienced.

This empiricism is much emphasised in Berkeley's private notebooks: 'Foolish in men to despise the senses. If it were not for them the mind could have no knowledge, no thought at all'; 'By *idea* I mean any sensible or imaginable thing'; 'Pure intellect I understand not' (C 539, 775, 810). He even sets out his empiricism in five simple propositions:

1 All significant words stand for ideas.
2 All knowledge about our ideas.
3 All ideas come from without or from within.
4 If from without it must be by the senses, and they are called sensations.
5 If from within they are the operations of the mind, and are called thoughts. (C 378)

Some philosophers of the seventeenth and eighteenth centuries had rejected empiricism of this kind. Thus Descartes and Leibniz claimed that since they had the idea of God, the idea of matter, the idea of soul or spirit, and since these were not obtainable in experience, there must, therefore, be what they called innate ideas, ideas which the human mind was so constituted as to frame and apply to experience without gaining them in experience. Such ideas were not sensible or picture-like. Since Locke had repudiated any such view, Berkeley did not think it necessary to argue against it; as the opening words of the *Principles*, quoted above, make clear, he himself thought it was evidently wrong. Locke, on the other hand, in spite of having expressly argued against innate ideas, still claimed to have the ideas of God, of substance, of matter and the like. This Berkeley attributed to Locke's recognition of a class of abstract ideas. In addition to the mind's compounding and dividing of ideas, which Berkeley allowed, Locke attributed to the mind a further power of forming ideas by abstraction, and it was this that Berkeley thought to be the cause of what he regarded as Locke's mistake. As for Berkeley, since he was an extreme empiricist he denied that he had any idea of an inherently imperceptible matter, an imperceptible God or even of imperceptible 'finite spirits'; just how Berkeley managed to combine this empiricism with his undoubted and undoubting Christian orthodoxy we shall obviously have to inquire in due course.

Let us try to understand the basic grounds for the rejection of matter as unintelligible a little more fully before we examine the detail of Berkeley's arguments, which vary greatly in cogency. It is clear that, for Berkeley, what we can think of must be imaginable; for all objects of the mind are ideas and by an idea Berkeley means what is sensible or imaginable, and what is sensible is imaginable. But matter is said by its adherents to be something which is not coloured, not warm or tepid or cold, odourless, tasteless etc.—the ideas of secondary qualities resemble nothing in matter. So if we try to imagine matter it is impossible, since we cannot imagine anything that lacks all secondary qualities. If I visualise something it must have some colour, however dingy and nondescript; it cannot just be a shape of no colour at all if I am to see it. If I imagine myself touching something it must feel hard or soft, and clearly the senses of hearing, taste and smell are concerned exclusively with secondary qualities. So one cannot perceive something having only primary qualities, nor can one imagine such a thing; yet that is what matter is supposed to be. So one cannot have an idea of matter, it cannot be an object of one's mind, it is unthinkable; we can attach no meaning to the word 'matter'. Perhaps at this stage of the argument some will be inclined to protest that though we cannot *imagine* matter as defined by Newton and Locke we can *conceive* of it in abstraction from secondary qualities. But Berkeley is prepared for this move; it involves, he thinks, Locke's doctrine of abstract ideas, and this, he believes, he can show to be absurd.

But let us not yet pursue the details of Berkeley's argument. First we should see that the line he takes is quite persuasive, independently of the particular form in which he presents it. Three-quarters of a century later, Kant will attack Berkeley's presentation of the argument as he understands it; but he too will argue that concepts can be applied only to phenomena and not to things in themselves, that we can think only about objects of possible experience, which certainly do not include matter. In the present century many have argued that of statements that purport to describe the world those alone were meaningful which were capable of verification and falsification by empirical means; but statements to the effect that what we experience is caused by an imperceptible matter are certainly unverifiable experimentally.

The argument may be put, as it was sometimes put by Berkeley, in a linguistic form. If we ask how we can come to understand, say, the word 'red', it would seem that, in principle, it can only be by somebody pointing to something red and saying 'That is red'—in principle, since clearly we learn such words by a less formal version of the same process; perhaps we hear somebody say to somebody else 'I do hate that shocking pink dress that that girl is wearing', we take a look at the dress, and say to ourselves 'So that is shocking pink, is it?' If one were ignorant of the game of rugby football, one could learn the meaning of the word 'scrum' by observing in what circumstances it is proper to say such things as 'A scrum has been formed' and so on. Of course, it is much more likely that we shall learn the meaning of such words at least partly by verbal explanation; but to verbal explanation an end must come. Some basic stock of words, it seems clear, must be learnt by confrontation with experience, before verbal explanation can begin.

But language can be abused. In Berkeley's own words, 'there are many names in use among speculative men which do not always suggest to others determinate, particular ideas, or in truth anything at all' (P, introduction, para. 19). The abuse may be conscious and in jest, as when a modern philosopher, being teased for requiring more sleep than most people, replied that she did not sleep more than other people, she simply slept more slowly. It may be hard to determine whether a use of words is an abuse; thus Newton spoke of absolute motion and contrasted it with relative motion; Berkeley in the *Principles* claimed that this was an abuse of words and that no meaning could be attached to the expression 'absolute motion'. Most scientists and philosophers since have followed Berkeley in this, but what Newton could not see could not be *obviously* right. But it is very hard to doubt that in some abstract disciplines, such as philosophy, meaning can become so rarified as to be undetectable.

It is clear that the word 'matter' has uses in which it is readily intelligible. As Berkeley represents Philonous as saying in the *Dialogues*: 'If by *material substance* is meant only *sensible body* . . . then I am more certain of matter's existence than you or any other philosopher pretend to be' (L ii 237). But the argument is that if matter is to be regarded as something inherently imperceptible then 'the Matter philosophers contend for is an incomprehensible Somewhat' (L ii 233). The word is familiar and so we overlook the fact that we have attenuated its meaning until it has vanished into thin air.

There is another argument that Berkeley uses against the intelligibility of matter which is rather more obviously unsatisfactory and rests on a confusion between the notions of substance and of matter. In this argument Berkeley very significantly refers to material substance rather than simply to matter. The essentials of this argument can readily be given in Berkeley's own words.

If we inquire into what the most accurate philosophers declare themselves to mean by *material substance*, we shall find them acknowledge they have no other meaning annexed to those sounds but the idea of Being in general, together with the relative notion of its supporting accidents. The general idea of Being appeareth to me the most abstract and incomprehensible of all other [, while] it is evident *support* cannot here be taken in its usual or literal sense, as when we say that pillars support a building. In what sense therefore must it be taken? For my part I am not able to discover any sense at all that can be applicable to it. (P 17)

In referring to 'the most accurate philosophers' Berkeley clearly has in mind principally John Locke and, indeed, the following passage from Locke's *Essay on Human Understanding*: 'If any one will examine himself concerning his notion of pure substance in general, he will find he has no other idea of it at all, but only a supposition of he knows not what support of such qualities which are capable of producing simple ideas in us.' But this is an admission, or, rather, a claim, that the notion of substance is ultimately unintelligible, not an admission that the notion of matter is in any way defective. Locke sees the same difficulty in the notion of substance whether we are talking about bodily or mental substances, as the following quotation shows: 'we have as clear a notion of the substance of spirit as we have of body: the one being supposed to be (without knowing what it is) the *substratum* to those simple ideas we have from without; and the other supposed (with a like ignorance of what it is) to be the *substratum* to those operations which we experiment in ourselves within'.

It is surely clear that the dubious intelligibility of the notion of substance as the mere somewhat that is the bearer of the qualities attributed to it cannot be properly taken to throw doubt on the concept of matter. Matter is not an indescribable somewhat supporting qualities but an imperceptible cause of perceptible ideas; both these views may be unacceptable, but, if so, the unacceptability of matter cannot be derived from the unacceptability of substance. The doctrine of matter is independent of the substance—attribute analysis of things, which appears only in Locke among the authorities we have quoted. By speaking of material substance so often Berkeley allows himself to confuse two distinct issues.

The superfluity of matter

We have seen Berkeley's reasons for wishing to maintain that the corpuscularian philosophers had been unsuccessful in their attempts to make their concept of an inherently imperceptible matter intelligible. It might have been the case that if matter were rejected a gap would be left and it would be necessary to postulate something else to fill the gap thus left. But Berkeley thought that this was not so; not only was matter unintelligible, but there was no gap to be filled: a complete and satisfying account of the world could be given without invoking it or any substitute for it.

If we look at Locke's inventory of the furniture of the world it would seem to include four elements:

1 God, the creator of everything else and the law-maker who determines the character and history of his creation.
2 Matter, which for certain purposes we may divide into that which impinges on our sense-organs to cause ideas and that which constitutes the sense-organs and nervous system on which other matter acts. But there is here no fundamental difference.
3 Ideas, which are mental but caused by the action of matter on the nervous system.
4 The mind that is aware of these ideas and operates on them and with them in thinking.

This ontology, which was shared in all essentials by Newton, most conspicuously lacks the physical object of common, everyday thought and discourse. We can, of course, still speak of chairs and tables; but on the physical side they are but dense collections of elementary corpuscles, and our seeing a chair or table is merely the occurrence of certain ideas caused by the particles emitted by such a collection. A further point to be noted is that the causal links between the elements in Locke's ontology are inexplicable. That the actions and purposes of God are inscrutable we may take for granted; but also the way in which matter acts on mind to produce ideas is scientifically inexplicable. A causal story in mechanistic terms can be given of particles being emitted from those collections of particles which constitute physical bodies; these particles strike on the eye or other sense-organs and by impact on the nerve-endings cause motion in the 'animal spirits' which were conjectured to be contained in the nerves; the motions of the animal spirits in the nerves is itself communicated to the brain; but how the motions of the particles that constitute the relevant portion of the brain cause the occurrence of ideas in the mind is not mechanically explicable (and perhaps modern physiology is equally powerless to offer an explanation). Locke gives an example: 'a violet, by the impulse of such insensible particles of matter of peculiar figures and bulks, and in different degrees and modifications of their motions, causes the ideas of the blue colour and sweet scent of that flower to be produced in our minds; it being no more impossible to conceive that God should annex such ideas to such motions with which they have no similitude, than that he should annex the idea of pain to the motion of a piece of steel dividing our flesh'. So Locke has to appeal to the direct action of God, without any scientific explanation of how the links in the causal chain are joined together.

If we look to see what reasons Locke had to offer for his belief in matter, we are bound to be disappointed. In the chapter entitled 'Of our knowledge of the existence of other things' in Book IV of his *Essay* he tells us that it can be gained only by sensation; but it is far from clear how knowledge of the existence of imperceptible matter could thus be gained. He tells us that our certainty is as great as our condition needs and, assuming that unless we posit matter we must consider waking to be indistinguishable from dreaming, tells the doubter that he 'doth but dream that he makes the question; and so it is not much matter that a waking man should answer him'. But knockabout humour is scarcely an adequate substitute for argument on such topics as these.

But Locke also says that 'it is plain those perceptions are produced in us by exterior causes affecting our senses', and it is this that Berkeley assumes to be the main argument that leads to a belief in matter. God, on this view, created matter to be the causal agency through which ideas are caused in sentient creatures. Thus, in the dialogues between Hylas and Philonous, when Hylas is driven to admit that he cannot sustain the notion of matter as conceived of by Locke and Newton, he falls back on the claim that matter is 'an instrument, subservient to the supreme Agent in the production of our ideas', and argues that he has some understanding of matter since 'I have some notion of *instrument in general*', which I apply to it.'

To this move Berkeley has a blistering retort, the essence of which can be given in the words given by Berkeley to Philonous:

'Is it not common to all instruments, that they are applied to the doing those things only which cannot be performed by the mere act of our wills? . . . How therefore can you suppose that an All-perfect Spirit, on whose Will all things have an absolute and immediate dependence, should need an instrument in his operation, or, not needing it, make use of it? . . . And the use of an instrument sheweth the agent to be limited by rules of another's prescription, and that he cannot obtain his end but in such a way, and by such conditions. Whence it seems a clear consequence, that the supreme unlimited Agent useth no tool or instrument at all.' (L ii 218–19)

This argument, of course, assumes that there is a God who is the omnipotent first cause; but, since those he was arguing against conceded it, Berkeley was entitled to make the assumption when arguing against them, especially as he had arguments for the existence of God in reserve. Given this basic assumption, the argument seems good. To postulate both God and matter as an explanation of our sense-experience seems to be superfluous, especially when it is agreed to be totally obscure why the hypothetical matter should cause sensations of the character that they do in fact have. Thus Berkeley at this point seems justified in claiming that the ontology of Locke is redundant and matter is superfluous. In the next two chapters we shall examine Berkeley's positive accounts of science and common sense without the aid of the concept of matter; but first we must consider one more attack on the materialists to which Berkeley attached great importance.

Abstract ideas

We have seen that it is basic to Berkeley's attack on matter to hold that to think of something is, ultimately, to imagine it.

Matter is unintelligible precisely because one could not see or imagine anything of the kind that matter is supposed to be, having primary qualities but lacking colour, smell, taste or sound. Berkeley is aware that at this stage some of his opponents, then as in our day, will want to claim that Berkeley's criteria of intelligibility are too restrictive. In the jargon of the philosophy of Berkeley's time the objection takes the form that while matter is not imaginable we can none the less have an abstract idea of matter. This Berkeley denies. Before we can consider the controversy we must try to understand the theory of abstract ideas, and this will be the objective of the next few pages.

It was a rarely questioned orthodoxy among the principal philosophers of the seventeenth and eighteenth centuries that thinking was primarily having ideas before the mind. That one can think in words was, of course, recognised, but language was regarded as being actually necessary only for purposes of communication with others. In Locke's typical words: 'The comfort and advantage of society not being to be had without communication of thoughts, it was necessary that man should find out some external sensible signs, whereby those invisible ideas which his thoughts are made up of might be made known to others.' One could think privately in words; but words stood to ideas as cheques do to real money, and cheques could be returned to drawer. All agreed that thinking in words could be dangerous—'Words often used without signification' is one of Locke's section headings.

With this view of the relation between thinking in ideas and thinking in words, which can indeed be traced back to Aristotle's *On Interpretation*, Berkeley was in full agreement. Moreover, he was convinced that most of the unintelligible metaphysics that he was attacking resulted from bogus thinking in meaningless words; the last eight paragraphs of his introduction to the *Principles* are devoted to explaining that this is so. In paragraph 21 of this introduction he writes:

Most parts of knowledge have been so strangely perplexed and darkened by the abuse of words, and general ways of speech wherein they are delivered, that it may almost be made a question whether language has contributed more to the hindrance or advancement of the sciences. Since words are so apt to impose on the understanding, I am resolved in my inquiries to make as little use of them as possibly I can: whatever ideas I consider, I shall endeavour to take them bare and naked into my view; keeping out of my thoughts, so far as I am able, those names which long and constant use hath so strictly united with them.

But what is it to think in bare and naked ideas? It is clear that basically ideas were thought of as mental images, and 'image' or 'picture' was the normal seventeenth-century meaning of 'idea' in non-philosophical writing also. Even the rationalistic Descartes, who was mainly responsible for the wide currency of the word 'idea' in philosophy, said that 'some of our thoughts are like pictures of things, to which alone the name idea is properly suited'. Both Berkeley and Hume clearly regard thinking in ideas to consist in having mental images, and for Locke too, at least when alleged abstract ideas are not involved, it seems that ideas are normally mental images; he can speak of 'ideas or images' as if the terms were interchangeable.

But it is not clear what thinking in mental images is supposed to be. Just having a mental image does not seem to be enough. One may, for example, have a mental image which is approximately round and red, but this on its own scarcely seems to be a thought about anything. Let us suppose that this red and round image has a close resemblance to a tomato, since there is no doubt that the philosophers with whom we are concerned believed that resemblance made the idea an appropriate way of thinking about some object. But if the occurrence of the idea is a thought, and indeed a thought having some reference to tomatoes, it remains unclear what thought about tomatoes it is. Let us make a list of possible candidates, expressed in verbal form:

This is a tomato; Tomatoes are red; That tomato was red and round; Some tomatoes are red; The tomato is a fruit; Is this a tomato? Some round objects are red.

Which, if any, of these, and of countless other possible candidates, is the appropriate verbalisation of the thought one thinks when one has before one's mind the round, red image resembling a tomato?

The difficulty can be approached from the opposite direction. Let us suppose that one is to have the thought 'This is white' in the form of an idea or mental image. Now if we summon up a white mental image it cannot be just white and have no other characteristics; it must presumably be bright or drab, round or of some other shape, with this or that background. Let us suppose that it is bright and round as well as white, and now the problem is what determines that the occurrence of the idea constitutes the thought 'This is white' rather than the thought 'This is bright' or 'This is round', if, indeed, it constitutes any of them.

These difficulties were to some extent seen, though not with exemplary clarity, by Locke among others. He, relying heavily on *The Art of Thinking* by Descartes' friend and collaborator, the theologian Arnauld (1612–94), made use of the notion of abstract ideas to try to solve some of them. Most of our thinking requires abstract ideas, according to Locke. He holds that of the words of the English language only proper names signify concrete or particular ideas; all other words which stand for any idea at all stand for abstract ideas. So abstract ideas are as essential to non-verbal thought as words other than proper names are essential to its verbal expression.

What then is an abstract idea? Locke tells us four times in his *Essay*, in Book II, Chapter xi, Section 9, Book II, Chapter xii, Section 1, Book III, Chapter iii, Sections 6 and 10 and Book IV, Chapter vii, Section 9. Of these the first three are very similar to each other; since Berkeley in his violent attack on abstract ideas quotes only the final and most paradoxical account from Book IV, we should perhaps note what these other concurring accounts say. In Book II Chapter xi we read:

The mind makes the particular *ideas*, received from particular objects, to become general; which is done by considering them as they are in the mind such appearances, separate from all other existences, and the circumstances of real existence, as time, place, or any other, concomitant *ideas*. This is called ABSTRACTION, whereby *ideas* taken from particular beings become general representatives of all of the same kind; and their names general names, applicable to whatever exists conformable to such abstract *ideas*. Such precise, naked appearances in the mind, without considering how, whence, or with what others they came there, the understanding lays up (with names commonly annexed to them) as the standards to rank real existence into sorts, as they agree with these patterns, and to *denominate* them accordingly. Thus the same colour being observed today in chalk or snow, which the mind yesterday received from milk, it considers that appearance alone, makes it a representative of all of that kind; and having given it the name *whiteness*, it by that sound signifies the same quality wheresoever to be imagined or met with; and thus universals, whether *ideas* or terms, are made.

This is not entirely unambiguous, for it is not clear what considering whiteness separately involves. If it is simply a matter of disregarding all other features of the idea, then a white, bright and round image can be used as the abstract idea of white by simply ignoring the other features and treating it as the general representative of everything having this feature. Similarly the same image could have been made the abstract idea of brightness, if we had chosen to disregard the whiteness and other features. Presumably it could have been made the general idea of colour by disregarding the differences between it and red or green images. While this is by no means a full and adequate explanation, we do have here some indication of how having a red and round mental image could constitute the occurrence of a thought and of one particular thought rather than another. In principle, the answer is that it becomes such as a result of some rule-like decision; a red and round image may become the thought of a tomato if we decide to treat this image as the general representative of all things having the characteristics of a tomato.

But there is another possible interpretation of Locke's words, in which the word 'separate' is taken more literally. On this interpretation, when Locke speaks of separating the colour of milk from all other circumstances and ideas he is demanding that we should have an image of which the only possible description is that it is white. On this interpretation it would seem that he is demanding the evidently impossible and, since it is better to interpret an author as making sense when it is possible plausibly to do so, we may well prefer the first interpretation.

Berkeley, however, quotes only the perplexing words of Book IV of Locke's *Essay*, in which the following extract occurs:

Does it not require some pains and skill to form the *general idea* of a *triangle* (which is yet none of the most abstract . . .), for it must be neither oblique nor rectangle, neither equilateral, equicrural, nor scalenon; but all and none of these at once. In effect, it is something imperfect that cannot exist, an *idea* wherein some parts of several different and inconsistent ideas are put together.

Berkeley has a good deal of fun from this. In his notebooks he had written: 'Mem. To bring the killing blow at the last, e.g. in the matter of abstraction to bring Locke's general triangle in the last' (C 687). He refers to it sarcastically as sublime speculations. It seemed to him to be self-evidently absurd.

But, once again, it is possible to interpret Locke here as making better sense, regarding the literal absurdities in his account as rhetoric in a purple passage glorifying the rational powers of mankind. If we ask whether the concept of a triangle includes being isosceles or scalene, the answer is that it includes neither, since it is possible to deny either of them of some triangles; in this sense the abstract idea of *triangle* is of something neither scalene nor isosceles. If we ask whether the concept of a triangle excludes being isosceles or scalene, the answer is that it excludes neither, since it is possible to assert either of them of some triangles; in this sense the abstract idea of triangle includes both being isosceles and being scalene. But since nothing can be merely triangular without being either equilateral, scalene or isosceles, being *triangular* cannot be a complete account of any existent thing. Thus Locke's rhetoric may be taken as illustrating the character of a generic concept which covers several species, though it must be owned that his wording invites misunderstanding if I have correctly interpreted him.

Rightly or wrongly, however, Berkeley regards the doctrine of abstract ideas as requiring there to be mental image of an essentially indeterminate nature, and this he regards as absurd. Even if there is the possibility of some degree of indeterminacy of images (if we imagine a speckled hen must it have some definite number of speckles?), still the notion of an image which is merely, say, white and nothing else is indeed absurd, and Berkeley is surely right in rejecting the doctrine of abstract ideas as he interprets it.

Given this view of the theory of abstract ideas, two points now need to be discussed. First, why does Berkeley think that the theory aids and promotes the metaphysics of materialism; secondly, what account does Berkeley give of thinking non-verbally without the aid of abstract ideas?

It is basic to Berkeley's position to claim that matter as described verbally by the corpuscularians is unintelligible since we cannot imagine anything which has primary qualities but including no ideas of secondary qualities. We cannot, for example, visualise a colourless expanse. He also thinks that, while some would claim to think of unperceived objects, it is obviously impossible to imagine an unperceived object, to separate existence from being perceived. What Berkeley is doing in his attack on abstract ideas is to counter the move that, while matter is not imaginable, it is none the less conceivable, since we can have an abstract idea of extension without colour, just as we can have, as Locke explained, an abstract idea of whiteness. In the same way, says Berkeley's imaginary opponent, we can conceive of an object existing unperceived, since we can abstract existence from perception and imagination.

Given Berkeley's interpretation of abstract ideas, which surely does make them indefensible, it is clear that he is right in thinking that the intelligibility of matter cannot be defended by an appeal to them. What I find odd is the claim of Berkeley that the doctrine of abstract ideas was closely connected with the belief in matter. I can think of no place where Locke or any other philosopher made use of the doctrine of abstract ideas to defend the intelligibility of matter. Moreover, if the alternative account of this doctrine which I have put forward is correct, the doctrine could not be used in this way. As I understand Locke, he is explaining not how whiteness, for example, can be conceived of as existing on its own, but how we can think of whiteness as distinct from the other features that any white thing would have; so the fact that we can think of the primary qualities without thinking of colour or taste could not be consistently regarded by Locke as a ground for believing in the existence of colourless and tasteless matter. It is not clear that Locke ever saw the problem of the intelligibility of matter on an empiricist hypothesis, or *a fortiori*, that he ever defended it. It was one of Berkeley's achievements to see the problem.

So Berkeley will have no truck with abstract ideas. But he does recognise that he must give some account of generality. If, as Berkeley seems to think, we can give an adequate account of thinking of a triangle—some particular triangle—in terms of having an image of it, what account is he to give of the thought of all triangles? He starts to do this in the introduction to the *Principles* by making a distinction between a special kind of idea, called an abstract idea, which cannot exist, and a general idea which is not a special kind of idea, but simply an ordinary idea or mental image that fulfils a special function. Generality, he holds, is a kind of role, not an internal characteristic. An idea is made general 'by being made to represent or stand for all particular ideas of the same sort' (para. 12). He illustrates his meaning with an example drawn from geometry. A geometer will prove some theorem with reference to some particular line; but the proof is general because, though it is one particular line, 'as it is there used, it represents all particular lines whatever', and Berkeley takes this proof to be the same as one concerning 'a line in general'. General ideas are on a par with the drawn line of the geometer.

Berkeley is surely right in claiming that a sign becomes general not by acquiring a peculiar character but by being used in a certain way. A full discussion is impossible here, but one or two difficulties may be mentioned. First, Berkeley says, in a quotation given in our previous paragraph, that the general idea is to represent all particular ideas 'of the same sort'. But, if I have before my mind some particular idea of, say, a line, how am I to know whether it is representative of all lines or of all short lines, or of all straight lines, or of all geometrical figures, or . . .? If it is to be representative of all *lines*, do I perhaps need to have the general idea of a line already to determine what is of the same sort and so what the line represents? But this clearly leads to a vicious regress.

The second difficulty is one which beset all the theorists who used the terminology of ideas. If we consider verbal thought we can readily distinguish between the words we use, which we may call the thought-vehicle, and the object of thought. If I think 'The cat is on the mat', the thought-vehicle is that set of five words, and the object of thought an animal. I can, of course, think about words in words, as when I think of 'The cat is on the mat' that it contains five words. But still the words which are the thought-vehicle are readily distinguished from the words which are the object of thought. Now if we regard the objects of our experience as being really ideas and not cats and mats, and if we call thinking the having of ideas, then we call the thought-vehicle and all objects of thought by the same name, 'idea'. Confusion can easily result, and historically it did.

Will an image in the mind of Berkeley's geometer, working 'in his head', be a thought-vehicle or the object of thought? Will the line be the non-verbal equivalent of the word 'line'? But the proof in words is not about the word 'line', and so the proof in non-verbal form should not be about the non-verbal equivalent of the word; *a fortiori*, the proof in neither case should be about it and everything of the same sort. We have got to distinguish between a line used as an iconic symbol to represent lines and one of the representative lines which it iconically represents. The word 'represent' is surely, as illustrated here, dangerously ambiguous in Berkeley's account.

So this chapter must end with two questions. First, does Berkeley succeed in giving an adequate alternative to Locke's account of general ideas in terms of abstraction? Secondly, if we take the alternative interpretation of Locke's theory which was suggested earlier in this discussion, does it not conform to Berkeley's requirement that generality be a question of function rather than of its internal character? Perhaps it is what Berkeley needs, when it is so interpreted. But generality is a very difficult subject which intensive modern study has still left full of difficulties. Nobody in the time of Locke and Berkeley had the conceptual apparatus to give an adequate account of it.

3

Immaterialism and common sense

S O BERKELEY has claimed that matter is unintelligible. We cannot imagine anything like it any more than we can observe it, and the invocation of abstract ideas by means of which we may think of the unimaginable involves absurdity. In so far as we allow matter to be vaguely intelligible as a tool or instrument of God we can see that, thought of as such a tool, it is superfluous: 'to what end should God take these roundabout methods of effecting things by instruments and machines, which no one can deny might have been effected by the mere command of His will, without all that apparatus?' (P 61). Moreover, even those who, like Locke, postulate the existence of matter acknowledge that they cannot explain the character of our experience by reference to matter; physics cannot explain why certain pulsations of the air cause heard sound or why in certain physical conditions we see one colour rather than another, or, indeed, why we see any colour at all. The most that Locke can plead is that it is 'no more impossible to conceive that God should annex such ideas to such motions with which they have no similitude, than that he should annex the idea of pain to the motion of a piece of steel dividing our flesh'; but, says Berkeley 'how Matter should operate on a Spirit, or procure any idea in it, is what no philosopher will pretend to explain' (P 50). Berkeley also wished to claim that the only causal agency that was intelligible was of the kind we know in acting ourselves, as when we summon up one idea or another; all we witness in the physical world is succession, regular or irregular, so that the causal agency of matter was yet another unintelligible postulate.

So on all counts it seemed clear to Berkeley that in the ontology of Locke, Newton and their associates matter was indefensible and superfluous. They themselves were ready to admit that matter without God yielded no satisfactory explanation of the world. So Berkeley claims that a complete account of the world can be

given in terms of the remainder of the Newtonian ontology—
God, finite spirits and their ideas. In a famous formulation of
this doctrine Berkeley said that to exist is either to perceive
(*percipere*), which consitutes the existence of spirits, or to be
perceived (*percipi*), which constitutes the existence of the inanimate, of ideas. These perceived ideas are objects of the mind
which have no existence independent of the mind. So the world
is ultimately spiritual; there is nothing beyond minds and their
contents.

At least at first sight, this is an outrageous doctrine, one which
is incompatible not only with the presuppositions of science but
also with common sense. It seems to deny the existence both of
the matter which the physical sciences investigate and of the
familiar objects of the everyday world, the chairs and tables, the
mountains, plains and rivers which surround us and which we all
believe to exist independently of ourselves. It is manifestly contrary to common sense to say that bodies do not exist when we
do not observe them.

Berkeley was prepared to agree that if his views were incompatible with common sense and made science impossible they
would be unacceptable. What makes his philosophy interesting
is that he claims that his ontology is perfectly compatible with
both common sense and religious beliefs and that, while it admittedly contradicts a metaphysical presupposition of the scientists, he can give a satisfactory account of the nature and value
of the sciences without invoking the hypothesis of matter. Moreover, he develops this claim with such ingenuity that it has always
been notoriously difficult to refute him.

We shall start by expounding in this chapter Berkeley's arguments designed to show that he can on his basis account for all
that common sense requires. In the next chapter we shall look
to see what account he can give of the nature of science on his
immaterialist hypothesis. Finally we shall consider what account
he can give of God and of finite spirits. Since this topic is being
so long postponed for full treatment one or two preliminary
words on it are perhaps desirable now. One of the first objections
to Berkeley which are likely to occur to his readers is that if
matter is unimaginable and if for this reason we can have no idea
of it, so also is God unimaginable and even finite spirits. So is
not God also an unintelligible absurdity on Berkeley's own prin-

ciples? This is a difficulty; Berkeley was aware of it and he tried to meet it. So the reader is asked for the present not to question Berkeley's acceptance of God and finite spirits but to consider only whether he can give a satisfactory account of commonsense belief and of science in terms of these spirits, their activities and their ideas.

Berkeley consistently claims that one of the great merits of his position is that it is wholly compatible with common sense. In his private notebooks he frequently reminds himself that he must emphasise this in his published work, as is clear from the following quotations:

All things in the Scripture which side with the vulgar against the learned, side with me also. I side in all things with the mob.

I must be very particular in explaining what is meant by things existing... when not perceived as well as when perceived; and shew how the vulgar notion agrees with mine.

Mem. To be eternally banishing Metaphysics, etc., and recalling men to common sense.

Mem. That I take notice that I do not fall in with the sceptics... in that I make bodies to exist certainly, which they doubt of. (C 405, 408, 751,79)

In this claim he never wavers. Thus in the first of the dialogues between Hylas and Philonous he even makes conformity to common sense the touchstone of acceptability. 'Well then,' says Philonous, 'are you content to admit that opinion for true, which upon examination shall appear most agreeable to Common Sense, and remote from Scepticism?' (L ii 172). To this Hylas agrees.

In claiming that he is in accord with common sense Berkeley clearly cannot mean that the common man has always been aware of and has always accepted a philosophical position identical with his own. He himself says that while we should 'speak with the vulgar' we should 'think with the learned', and he acknowledges that 'it is indeed an opinion strangely prevailing among men, that houses, mountains, rivers, and in a word all sensible objects, have an existence, natural or real, distinct from their being perceived by the understanding' (P 4). This view, as distinct from the philosophical doctrine of matter, is clearly attributed to the common man by Berkeley, and with good reason. Rather, it appears, he is making the following twofold claim: first, that Berkeley himself is committed to no positive claims about the world which are not already assented to by common sense, unlike the followers of the corpuscularian philosophy, who have introduced imperceptible matter; secondly, that given any belief of common sense expressed in the common non-technical language of everyday life, he can provide an alternative statement of that belief in terms of his basic hypothesis, equivalent to the commonsense statement in the sense that it would be impossible to imagine a state of the world which would make one of them true when the other was false. Berkeley, it seems clear, was not claiming that the common man was already aware of these equivalent formulations before Berkeley formulated them. As we shall see, he himself had at times considerable difficulty in deciding what reformulation was most acceptable and accurate. He was claiming to be able to provide what such more modern philosophers as Susan Stebbing and John Wisdom would have called a metaphysical or new-level analysis of the statements of common sense, and, as G. E. Moore constantly said, one may know the truth of a statement and understand it without being able to give its analysis.

Berkeley, then, claims that he can give an adequate analysis of commonsense beliefs in terms of an infinite spirit—God—finite spirits and mind-dependent ideas. He is well aware of the apparent difficulties in this position and lists them in paragraphs 34 onwards in the *Principles*:

First, then, it will be objected that by the foregoing principles all that is real and substantial in nature is banished out of the world, and instead thereof a chimerical scheme of *ideas* takes place.

Secondly, it will be objected that there is a great difference betwixt real fire, for instance, and the idea of fire, betwixt dreaming or imagining oneself burnt, and actually being so.

Thirdly, it will be objected that we see things actually without or at a distance from us, and which consequently do not exist in the mind.

Fourthly, it will be objected that from the foregoing principles it follows things are every moment annihilated and created anew.

We can learn to understand Berkeley's position no better than by considering why, in his view, it is immune to these objections.

How, then, if there are but spirits and their ideas, can there be a distinction between a real world and the world of dreams, of fantasy and of illusion? Surely the difference is that the world of dreams or fantasy or illusion is indeed only within our minds, and the real world independent of them? But Berkeley denies this. The difference is not between mind-dependent ideas on the one hand and something outside the mind on the other but between ideas having a certain nature, relation to each other and relation to ourselves, and ideas having a quite different nature, relation to each other and relation to ourselves. First, they differ normally in their nature; the ideas of imagination or dreaming or memory are less strong, lively and distinct than those of sense which constitute the real world. Secondly, they differ in their relation to us; the ideas of imagination and memory are brought before our minds by our own decision, whereas the ideas of sense are independent of our will. I can decide to think about trees, for example, but whether I see a tree when I open my eyes is quite beyond my control. Thirdly, the ideas of sense have 'a steadiness, order and coherence, and are not excited at random, as those which are the effects of human wills often are, but in a regular train or series' (P 30). In dream, imagination or illusion anything can happen, but in the real world the train of ideas is determined by the laws of nature.

Berkeley cannot claim, nor does he need to claim, that all these three types of difference are always observable; unlike imagination, dream and illusion have a content over which we have no control, for example. But he does want to claim that at least one of these differences will always be present and that awareness of them is the way, the only way, in which reality can be distinguished from illusion or other forms of unreality. How, for example, does Macbeth determine that the dagger that he sees is unreal? Here are Shakespeare's words that he puts into the mouth of Macbeth:

> Is this a dagger which I see before me,
> The handle toward my hand? Come, let me clutch thee!
> I have thee not, and yet I see thee still.
> Art thou not, fatal vision, sensible
> To feeling as to sight? or art thou but
> A dagger of the mind, a false creation
> Proceeding from the heat-oppressed brain?

Clearly Macbeth determines that the dagger is an illusion, not by finding (how could he?) that it has a status independent of his mind, but by finding that his ideas of sight and touch lack the coherence which would be necessary for the experience to count as experience of reality. Berkeley wants to claim that he can make the distinctions that common sense makes in his own terms and that in fact common sense makes the distinctions in precisely the ways that he describes. So the distinction between reality and the merely subjective is not just *detected* by the features Berkeley has mentioned, acting as clues; certain trains of ideas *count as* experience of reality while others do not, 'by which is meant', Berkeley claims, 'that they are more affecting, orderly and distinct, and they are not fictions of the mind perceiving them' (P 36). To be real and to have these features are, for Berkeley, one and the same thing. Berkeley is giving a reductionist analysis, not giving us hints on how to check up on our experience.

This is an appropriate place to pause and make for the first, but not the last, time the point that there is an important distinction to be made between Berkeley's analysis of commonsense beliefs in terms of ideas and his metaphysics. Berkeley certainly thinks that the metaphysical explanation of why some ideas have coherence, liveliness and independence of our wills is because God, the infinite spirit, causes them. Thus metaphysically reality is to be explained in terms of the activity of God; but the analysis of what we mean when we ascribe reality to something does not contain, as we have seen, any reference to God. This distinction is often ignored and Berkeley is frequently represented as bringing God into his analysis when he does not. Berkeley gives on the whole what may be counted as a positivistic analysis of commonsense beliefs, a fact which is perfectly compatible with the fact that he offers a theocentric metaphysic to explain why our experience has the character that it has. We should not underestimate the importance of God in Berkeley's thought, but we also should not misrepresent Berkeley as holding that talk about chairs and tables is to be analysed as talk about the deity.

Berkeley's treatment of the third objection, that what we see is at a distance from us and therefore cannot be within our minds, is the occasion for us to consider very briefly Berkeley's *A New Theory of Vision*, in which he is concerned to state how by the sense of sight we are able to judge distance. Berkeley was clear that distance had to be judged and could not be seen: 'For, distance being a line directed endwise to the eye, it projects only one point in the fund of the eye, which point remains invariably the same, whether the distance be longer or shorter' (V 2). If we judge distance it is not, he holds, as some have thought, in virtue of the difference of the angles of the eye in binocular vision, for we are not aware of the angles of the eyes when we judge distance, nor do we need to be. Nor do we ultimately judge from sensations in the eye, such as, perhaps, a sense of strain when we look at a thing close up. For we rather learn from experience that we experience the strain when the object is close and so must have another means of determining that the object is close.

Berkeley's own solution to this problem is in terms of a correlation between sight and touch. In the *New Theory of Vision* he gives this solution as though by touch we were aware of objects outside us in a real physical space, since, as he says in the *Principles*, he is there concerned with vision alone and not with the fundamentals of epistemology. More accurately, we should speak of a correlation of ideas of touch with ideas of vision. Though we speak of being aware of shape by both sight and touch, Berkeley maintains that the visual idea of, say, a rectangle and a tactual idea of a rectangle are quite distinct and we learn only from experience that given the one idea the other will accompany it. A great controversy raged about a question which the Dublin lawyer Molyneux set in a letter to his friend Locke:

Suppose a man born blind and now adult, and taught by his touch to distinguish between a cube and a sphere of the same metal, and nighly of the same bigness, so as to tell, when he felt one and the other, which is the cube, which the sphere. Suppose then the cube and sphere placed on a table, and the blind man to be made to see; query, whether by his sight, before he touched them, he could now distinguish and tell which is the globe, which the cube?

To this question Berkeley, like Locke and Molyneux himself, gave the unequivocal answer 'No.' Now if we suppose that it will take more time, in similar conditions, to get the tactual idea of something round than to get the tactual idea of something rectangular, then the visual idea of the rectangular will be regarded as more distant than the visual idea of the round. This correlation of sight and touch is fundamental, in Berkeley's view. But on this basis we learn to judge distance in terms of the visual appearances of things; thus if one thing having the general look of a ping-pong ball looks larger than something that looks like a tennis ball we shall judge the ping-pong ball to be much nearer.

Thus Berkeley claims that the judgement of distance does not require us to posit an external space. Furthermore the appearance of relative distance from us can be exhibited by objects of imagination, which no one supposes to be in some real space, just as much as by the objects of the senses.

What then of the fourth difficulty that Berkeley mentioned, about the continued existence of ordinary physical bodies like chairs and tables and mountains and rivers? This difficulty has been expressed in a well-known limerick:

> There was a young man who said 'God
> Must think it exceedingly odd
> If he finds that this tree
> Continues to be
> When there's no one about in the Quad.'

The author of this limerick, Monsignor Ronald Knox, also produced another limerick which purports to offer Berkeley's solution to the problem and runs as follows:

> Dear Sir:
>   Your astonishment's odd;
> I am always about in the Quad.
> And that's why the tree
> Will continue to be,
> Since observed by
>   *Yours faithfully*,
>   GOD.

This view, which makes Berkeley locate the continuous existence of bodies in their eternal and continuous perception by God, is, I suppose, the orthodox interpretation of Berkeley on this topic. But it is at best a misleading and inadequate account of Berkeley's view. Certainly Berkeley held that metaphysically the existence of unobserved trees depended on the activity of God; but then he held that metaphysically the existence of observed trees and finite observers depended on the activity of God. But, as has already been said, we must distinguish between Berkeley's metaphysical view that all existence was dependent on God and his analytical views about the meaning of statements. There is very little, if any, evidence that Berkeley believed that, when we assert the existence of some unobserved object, what we mean is something about the observations of God; there is, on the contrary, a lot of evidence that he did not. So the rest of this chapter will be devoted to the discovery of what his views on this topic were. How could Berkeley, the immaterialist, allow the commonsense assumption that bodies exist continuously, whether perceived or unperceived?

This inquiry is both instructive and amusing. For Berkeley's great insight had been the negative one of the non-existence of matter. His initial claim that this insight was compatible with common sense was an act of faith, for he had at that stage no idea what account he should give of bodies. He tried out many theories, some plausible and ingenious, some very crude and unconvincing, before giving his final answer to the question in the third and last of the dialogues between Hylas and Philonous.

We find a number of mutually incompatible and unplausible suggestions about the nature of body in the private notebooks. Here, for example is a particularly ill-conceived one:

We see the house itself, the church itself; it being an idea and nothing more. The house itself, the church itself, is an idea, i.e. an object—immediate object—of thought. (C 427, 427a)

But, clearly, to identify an object with some single idea will not do. For if I look three times at what common sense would call a house I have, in Berkeley's terminology, three separate ideas; if we identify the house with the ideas then I shall have seen not one but three houses, each of which will have only a fleeting existence.

Here is another suggestion from the same notebooks, one almost as unfortunate as the one just considered:

You ask me whether the books are in the study now, when no one is there to see them? I answer, Yes. You ask me, Are we not in the wrong for imagining things to exist when they are not actually perceived by the senses? I answer, No. The existence of our ideas consists in being perceiv'd, imagin'd, thought on. Whenever they are mentioned or discours'd of they are imagin'd & thought on. Therefore you can at no time ask me whether they exist or no, but by reason of that very question they must necessarily exist. (C 472)

The ghost of this argument continued to haunt Berkeley in later writing; but he had no sooner written it down than he began to feel uneasy about it. The next note reads as follows:

But, say you, a chimaera does exist? I answer, it doth in one sense, i.e. it is imagin'd. But it must be well noted that existence is vulgarly restrain'd to actual perception, and that I use the word existence in a larger sense than ordinary. (C 473)

This is, at best, a very half-hearted defence from one who claims to side with the vulgar against the learned.

But, on the whole, these early notebooks incline to phenomenalism. Bodies are to be what they were for Mill in his classical formulation of phenomenalism, permanent possibilities of sensation. Just how honestly one could claim that phenomenalism coincided with common sense did worry Berkeley, as it has worried many other phenomenalists, but he tried to stifle these doubts, as the following quotation shows:

Mem. To allow existence to colours in the dark . . . but not an actual existence. 'Tis prudent to correct men's mistakes without altering their language. This makes truth glide into their souls insensibly. Colours in the dark do exist really, i.e. were there light, or as soon as light comes, we shall see them, provided we open our eyes; and that whether we will or no. (C 185, 185a)

What he says about colours he also says about bodies:

Bodies &c. do exist whether we think of 'em or no, they being taken in a twofold sense—
   1. Collections of thoughts.
   2. Collections of powers to cause these thoughts. (C 282)

If an explanation of what he means here by powers is needed, he immediately gives it, again in a purely positivistic vein:

Bodies taken for powers do exist when not perceived; but this existence is not actual. When I say a power exists, no more is meant than that if in the light I open my eyes, and look that way, I shall see it, i.e. the body &c. (C 293a)

Even when Berkeley was writing the *Principles* he had still not really made up his mind what to say about the continued existence of bodies. Here we have a thoroughly phenomenalistic story:

The table I write on I say exists; that is, I see and feel it; and if I were out of my study I should say it existed; meaning thereby that if I were in my study I might perceive it, or that some other spirit actually does perceive it. (P 3)

Here 'some other spirit' is written without the capitals which Berkeley always uses when referring to God—it surely means merely 'somebody else' and not God specifically. But over the page in the sixth paragraph we get the one case that I have noticed of Berkeley putting forward the view assigned to him by Ronald Knox in the limerick quoted above. Having reaffirmed that nothing exists outside a mind, he says of bodies:

Consequently so long as they are not actually perceived by me, or do not exist in my mind, or of any other created spirit, they must either have no existence at all, or else subsist in the mind of some Eternal Spirit. (P 60)

Here we do have the capital E and capital S. It is unambiguously stated that, when not perceived by finite spirits, bodies, if they exist at all, must be in the mind of God; and this obviously and flatly contradicts the phenomenalistic story he has already given, unless we can claim that Berkeley has without warning moved from analysis to metaphysics.

There are two principal objections to the analysis of statements about physical objects in terms of the ideas in the mind of God, independently of doubts about God's existence. First, it is surely clear that the statement that God does not exist but that there are unobserved physical objects is not self-contradictory, even if it is false; when we speak of physical objects we do not thereby say anything about God. The second objection arises from the Christian theology which Berkeley accepted and needs explaining at a little more length.

It is a commonplace of theology that God is eternal and un-changing. The notion of an unchanging person may be difficult, but for the present all we need to understand by it is that God does not in time come to have ideas or thoughts which he had not had previously. It is another commonplace of theology, based theologically on the first chapter of the book of Genesis but no doubt confirmable by paleontological investigation, that God created the inanimate—the earth, the sea and the heavenly bodies—before he created on earth any living creatures. But if the existence of physical bodies consists in their being objects in the mind of God, then physical objects have existed from all eternity and were not created at all; and the existence of physical objects can also not consist in their being actually ideas of finite spirits, since they were created before finite spirits.

So it would seem that if we accept the doctrine of creation, as Berkeley certainly did, the permanent existence of physical bodies cannot consist in their being actual objects of thought or perception either by an infinite or by finite spirits. It seems that Berkeley did not become fully aware of this problem until he wrote the three dialogues between Hylas and Philonous; there he meets it squarely in the third dialogue, and in doing so comes up with what, given his basic positions, philosophical and theological, must be the most satisfactory answer possible. The solution, stated baldly, is this; God has, indeed, all his ideas from all eternity, and this in no way constitutes the existence of physical bodies. When God created the physical universe his creation consisted in his ordaining that from that time forward ideas of the physical should be available to finite spirits if any; this ordinance was valid even before there were finite spirits, just as criminal laws are valid even if there are no criminals. So the existence of physical objects consists in the relevant ideas being available. Physical objects are permanent possibilities of sensation—that is the analysis—and this possibility exists because God ordains that it should—that is the metaphysical explanation of this possibility.

Thus the phenomenalist analysis prevails in the end, and in a form superior to earlier versions. Berkeley's phenomenalist analysis at the beginning of the *Principles*, already quoted, starts: 'The table I write on I say exists; that is, I see and feel it' (P 3). He goes on to allow for its existence when he is not in his study; but it surely is clear that we never (*never*) assert that we are actually observing an object when we assert its existence, even if as a matter of fact we are observing it. So as an analysis the account in terms of the possibility of ideas alone is clearly preferable and seems to be about the best version of phenomenalism that it is possible to formulate. On the whole it is true that the *Three Dialogues* are largely a more popular version of ideas that are more accurately and fully developed in the *Principles*. But when Berkeley, in the third dialogue, wrote: 'things, with regard to us, may properly be said to begin their existence, or be created, when God decreed they should become perceptible to intelligent creatures, in that order and manner which He then established, and we now call the laws of nature' (L ii 253), he was surely making an advance on what he had previously written.

We may close this chapter on Berkeley's view of the physical world with a look at a famous, or perhaps notorious, attempt by Berkeley to prove that it is impossible to conceive of bodies existing independently of minds. He repeats it more than once in very similar language and I quote it now from paragraph 23 of the *Principles*:

But, say you, surely there is nothing easier than for me to imagine trees, for instance, in a park, or books existing in a closet, and nobody by to perceive them. I answer, you may so, there is no difficulty in it. But what is all this, I beseech you, more than framing in your mind certain ideas which you call *books* and *trees*, and at the same time omitting to frame the idea of any one that may perceive them? But do you not yourself perceive or think of them all the while? This therefore is nothing to the purpose; it only shews you have the power of imagining, or forming ideas in your mind; but it does not shew that you can conceive it possible the objects of your thought may exist without the mind. To make this out, it is necessary that you conceive them existing unconceived or unthought of; which is a manifest repugnancy.

This is surely fallacious; certainly it is not possible that a body be conceived of and at the same time both exist and not be conceived of, just as God cannot be conceived of and at the same time exist and not be conceived of, and just as a chair cannot be kicked and at the same time exist unkicked. If one is thinking of a chair then it does not exist unthought of. But this has no tendency to show that the concept of an unthought-of chair has any logical deficiencies.

So Berkeley cannot prove that it is logically necessary to concede that body is ultimately mind-dependent. But he can surely claim to have made a very plausible effort to show that his view gives common sense everything it needs. Our experience of the world, as it actually occurs, cannot be different from how it would be on a Berkeleian view, since our experience of it just is the sequence of ideas of which Berkeley speaks. Any apparent discrepancy will not disprove Berkeley's view in principle, but will merely show that it has been mis-stated. We might perhaps believe that we could catch Berkeley out by taking a photograph of the interior of a room by remote control when there is nobody in the room. But Berkeley is perfectly able to accept that we shall have the requisite series of ideas called looking at a photograph of an empty room in the given circumstances; that is part of the order of nature. Berkeley can well ask what more we want. Occam's razor tells us not to multiply entities beyond necessity, and all that Berkeley is taking away from us, he claims, is a hidden machinery which is a totally superfluous hypothesis, in so far as it is at all intelligible.

If we do imagine that Berkeley speaks to us in some such words as those we may be tempted to reply as follows: even if it be true that the hypothesis is superfluous at the level of everyday life, in science it is not superfluous. So far from the material world being a something we know not what, science is continually discovering more and more about it and, in virtue of our knowledge of its nature, we are able to predict and engineer new marvels which would otherwise be unknown. How could man make the atom bomb if there were no atoms, and how could he predict it from a superfluous and empty hypothesis? We might be tempted to say this because it is a very natural, not to say obvious, thing to say at this stage. Being natural and obvious, the thought has occurred to Berkeley also. Our objection would not have caught him unprepared and he answered it in advance to his own satisfaction. In the next chapter we shall examine what account of the nature of the empirical sciences Berkeley was able to give on his principles.

4

The nature of empirical science

'MEM. Much to recommend and approve of experimental philosophy' said Berkeley in his private notebooks (C 498). This was no piece of window-dressing. Berkeley's interest in experimental science, or experimental philosophy as he called it in accordance with normal seventeenth- and eighteenth-century usage, was intense and genuine. His great admiration for Newton is expressed over and over again in his writings, and not only in those intended for publication. He had studied Newton's *Principia*—a very difficult work which very few could claim to understand with any ease—and probably the *Optics*. He never doubted that most of the experimental discoveries of Newton were true and valuable additions to human knowledge. So on the whole Berkeley had no desire to argue with the experimental scientists; most of his endeavours were directed to showing that the findings of science could and should be interpreted in a way which made them perfectly in accord with his philosophy and did not demand a belief in the independent material world. Criticism of Newton's experimental work is almost entirely confined to that small portion in which Newton claims to find empirical grounds for asserting the existence of absolute space and motion. Berkeley also criticised the mathematics that Newton had developed to state his arguments, in particular the theory of fluxions, but this topic will be discussed in a later chapter. The most important parts of Berkeley's works to consult on experimental philosophy are *Principles* 101–17 and the essay *De motu* (*On Motion*), which was originally published in Latin, but of which translations are available. There are also, as we shall see, some important remarks on the topic in Berkeley's very late work intriguingly entitled *Siris: a Chain of Philosophical Reflexions and Inquiries concerning the Virtues of Tar-Water*.

The complete title of the work we call the *Principles* ends with the phrase: 'wherein the chief causes of error and difficulty in the sciences, with the grounds of scepticism, atheism, and irreligion, are inquired into'. The scepticism Berkeley has in mind is not so much religious doubt, which he here calls irreligion, but doubt about the possibility of knowledge about the world, or scientific scepticism. The most obvious place for doubt is concerning the reality of the physical world. Berkeley claims that on his view the physical world is immediately available to the senses, so that there is no cause to doubt its existence; but if the world is to be an imperceptible and unimaginable matter distinct from the ideas we have, then there is cause for doubt of its existence. As we have seen already, Locke's official doctrine that 'since the mind . . . hath no immediate objects but its own ideas . . . it is evident that our knowledge is only conversant about them' is plainly incompatible with knowledge of a reality beyond our ideas; when in Book IV, Chapter iv of his *Essay*, entitled 'Of the Reality of Human Knowledge', he tries to meet the objection that on his principles 'knowledge placed in ideas may be all bare vision', the argument is notoriously weak, being little more than the claim that our simple ideas must have some cause.

Furthermore, if we pass over the doubts concerning the reality of matter, Locke himself insists that knowledge in the physical sciences is virtually impossible. On Locke's view, the true nature, or real essence, of physical things, depended on the organisation of the basic atoms that composed them; but since we do not have microscopic eyes, as he himself puts it, we can never know this organisation and therefore never know why bodies are as they are. And, he continues, even if we could observe these insensible parts,

we are so far from knowing what figure, size, or motion of parts produce a yellow colour, a sweet taste, or a sharp sound, that we can by no means conceive how any size, figure, or motion of any particles can possibly produce in us the idea of any colour, taste, or sound whatever; there is no conceivable connexion betwixt the one and the other. In vain therefore shall we endeavour to discover by our ideas (the only true way of certain and universal knowledge) what other ideas are to be found constantly joined with that of our complex idea of any substance.

So Berkeley's first point in defence of his conception of science is in effect a preventive or spoiling attack. If the physical world is a transcendent reality inaccessible to our investigation scientific knowledge is impossible. Since on Berkeley's view the physical world was directly accessible, the possibility of knowledge about it did not meet such basic problems.

Locke's theory not only made physical reality inaccessible; it also ascribed causal agency to this inaccessible organisation of particles. Berkeley denied all causal efficacy to anything in the physical world, which was, on his analysis, ultimately composed of ideas alone. Paragraphs 25 and 26 of the *Principles* contain the clearest statement of his grounds for this view, which is revealed in the following quotations from those paragraphs:

All our ideas...are visibly inactive...so that one idea... cannot produce or make any alteration in another... For, since they and every part of them exist only in the mind, it follows that there is nothing in them but what is perceived; but whoever shall attend to his ideas, whether of sense or reflexion, will not perceive in them any power or activity... Whence it plainly follows that extension, figure and motion cannot be the cause of our sensations ... We perceive a continual succession of ideas.

Since these ideas do not cause each other they must be caused by the only kind of agency we know, a spirit.

It is worthwhile to compare this claim with the views of Hume. Hume agrees with Berkeley that we can find in nature nothing beyond succession; there is in nature no causal relation beyond succession. But whereas Berkeley goes on to claim that we must therefore locate true causal agency elsewhere, in spirits, Hume takes a different line; since we can find no causal agency in nature beyond succession we must analyse causation in terms of succession; causation is nothing more than the regular succession which we observe in nature; the constant conjunction of ideas which we experience produces an inevitable expectation in our minds of the continuance of the regularity and we transfer this inevitability into the realm of nature by a kind of illusion. Here Hume is carrying the line of reductionist analysis started by Berkeley further than Berkeley (whom Hume greatly admired) was prepared to go. Part of the explanation is that Hume denied Berkeley's claim, vital to his metaphysics, that he could distinguish a genuine activity in spirits going beyond mere succession; we shall have to consider this problem carefully when we come to look closely at Berkeley's account of spirits and their powers.

Science, then, for Berkeley, is not investigating a nature beyond our ideas or discovering causal connections, either between matter and matter, or matter and ideas, or ideas and ideas. What then is the role of the scientist or experimental philosopher? Berkeley's basic answer is given in paragraph 105 of the *Principles* :

If therefore we consider the difference there is betwixt natural philosophers and other men, with regard to their knowledge of the phenomena, we shall find it consists, not in an exacter knowledge of the efficient cause that produces them—for that can be no other than the *will of a spirit*—but only in a greater largeness of comprehension, whereby analogies, harmonies, and agreements are discovered in the works of nature, and the particular effects explained, that is, reduced to general rules.

At this point we must insist once again on the distinction between Berkeley's analytic theories and his metaphysics. Metaphysically the explanation of why the world is as it is, the causal agency which maintains it as it is, the ground which permits us to ask for final causes (What is it for?) in nature, must be a spirit, whom Berkeley calls God. Metaphysically, therefore, scientists are investigating the handiwork of God, reading the divine handwriting, as Berkeley sometimes puts it, discovering the designs of God. But, given this metaphysical basis, we must give a different analytical account of what the scientist is doing. Metaphysically all scientists are investigating the activity of God, but analysis must allow that one is investigating an alkali and another an acid; metaphysically the explanation of every phenomenon is God, but we must give an analytic account of science which allows that the explanation of one natural phenomenon will often be very different from the explanation of another.

If we now ask for an account of Berkeley's basic analysis of the nature of empirical science, the answer is that the scientist is discovering regularities in the succession of our ideas. In so doing he is doing nothing different in principle from what all men do when they learn from experience. He is merely doing it in a much more systematic way. But Berkeley also gives an analytic account of scientific explanation which, simply stated, is the reduction to general rules. We may usefully clarify and explain this doctrine with the use of one of Berkeley's own examples.

That apples, and not only apples, fall to the ground, that tides are affected by the moon, that the moon circles the earth and

that the planets rotate round the sun—these and similar phenomena were all well known and familiar to men before Newton.
What Newton did was not to discover these phenomena but to
explain them. He explained them by showing them all to be special
cases of a single regularity—gravitational attraction. Unlike Newton,
but like many of Newton's earliest and closest disciples, we may be
tempted to regard this as explanation by reference to some efficient
cause, some force called the force of gravitation. But as an efficient
cause the force of gravitation would be a mere something we knew
not what; to say that apples accelerate towards the earth at a rate
of thirty-two feet per second per second because there is a force
that accelerates them at that rate is empty talk, as it would be to
say that petrol in an internal combustion engine ignites because it
has a power of combustion. What Newton did to explain these and
related phenomena was to show that they were all cases of the same
few basic principles. Gravitational attraction is a concept which has
explanatory power because it is a shorthand way of referring to the
common feature exhibited by all these phenomena, not because it
names an efficient cause of them. So explanation is neither the
giving of an efficient cause or mere description but, in Berkeley's
words, 'reduction to general rules'.

If we turn to *De motu*, we shall find a further amplification of
this analysis of science, an analysis which in recent years has
attracted more attention than earlier, since philosophers have
noticed in it similarities to the positivist analysis of the nature of
mechanical science by the nineteenth-century Austrian philosopher and physicist, Mach. In *De motu* Berkeley is mainly concerned with the science of mechanics, the only part of science
which in his day had achieved a mathematical formulation and
systemisation. In mechanics one uses constantly such terms as
'mass', 'force', 'momentum' and 'energy'; are we to say that this
is illegitimate, and how can we avoid doing so, if we start from
Berkeley's immaterialist basis? Since *De motu* is not so easily
accessible as the *Principles* and the *Dialogues*, let us read Berkeley's solution so far as possible in a translation of his own words:

Force, gravity, attraction, and words of this sort are useful for reasoning
and computations concerning motion and bodies in motion; but not for
understanding the simple nature of motion itself or for designating so
many distinct qualities. (M 17)

For understanding the true nature of motion it will be of the greatest assistance first, to distinguish between mathematical models and the nature of things: secondly, to beware of abstractions: thirdly, to consider motion as something sensible, or at least imaginable; and to be content with relative measurements. If we do these things, not only will all the celebrated theorems of mechanics, by which the secrets of nature are revealed and the system of the world is subjected to human calculation, remain unimpaired, but also the study of motion will escape free from a thousand pedantries, subtleties and abstract ideas. (M 66)

All forces attributed to bodies are as much mathematical hypotheses as attractive forces in the planets and the sun. Moreover mathematical entities have no firm essence in the world of nature, but they depend on the notions of him who defines them, so that the same thing can be explained in various ways. (M 67)

The mechanical principles and universal laws of motion so happily discovered in the last century, stated and applied with the aid of geometry, introduced a remarkable clarity into science. But the metaphysical principles and the true efficient causes of motion and of the existence of bodies or the properties of bodies are in no way part of mechanics or experimental science. (M 41)

Thus we find Berkeley giving a completely positivistic analysis of science, while maintaining a theistic explanation at the metaphysical level. In so far as science is talking about observed phenomena (sensible ideas) or, at least, objects of possible experience (the imaginable), we may take it literally. Berkeley does not wish to doubt the existence of small particles, regarded in the way he regards all bodies, as permanent possibilities of sensation. But in so far as science wishes to talk of inherently imperceptible bodies, this is legitimate for computational purposes but must not be taken literally.

What Berkeley has in mind when he speaks of mathematical models or hypotheses as having no real existence and as depending for their content on the arbitrary definition of the scientist can be explained by reference to an illustration he himself uses in *Siris*. Ptolemy in his geocentric astronomy accounted for the motion of the heavenly bodies by means of a theory of cycles and epicycles (circles revolving round a circle). This he did so successfully that users of the heliocentric astronomy did not succeed in accounting significantly better for the motions of the stars and calculating their courses until about the time of Newton. Now the hypothesis of epicycles can be indefinitely refined to account with increasing accuracy for celestial motions. Is, then, the heliocentric or the geocentric hypothesis correct? Are there or are there not epicycles? Berkeley's answer to this question would be that both theories are mathematical hypotheses and, in so far as they answer equally well empirical questions about what we shall observe, it is senseless to ask which is true. It is legitimate to talk about epicycles, or gravity, provided that we realise that to do so is merely to adopt one framework for computation rather than another. Here are Berkeley's own words on this topic:

It is one thing to arrive at general laws of nature from a contemplation of the phenomena; and another to frame an hypothesis, and from thence deduce the phenomena. Those who suppose epicycles, and by them explain the motions and appearances of the planets, may not therefore be thought to have discovered principles true in fact and nature. And, albeit we may from the premises infer a conclusion, it will not follow that we can argue reciprocally, and from the conclusion infer the premises. (S 228)

There is much of interest in *Siris* for the student of Berkeley's philosophy of science, particularly in sections 247 and following.

Berkeley, then, thought that he could give an adequate analysis of science in terms of his basic phenomenalistic view. This analysis has to be supplemented according to Berkeley by a metaphysic. Since there is no causal agency within nature we must account for the regularity and very existence of the world of nature by an agency lying outside it, which is, according to Berkeley, an incomparably powerful spirit that he calls God. Berkeley's view of spirits and of the Infinite Spirit on which his metaphysical explanation of the possibility of science depends will be considered in detail later. But one consequence of this metaphysic may be considered now, Berkeley's defence of seeking final causes within science.

Plato and Aristotle, and their medieval followers, had insisted on the importance of final causes in science. An important part, they would have said, of understanding, say, the heart or the liver is understanding what purpose it serves. Just how far teleological explanation is to be sought was not clear; Aristotle himself explicitly said that there was no teleological explanation of such facts as that rain fell at some particular place and time. But certainly some teleological explanation was part of science. That teleological explanation was possible was not doubted by the Christian philosophers and scientists of the late seventeenth century; but the pious Boyle himself laid it down that there should be no reference to God in the explanation of particular phenomena. God had created matter which behaved according to immutable laws, and it was illegitimate to explain the behaviour of anything in science except by reference to matter and the universal laws of its behaviour. But Berkeley was dissatisfied with this. It would be an extreme behaviourist who rejected teleological explanation of intelligent human activity; to ask to what end you or I acted in a certain way seems obviously justified and an answer is surely needed if we are to understand that action. But if we regard the natural world as the direct and immediate activity of God surely the same teleological question will be appropriate here, even if we cannot always find the answer. Why should the fact that God acts in a reliably predictable manner prohibit the question? It is not that Berkeley wants questions about God to be regarded as part of natural science; we know that he did not. But he thought that the metaphysical propriety of speaking of God's purposes meant that it was appropriate to ask within science to what end the liver or heart behaved as it did and to regard it as possible to answer such questions. The modern scientist seems to preach the doctrine of Boyle rather than that of Berkeley on this topic, though whether in fact we shall ever cease to ask and answer such teleological questions about natural phenomena, or some of them, is another matter.

So far Berkeley has been giving his interpretation of the activities of Newton, not condemning them. He has censured Newton's followers for thinking of attraction as a real entity to explain motion, but he has explicitly excepted Newton from this error. But to some of Newton's doctrines Berkeley did take exception, and on topics about which modern scientists are more likely to agree with Berkeley than with Newton. In particular Newton had distinguished absolute time and space from relative time and space in a celebrated scholium in the *Principia*:

Absolute, true, and mathematical time, of itself and from its own nature, flows equably without relation to anything external . . .

Absolute space in its own nature, without relation to anything external, remains always similar and immovable . . .

How it can even make sense to speak of time flowing with a speed, constant or inconstant, Newton does not tell us. But he not only claims to be able to make the distinction conceptually between, say, our movement relative to the earth and the movement of the earth through absolute space; he even produces the celebrated bucket experiment as an empirical proof of the difference between the two. He claims that the varying behaviour of water in a bucket which is suddenly set into circular motion, the surface gradually becoming concave, has to be analysed by a distinction between the movement of the water relative to the bucket and its absolute motion.

Among scientists Newton's authority was so great that these distinctions were not challenged by them until the late nineteenth century, when Clerk Maxwell, Mach and then Einstein demolished them, presumably for ever. Leibniz had attacked them in a celebrated correspondence with Clarke, a close follower of Newton, but without much effect. Berkeley, too, saw that he had to attack Newton on this point, for a real absolute space, which Newton was even heretically willing to call the sensorium, or organ of perception, of God, could by no means be incorporated into a phenomenalistic account of science. Berkeley's attack is to be found in *Principles* 110–18; and it is what one would expect. He claims that the concepts of absolute space and time are empty and that what Newton regards as cases where the distinction between the absolute and the relative is required are shown to be cases where we have space or time relative to two different frames of reference. He in effect offers the modern solution to Newton's bucket experiment, that what Newton calls absolute motion is in fact motion relative to the fixed stars, so called. It is hard not to accept Berkeley as clearly right on this point, and hard to understand why his arguments were so long ignored.

Berkeley's philosophy of science was in his day totally novel. Few if any concurred with him until the rise of positivism in the late nineteenth century, but many philosophers and not a few scientists have accepted positions not unlike his in the twentieth century. As modern physics began to ascribe to its basic particles a character more and more unlike that of any objects with which we are acquainted with in experience, it became more and more satisfying to say that so long as the mathematical calculations led to correct predictions we should not ask for more and should regard the bewildering descriptions of fundamental particles as the inevitable result of trying to express non-mathematically what could only be expressed in mathematical terms. We should not regard a mathematical model as a factual description. Perhaps this is an over-simple view which sees too sharp a distinction between model or mathematical hypothesis and mere factual description; but certainly we cannot regard Berkeley's views as the eccentric dream of a crazy metaphysician.

5

God and finite spirits

THERE is surprisingly little said about spirits and their nature in either the *Principles* or the *Dialogues*. Why this is so is unclear. In the private notebooks Berkeley wrote: 'Mem. Carefully to omit defining of person, or making much mention of it' (C 713). Since he wrote just below: 'N.B. To use utmost caution not to give the least handle of offence to the Church or Churchmen' (C 715), it might be conjectured that it was out of prudence that he pursued this policy. But, again, when the first edition of the *Principles* appeared it was called 'Part I', though no Part II ever appeared. In a letter to an American friend named Samuel Johnson, Berkeley said that he had 'made considerable progress on the Second Part', adding that the manuscript 'was lost about fourteen years ago, during my travels in Italy; and I never had leisure since to do so disagreeable a thing as writing twice on the same subject'. Some have conjectured that we should have learnt more about spirits from this second part, though Berkeley alleges that *Principles* I, 135 to the end, deal with this topic.

The little that is said has often been thought to be unsatisfactory, so that the, surely unworthy, suspicion has been entertained that Berkeley says so little about spirits because he sees that his views on the topic are indefensible and inconsistent with what he says on other topics. It would be as well to start by indicating what the grounds for this dissatisfaction are.

It will be remembered that Berkeley opened the *Principles* with the assertion that it is evident that the objects of human knowledge are limited to ideas of sense, ideas of passions and other operations of the mind, and ideas of memory and imagination. But while we may observe our passions, our thoughts and our planning, and other 'operations of the mind', we never observe, that is, have an idea of, the mind itself. Some twenty-two or twenty-three years later Hume was to write: 'For my part, when I enter most intimately into what I call *myself*, I always stumble on some particular perception or other, of heat or cold, light or shade, love or hatred, pain or pleasure.' So Hume, on the same phenomenalist principle that Berkeley follows in analysing physical bodies, reduces the person to a series of ideas and sensations. How can Berkeley do otherwise? And, if he does so, is he to give a similar phenomenalist account of the infinite spirit who may be called God?

Berkeley is perfectly well aware of this problem. But he has no thought of trying to avoid it by claiming that he has an idea of himself. He agrees entirely with Hume that there is nothing that can be an object of attention which could be called the thinker of the thought or the feeler of the pain as one is aware of the thought or the pain. Berkeley states the problem in this way in the *Principles*: 'But it will be objected that, if there is no *idea* signified by the terms *soul*, *spirit*, and *substance*, they are wholly insignificant, or have no meaning in them' (P 139). Then in the next paragraph he says: 'In a large sense indeed, we may be said to have an idea or rather a notion of *spirit*. That is, we understand the meaning of the word, otherwise we could not affirm or deny anything of it.' This is very easily seen as a mere evasion of the problem. It is not clear why Locke and Newton should not reply to Berkeley that perhaps they have no idea of matter in a narrow sense but that in a larger sense they have an idea or rather notion of it in so far as they understand the word *matter* as readily as Berkeley understands the word *spirit*. Moreover it is not clear that God as an ultimate metaphysical explanation of things is essentially different from matter; in each case the metaphysical source of ideas is to be a something that causes ideas of which itself we can have no proper idea. An appeal to a transcendent something we know not what is perhaps equally futile by whatever name we call that something. Such is the difficulty; we must look carefully to see whether Berkeley's position is really as weak as it can certainly appear.

If we read the entries in Berkeley's private notebooks that are concerned with minds, souls or spirits, it is clear that he was initially in some doubt what line to take. This wavering can be graphically illustrated. At one point he writes: 'We think we know not the soul, because we have no imaginable or sensible idea annex'd to that sound. This the effect of prejudice' (C 576). But then in the very next entry he contradicts himself: 'Certainly we do not know it' (C 576a).

At this point Berkeley adopts a position he will later abandon, one which anticipates the Humean notion of the mind as a bundle or series of ideas. The passage deserves an extended quotation:

The very existence of ideas constitutes the Soul. Consciousness, perception, existence of ideas, seem to be all one . . .

Consult, ransack your understanding. What find you there besides several perceptions or thoughts? What mean you by the word mind? You must mean something that you perceive, or that you do not perceive. A thing not perceived is a contradiction. To mean (also) a thing you do not perceive is a contradiction. We are in all this matter strangely abused by words. Mind is a congeries of perceptions. Take away perceptions and you take away the mind. Put the perceptions and you put the mind. (C 577, 579–80)

At this stage he is so bold as to say that 'in sleep and in trances the mind *exists not*', since its existence is identical with the occurrence of ideas.

We have seen that Berkeley has shown himself well aware of the problem how spirits can be accounted for on his basic premises; and we have seen him willing to canvass a view of the mind which has often been regarded as one of Hume's most daring innovations. This being so, we can scarcely explain his apparently weak claim in the *Principles* that we have a notion of spirit, though no idea of it, as arising from either an inability to see its apparent weakness or from a mere timid evasion of the problem. In fact he does seem to have believed himself to have discovered a true theory of the nature of spirits which does overcome the basic difficulty, and this view we must now examine.

Perhaps the shortest way to put Berkeley's position, though it is not Berkeley's own, is to say that we know ideas as objects of observation; we cannot observe ourselves and so we are not ideas and we have no idea of ourselves; but we do act, and will and observe, and it is this activity which constitutes our existence as spirits. In Berkeley's language, the existence of ideas consists in their being perceived (their *esse* is *percipi*), whereas the existence of spirits consists in acting, willing and perceiving (their *esse* is *agere, velle, percipere*). 'By the word *spirit* we mean only that which thinks, wills and perceives' (P 138).

So we are aware of ourselves as acting, not by observation but simply because action is a conscious activity. Berkeley claims that we are actually aware of our causal agency, of our exertion of power. Hume will deny this, partly by claiming that we have no idea of power or force—which Berkeley himself urges—and partly by pointing out that even when we will to perform some simple action we may fail to do so (our arm may be paralysed when we try to move it). But the cases that Berkeley has in mind are not of bodily events but of our summoning up ideas in our minds. We are not aware of some phenomenon called the exertion of power, but we consciously exert power when we call any train of thought or imagination before our minds.

So we understand the word 'spirit', which Berkeley calls 'having a notion of spirit', though we have no idea of spirit in the strict sense of idea. Spirits are substances; they are that in the world which acts and ideas are the field of their actions, totally inert and mind-dependent.

This immediate awareness of ourselves as spirits is unique. We are not aware even of other spirits in this way. Berkeley says very little about our knowledge of other minds, a topic which has received much very sophisticated attention from recent philosophers. He is content with a simple argument from analogy—we attribute an active finite spirit which governs it to each body which behaves like ours. This has been much attacked as a form of argument—by F. H. Bradley on the ground that we do not want as friends inferred beings who are mere hypotheses to explain physical phenomena, and by others on the ground that the analogy is weak, being from one case to all, or illegitimate in principle. This is not the place to go into this question, to which Berkeley allowed only a few perfunctory words.

Berkeley uses this conception of finite spirits to argue for the natural immortality of the soul in a manner reminiscent of Plato's *Phaedo*. When bodies cease to exist what happens is that they are dissolved into their constituent parts or elements in accordance with the laws of nature. Since to perish is the dissolution of a complex into its simple parts, we can have no idea of the perishing of something simple. But the soul is 'indivisible, incorporal, unextended'; it is therefore, not being part of nature, not subject to the laws of nature, and, being simple, is not capable of dissolution. God can create a soul or annihilate it, but apart from the creative power of God nothing comes to be out of nothing or becomes nothing. Once again, Berkeley gives this argument without any attempt at elaboration or defence against possible objections and we shall not pursue the topic here.

But what of the existence of God? For the whole of Berkeley's metaphysics depends on his existence. Berkeley's argument is basically very simple: he, Berkeley, is aware of ideas in his own mind and knows them to be essentially dependent on the mind. The notion of a pain or a sound or a tickle or even a coloured expanse existing independently of a mind is absurd. But while Berkeley is conscious that the existence of some ideas is dependent on his mind and on his will, it is manifest that the great bulk of ideas are not dependent for their existence or character on his own mind; nor could they be caused by another mind similar in capacity to Berkeley's own; nor, being clearly passive and mind-dependent, could they be permanent, independent and basic entities. The mind that must therefore be causally responsible for the existence of that regular sequence of ideas that we call reality must be immensely more powerful than our own.

This argument is clearly a version of the cosmological argument, an argument from the existence of the world to a cause of its existence. But it has its own special features. Thus, one common reply to the cosmological argument has always been to ask why we need to ask for a cause of the existence of the world, which might be treated as basic just as easily as a creator could be treated as basic. But Berkeley can reply to this that on his view the natural world is known to be essentially mind-dependent; the only question can be on what mind it is so dependent. Why Berkeley is entitled, if he is, to call the mind that is responsible for the natural order an infinite spirit rather than merely a very powerful spirit, why he should be entitled to call this spirit eternal, and why he should be entitled to identify it with the God of the Christian religion, are further and difficult questions. But the notion of some very powerful mind that must be responsible for the world-order is deeply embedded in Berkeley's views and it cannot be excised as a mere religious excrescence arbitrarily added by a future bishop.

I have emphasised the importance of the infinite spirit in Berkeley's philosophy as the cause of those regular sequences of ideas that are called reality. Berkeley is often represented as arguing that God is needed to keep the world in existence by perceiving it. That Berkeley did believe that God in some sense perceives the world is clear; but I do not believe that Berkeley held the view, which Malebranche held, that what we perceive is the ideas of God. What makes the natural world and its order is the will of God that men should obtain these ideas, not God's own perception of them from all eternity.

Berkeley often referred to the natural course of ideas as the language or handwriting of God. He wanted this to be taken very literally, so much so that it is a central element in an argument for the existence of God produced in the dialogue *Alciphron*. In this dialogue a Christian, Euphranor, and Alciphron, a free-thinker, or minute philosopher, as Berkeley prefers to call him, are the main characters. In the fourth of these dialogues Euphranor presses Alciphron to explain why he believes in other finite spirits, though imperceptible, but does not believe in God. Alciphron replies that though he cannot perceive other finite spirits he has empirical evidence for their existence since he can communicate with them; Alciphron, in effect, produces the argument from analogy on which Berkeley himself had relied in the *Principles*. Euphranor now says: 'But if it should appear plainly that God speaks to men by the intervention and use of arbitrary, outward, sensible signs, having no resemblance or necessary connexion with the things they stand for and suggest . . . will this content you?' (A iv 7). He then proceeds to claim that the relation between cause and effect, or between visible appearance and feel, is as arbitrary as between any word and its signification; 'you have as much reason to think the Universal Agent or God speaks to your eyes, as you can have for thinking any particular person speaks to your ears' (A iv 12); the look of fire is God's warning to us of potential danger in exactly the same way as is a human shout of 'Fire!'. So Alciphron is made to acknowledge that 'we see God with our fleshly eyes as plain as we see any human person whatsoever, and that He daily speaks to our senses in a manifest and clear dialect'. Whether Alciphron ought to have found this argument so convincing is another question, but it is interesting in its literal use of the notion of sensible ideas being literally a sign-language to warn and inform us of other experience, as well as for its novel use of the argument from analogy for the existence of other minds.

We should, in our consideration of Berkeley on minds or spirits, finally note a problem for Berkeley which is one facet of the problem of free will and determinism which besets all philosophers, whether idealist or materialist, theistic or atheistic. It will be remembered that Berkeley distinguished the world of imagination from the real world by claiming that, metaphysically, God was the cause of the occurrence of the ideas which constitute the real world while finite spirits are the cause of their own ideas or imagination; the same distinction can be made by the empirical observation that we can choose to imagine or not to imagine, whereas the ideas that constitute reality are beyond our control; that the ideas of imagination are fragmentary and disordered, whereas the ideas that constitute reality are orderly and continuous; and the ideas of imagination are less lively and vivid than the ideas that constitute reality. So the whole distinction between reality and the world of fantasy depends on the view that ideas constituting reality are caused by God, and are outside our control.

What, then, is Berkeley to say about our own bodily movements? It would seem that the series of ideas which constitute the history of a human body are philosophically on a par with the series of ideas which constitute the history of any other real body. So must not the series of ideas that constitute the movement of a part of my body be caused by God and so be outside my control? But if this is so, are we committed to the view that man has no control over his bodily movements, that as causal agents we can control only the activities of our imaginations?

Berkeley was not willing to accept this view. In the private notebooks, the first writings of Berkeley that we have, he wrote: 'We move our legs ourselves. 'Tis we that will their movement' (C 548), and in his very last book, *Siris*, there is some strange neo-Platonic speculation about how the soul moves the body. There is no place where he departs from this view, but also no place where he deals with the problems that it raises, so that we can only speculate on what answer he would give on this point if pressed.

Part of the difficulty could perhaps be fairly easily dealt with. It is clear that in one way we always have some control over the course of our ideas; we can open or shut our eyes, turn our heads in one direction or another, and so on. It is clear that in saying that we cannot choose what ideas of reality we shall experience Berkeley means that if we open our eyes or turn our heads in a particular direction we shall see what we shall see and cannot choose how things will look; he does not need to deny that we can choose whether to look in order to make the distinction between reality and the world of imagination. Perhaps Berkeley could argue that we can will to move our leg just as we can will to look or turn our heads, and what we shall then see, the ideas that we shall have, is in each case equally outside our control. To put the point another way, there are many different possible series of ideas which might occur in our life-histories, each of which would be equally part of reality. We may, for example, choose to sit and watch one television programme or another, or to watch no television at all; but, though we can, so to speak, choose between different programmes, we cannot determine the content of the programme which we have chosen; whereas in imagination the programme is indefinitely variable at will. Perhaps Berkeley could maintain that his answer to the objection that 'by the foregoing principles all that is real and substantial in nature is banished out of the world' might be justified in this way.

But serious difficulties remain. Berkeley would allow that God from time to time brought about a miracle which was an exception to the regularity of nature; but he held that in general nature was uniform and that this uniformity was part of the goodness of God, through which one experience could be reliably expected on the basis of another. How could a human decision to move or not to move a leg be compatible with such uniformity? This is the Berkeleian version of the ancient problem how free will can be compatible with the uniformity of nature. There is also the problem how a finite will is to cause the Infinite Spirit to bring about one series of ideas rather than another, which is the Berkeleian version of the problem of how a will could act upon nature.

As we know, Berkeley deliberately abstained from discussing these problems in his published works, and we do not know whether he would have discussed them in the projected second part of the *Principles*. I suspect that Berkeley, like everyone else, would have had no adequate solution to offer and that this fact would not have shaken him. In the dialogues between Hylas and

Philonous Hylas asks how Philonous can claim both that God was eternally unchanging and that God created the world; Philonous replies that he has no answer to this problem but does not need to answer it since it is a problem for all theists who accept the doctrine of creation and does not arise from the thesis of immaterialism. I suspect that on the problem of the freedom of the will Berkeley himself would have admitted that he had no clear answer to it but that it, too, was one which was common to all and in no way a special problem for him.

6

Mathematics

THERE are two distinct topics that must be considered in this chapter. First we shall consider Berkeley's own positive philosophy of mathematics, in which he attempts to give an account of the nature of mathematical propositions; secondly we must look at Berkeley's attacks on the mathematicians of his day, including the mighty Newton, for what Berkeley claimed were logical errors which invalidated both Newton's theory of fluxions and the equivalent infinitesimal calculus of Leibniz.

In his earlier writings, comprising remarks in his notebooks and paragraphs 118–32 of the *Principles*, Berkeley gave entirely different accounts of the nature of arithmetic and algebra on the one hand, and geometry on the other. The account of arithmetic and algebra he adhered to; the most implausible account of geometry he later abandoned in favour of an account which was very similar to that of arithmetic.

Berkeley held what would now be called a formalistic view of arithmetic and algebra. He held, as we have seen, that words stand for ideas—we can ask what they denote. But this is not so in the case of numerals; 'there are no *ideas* of number in the abstract, denoted by the numeral names'; arithmetical theorems have value because they can be applied, but 'can be supposed to having nothing at all for their object' (P 120). To say there are ten fish in a pool is nothing more than a compendious way of saying that there are as many fish in the pool as there are here strokes on the paper: //////////. If there are ten fish in that pool, seven in another and twelve in a third, the principles of addition give us a convenient, quick method of determining the total number of fish. 'Hence', Berkeley says, 'we may see how entirely the science of numbers is subordinate to practice, and how jejune and trifling it becomes when considered as a matter of mere speculation' (P 120). This view will be distasteful to pure mathematicians; Berkeley's libel may be mitigated by the fact that in his youth he was an addict of pure mathematics. He even published a short Latin work on mathematics in 1707 containing a description of an algebraic game that he had invented.

By the time that he wrote *De motu* Berkeley had come to hold a view of geometry very similar to his view of arithmetic. We have seen, in discussing Berkeley's view of science, that though such terms as *attraction, action* and *force* are held to denote nothing real they are of the utmost value in computations of motion. In paragraph 39 of *De motu* he says that geometers also 'bring in many things for the development of their science that they cannot describe or find in the realm of nature which are of similar utility for computational purposes'.

But in earlier years Berkeley had held that geometry was an empirical science having as its subject-matter physical lines, triangles etc. Since physical things are, for Berkeley, merely bundles of ideas, geometry is in the end about our ideas of lines and the like. So construed, a point must be what he called a *minimum sensibile*, the smallest perceptible area, and all lines must have a finite length. A line so thought of is made up of points. Berkeley was prepared to accept the consequences. A line consisting of an odd number of points could not be bisected, he held; in his notebook he wrote: 'I say there are no incommensurables'; of the proof of congruence by superposition: 'the under triangle is no triangle—nothing at all, not being perceiv'd'; 'particular circles may be squared, for the circumference being given a diameter may be found betwixt which and the true there is no perceivable difference'; 'the diagonal is commensurable with the side' (C 469, 528, 249, 286).

Berkeley was well aware that these views had the sound of absurd paradox. But he thought that it was less absurd to hold his view than to hold that, for example, the word 'line' named something real which had length but no breadth; we have already seen that he regarded the claim that we have an abstract idea of length without breadth as merely to pile one absurdity on another. Abstract ideas are philosophical monstrosities. But his views were very odd, and as soon as he saw how to give an account of geometry which did not lead to these absurdities, as he saw them, he abandoned his own paradoxes.

In Berkeley's own time his positive views on the nature of mathematics were given little heed. But in 1734 he published a polemical work on mathematics which in his lifetime was more celebrated than any other writing of his to that date, though *Siris* was later to outstrip it. This book was the occasion of a pamphlet war in which many of the leading mathematicians of the day took part. So though Berkeley's attack is of only historical interest and irrelevant to modern mathematics, we should pay some attention to it.

The full title of this book was *The Analyst; or a Discourse Addressed to an Infidel Mathematician wherein is examined whether the Object, Principles and Inferences of the Modern Analysis are more distinctly conceived, or more evidently deduced, than Religious Mysteries.* This title is significant; Berkeley's main aim is to show that free-thinking mathematicians, such as Edmund Halley, the famous astronomer, who mocked at the absurdities of Christian theology, were themselves guilty of logical errors of such seriousness that theology was of exemplary clarity in comparison with their mathematics. The subordinate aim, which was the means to the higher end, was to show that the mathematical analysis of his time was logically faulty; to achieve this he had to attack not only free-thinking mathematicians like Halley, but also such eminent theists as Newton, the inventor of the theory of fluxions, and Leibniz, who invented the equivalent theory of the infinitesimal calculus. The theory of fluxions, or of differential calculus, is a method of determining the rate of change of one variable in relation to another; since such concepts as that of acceleration are of rates of change, the theory was of vital importance to Newton's presentation of mechanics in mathematical form.

Berkeley objected in any case, as we have seen, to talk of infinitely short lines or extensionless points, but that is not the main point of attack in the *Analyst*; his objection here is that the mathematicians of his day were guilty of enormous logical howlers in their argumentation. It was for this that he despised them, so that in his notebook he wrote: 'I see no wit in any of them but Newton. The rest are mere triflers, mere nihilarians' (C 372). It is quite easy to set out the principle of Berkeley's main objection in a form intelligible even to readers who have only the most elementary acquaintance with algebra, and I shall do so by using a simpler example than those Berkeley used and employing a modern notation.

Let us see first how in more recent tradition a simple algebraic differentiation is done from first principles. Let us take the equation

(1) $y = x^2$

which gives y when x is given. Let δx be a small increment to x which gives a small increment δy to y; that is

(2) $y + \delta y = (x + \delta x)^2$.

Then

(3) $y + \delta y = x^2 + 2x\delta x + (\delta x)^2$.

Since $y = x^2$ from (1), this last equation becomes, after subtraction,

(4) $\delta y = 2x\delta x + (\delta x)^2$.

We now divide both sides by δx so that we have

(5) $\dfrac{\delta y}{\delta x} = 2x + \delta x$.

We now say that

(6) the limiting value of $\dfrac{\delta y}{\delta x}$, as δx tends to zero, is $2x$.

What this means is that as the value of δx gets nearer to zero the value of the ratio $\dfrac{\delta y}{\delta x}$ tends to a non-zero limit even though δy and δx both tend to zero. When (6) is true it is customary to write

(7) $\dfrac{dy}{dx} = 2x$.

Here dy and dx are not two mysterious new numbers; (7) is merely the conventional abbreviation of (6). It tells us that if $y = x^2$ then the rate of change of y is twice that of x.

Now if a seventeenth- or early eighteenth-century mathematician were to carry out this differentiation in this notation he would require in the first place that δx should be not merely a small, but an infinitesimally small increment. Berkeley protested that he could not conceive of the infinitesimally small, but that is not now the main point at issue. What is at issue is the move that the old mathematician made after reaching stage (5):

(5) $\dfrac{\delta y}{\delta x} = 2x + \delta x.$

He now said that since δx was infinitesimally small it could be neglected, so that we may simply cancel it out to write

(6) $\dfrac{\delta y}{\delta x} = 2x$

This is the move that aroused Berkeley's derision; if δx could be cancelled it must be a nothing; but to divide δy by nothing or nothing by nothing will never give the result $2x$. The doctrine of the Trinity seemed pellucid to Berkeley by comparison with this piece of argumentation.

It is clear that Berkeley's criticism is irrelevant to more modern presentations and equally clear that it is justified with regard to the type of procedure that we have just considered. There are, indeed, scholarly controversies about whether Newton's later formulations of what we now call the differential calculus are liable to Berkeley's objections; but certainly any formulation which requires us first to posit infinitesimal quantities and then to claim that they can be treated as zero is faulty, and Berkeley was justified in attacking it.

7

Moral and political philosophy

UNTIL very recently, Berkeley's contribution to moral and political philosophy was ignored by, and probably unknown to, all save a few specialists. But, though small in compass, Berkeley's views on these topics are original, clear and concerned with very fundamental issues. As we shall see, one of his achievements was to state with complete clarity a version of utilitarianism which has usually been thought to emerge only gradually in the nineteenth century and to have been stated and distinguished clearly only in the latter part of the twentieth-century.

The only important document we have has the full title: *Passive Obedience or the Christian Doctrine of not Resisting the Supreme Power, Proved and Vindicated upon the Principles of the Law of Nature in a Discourse Delivered at the Chapel of Trinity College, Dublin.* It was published in 1712, between the *Principles* and the *Three Dialogues.* The phrase in the title which runs 'Proved and Vindicated upon the Principles of the Law of Nature' is very important; it indicates that, though the discourse had the form of a sermon on the text 'Whosoever resisteth the Power, resisteth the ordinance of God', the argument is to be based purely on rational, philosophical considerations, with no appeal to authority or revelation. So, at the outset, he says that, in arguing for passive obedience, 'in order to lay the foundation of that duty the deeper, we make some enquiry into the origin, nature and obligation of moral duties in general, and the criterions whereby they are to be known' (O 4).

Every argument must start from premises. Here Berkeley's are first the existence of a good and omnipotent God, which he declares to be evident by the light of nature, and second the principle of self-love. This principle of self-love is the doctrine first stated by the Platonic Socrates and, to the disgust of Bishop Butler, embraced by most subsequent philosophers, that all men always aim at what they take to be most conducive to their happiness. Berkeley, indeed, says that we denominate things good or evil accordingly as they augment or impair our happiness. Since our happiness, our supreme good, must clearly depend on the will of the omnipotent God in the long run, whatever the short-term advantages of disobedience, Berkeley says that 'it plainly follows that a conformity to His will . . . is the sole rule whereby every man who acts up to the principles of reason must govern and square his actions' (O 6).

So the question now is whether, by reason and not by an appeal to revelation, we can know what the will of God is, at least in regard to our actions. Berkeley thinks that we can. Since God is supremely good he will wish the happiness or good of man, and not just of some men but of all men at all times and places. If this is God's will, then we must set ourselves to produce this general good if we are to conform ourselves to the will of God.

The next question, therefore, Berkeley says, is to find how we are to promote this general good that God wills. In order to answer it he starts by making, in paragraph 8, a historically most important distinction between what are now known as act- and rule-utilitarianism, which deserves quotation also for its economical clarity:

The well-being of mankind must necessarily be carried on in one of these two ways: - Either, first, without the injunction of any certain universal rules of morality; only by obliging everyone, upon each particular occasion, to consult the public good, and always to do that which to him shall seem, in the present time and circumstances, most to conduce to it; or, secondly, by enjoining the observation of some determinate, established laws, which if universally practised, have, from the nature of things, an essential fitness to procure the well-being of mankind; though, in their particular application, they are sometimes, through untoward accidents, and the perverse irregularity of human wills, the occasions of great sufferings and misfortunes, it may be, to very many good men.

Berkeley now opts firmly for the second method, which we now call rule-utilitarianism. Act-utilitarians protest that, if one is sure that violation of some traditional rule of morality will have the best results, then it is mere conditioned rule-worship to obey the rule; in cases of uncertainty, they will often concede, it is best to act in the way which in most similar circumstances has usually turned out to be for the best, but this is to treat the traditional rules as rules of thumb, prudential maxims, and not to allow them authority, as does the rule-utilitarian.

But Berkeley argues that, first, we have neither the knowledge nor the time to judge of the basic merits of an action, whereas it is easy to determine that it is a case of lying or theft, and, secondly, we need public standards of behaviour to give certainty to our judgements about what is permissible and what requires prohibition. Without general rules of conduct of manageable complexity 'there ensues the most horrible confusion of vice and virtue, sin and duty that can possibly be imagined' (O 10).

So we must, thinks Berkeley, conclude that the general welfare, which is willed by God, can best be achieved by recognition of determinate rules; 'whatever practical proposition doth to right reason evidently appear to have a necessary connexion with the Universal well-being included in it, is to be looked upon as enjoined by the will of God' (O 11). In general, he holds, these principles are evident to all men; they are eternal rules of reason and should be adhered to even when such desirable human feelings as tenderness and benevolence speak against so doing. To use an illustration drawn from Hume, though we all dislike the thought of a deserving poor man paying a debt to a rich miser, none the less, the principle of justice must prevail.

We have reached the conclusion that 'the Law of Nature is a system of such rules or precepts as that, if they be all of them, at all times, in all places, and by all men observed, they will necessarily promote the well-being of mankind, so far as it is attainable by human actions' (O 11). There are 'unalterable moral rules, which to violate to the least degree is vice or sin' (O 15). We all know what these rules are; Berkeley gives as examples 'Thou shalt not forswear thyself' and 'Thou shalt not steal', among others.

That is the moral theory put forward by Berkeley. It is on this basis that he has to defend and explain the principle of passive obedience. In modern times, when the question of the limits of civil obedience is often discussed, it is of interest to see how Berkeley attempted to defend this extreme position by rational argument and without appeal to such extravagant notions as the divine right of kings, which has been employed by his Jacobite predecessors.

Berkeley starts by stressing the miseries of anarchy. Hobbes had said that in a state of nature, which is a state of anarchy, we find 'no arts, no letters, no society, and, which is worst of all, continual fear and danger of sudden death, and the life of man solitary, poor, nasty, brutish, and short'. Berkeley echoes this; without the law of society 'there is no politeness, no order, no peace, among men, but the world is one great heap of misery and confusion' (O 15). So obedience to the law of society, and thus to those who make and enforce the law, is of the highest importance and cannot be left to individual discretion. Obedience is 'a rule of law of nature, the least breach whereof hath the inherent stain of moral turpitude'. Breaches of obedience lead to the dissolution of society with all its attendant evils.

The remainder of the discourse is devoted to defending this doctrine and explaining it. We shall consider only two points. First, Berkeley acknowledges that lawful authority may order one to act in a way that transgresses moral law; in such a case the principle of non-resistance does not require us so to act; but it does require us not to resist any penalty that the authority may impose on us if we do in these circumstances fail to comply. Berkeley bases this claim on a distinction that he makes between positive and negative precepts, only the latter of which have totally binding force. This is not an easy distinction to understand. If we take 'negative' and 'positive' to refer to mere grammatical form the distinction is untenable, since the positive 'Always tell the truth' has the same effect as 'Never lie.' On the other hand it does seem intuitively that there is a distinction between abstaining from thwarting the will and needs of others and actively co-operating with them. There is room for debate.

The second point to notice is that Berkeley agrees that 'by virtue of the duty of non-resistance we are not obliged to submit the disposal of our lives and fortunes to the discretion either of madmen, or of all those who by craft or violence invade the supreme power' (O 52). This is surely dangerous, and would not have been tolerated by Hobbes. Berkeley was loyal to the newly reigning house of Hanover: but might not a Jacobite have claimed that Berkeley's caveat justified him in rebellion? It is very hard for those who claim that there are principles which should absolutely never be transgressed to avoid both the Scylla of carrying it to absurdity (such as obeying a madman) and the Charybdis of inserting qualifying clauses that rob it of certainty of interpretation.

Finally, Berkeley was a sincerely religious man. He wished to propagate the Christian religion both because he thought it true and from a religious concern for the souls of men. But he also, as we have seen, makes it the basis of morality. We, who aim at our own happiness, are to aim at the general happiness that is willed by God because it is only by obeying the will of God that we can achieve our own happiness. So Berkeley thinks that without religion men have no rational motive to be moral; and since political obedience has a moral justification, the atheist will also have no inner drive to obedience but only at most fear of retribution from the civil power. So for Berkeley our temporal as well as our spiritual well-being is based only in religion. We find in Berkeley's apologetic writings, such as *Alciphron*, a continual awareness of and stress on the practical importance of combating atheism. Within limits Berkeley was an advocate of religious toleration; there exists an episcopal charge to the clergy of the diocese of Cloyne, which he delivered as Bishop, in which he exhorts them to friendship with and understanding of the many Catholics who surrounded them. But there could be no toleration for atheists, since they had no rational motive for the preservation of moral society, as did all theists, however misguided in their theological views. So, in his *Discourse Addressed to Magistrates and Men in Authority*, Berkeley warns them that 'obedience to all civil power is rooted in the religious fear of God'; so they should be aware that 'those pretended advocates for private light and free thought are in reality seditious men, who set up themselves against national laws and constitutions' (L vi 208). Magistrates, he concludes, should enforce the law against them.

8

Berkeley's later years

THE most important of Berkeley's views were formed, and
the most important and enduring of his works were written,
while he was a young Fellow of Trinity College, Dublin. *An Essay
Towards a New Theory of Vision* had appeared in 1709, the *Principles* in 1710, *Passive Obedience* in 1712 and the *Three Dialogues*
in 1713. Berkeley, as we shall see, published many further works
in later life, some of which then made more stir by far than those
we have mentioned. But today it is only the *De motu* of 1721
which is regarded as adding significantly to the previously mentioned publications.

The remainder of Berkeley's works were written against a background of more practical interests and were often directed more
to religious and social than to philosophical ends. After writing
the *Three Dialogues* Berkeley left Dublin for London in 1713 on
leave, and though he was to remain a Fellow for some years he
never resumed active work at Trinity College.

In London Berkeley met some of the foremost literary figures
of the day. These included Steele, to whose *Guardian* Berkeley
contributed a few articles, Pope, who presented Berkeley with a
copy of his poem 'Windsor Forest', and Addison. He became
closely associated with his fellow-Irishman Swift, and through
him with Mrs Vanhomrigh, the mother of Swift's Vanessa. There
was to be a curious sequel to this: Vanessa had intended to make
Swift her heir, but, angered by his marriage to Stella, she changed
her will and left a large legacy to Berkeley instead, though she
had never met him, a legacy which Berkeley received in 1723
when Vanessa died.

But Berkeley was not satisfied by his reception in London, for
it was not literary friendships but recognition of his philosophy
that he was seeking, and this eluded him. Already, before his
arrival in London, his influential friend Sir John Percival had
warned him in a letter of what was to come: 'I did but name the

subject-matter of your *Principles* to some ingenuous friends of mine, and they immediately treated it with ridicule, at the same time refusing to read it; which I have not yet got one to do.' On arrival Berkeley was faced with the same difficulty; the London intelligentsia to whom he had looked for comment and reasoned argument welcomed the man but refused even to discuss his views with him.

So Berkeley was not happy in London. In 1713 he took the opportunity to become chaplain to Lord Peterborough and toured France and Italy with him in that year and in 1714, and after another two years in London returned to Italy in 1716 for an extended tour which lasted until 1720. Berkeley wrote a journal on this tour, of which a portion dealing with the year 1717 survives. It was towards the end of this tour that he wrote his Latin treatise on mechanics, *De motu*, which he published on his return to England.

Berkeley returned to Dublin in 1721 and received the degree of Doctor of Divinity. But he was no longer happy in either Ireland or England, both of which he found decadent and corrupt, as such of his writings as *An Essay towards Preventing the Ruin of Great Britain* (1721) abundantly show. In 1723 he wrote to Lord Percival: 'It is now about ten months since I have determined to spend the residue of my days in Bermuda, where I trust in Providence I may be the mean instrument of doing good to mankind'; he added that a number of his friends were determined to go with him. The good that he proposed to do to mankind is made clear by the full title of a publication of 1725: *A proposal for the better supplying of Churches in our Foreign Plantations, and for converting the savage Americans to Christianity, by a College to be erected in the Summer Islands, otherwise called the Isles of Bermuda.*

In 1724 Berkeley was made Dean of Derry, but this seems to have had no effect on his plans, for he never took up residence in Derry, though nominally Dean until 1734. In 1724 he went to London to whip up support for the Bermuda project and, so far as words went, received strong backing for his impractical and unresearched project. Many private persons promised donations, the House of Commons voted a grant of twenty thousand pounds, George I gave Berkeley a charter for the college, and Walpole himself promised support. But little came of this promised aid; the parliamentary grant was delayed and Walpole temporised.

So Berkeley lost patience and in 1728, having married, he took ship for America. 'Westward the course of empire takes its way', he wrote in his only known poem, and Berkeley accompanied it. He landed at Newport in Rhode Island and, after a short stay there, bought a farm outside Newport and built a house which he called Whitehall. The house still stands and, after a period of neglect, was renovated and reopened to the public in 1980. Berkeley appears to have been happy and well liked in Rhode Island. He made contact with Yale College in New Haven and had close contacts with Samuel Johnson, a missionary living in Stratford, who, with Jonathan Edwards, became one of the first two American philosophers of note. Some of Berkeley's correspondence with Johnson survives, and that part in which he explains problems about the *Principles* to Johnson is useful reading. In Rhode Island Berkeley also wrote *Alciphron*, a philosophical defence of Christianity against free-thinkers. There is little in this work which still has philosophical or religious importance, though there are occasional passages, such as that in which Berkeley discusses how an empiricist can claim to know what he means by grace, which the specialist must read.

But Berkeley was living in virtual retirement, not carrying out his philanthropic projects. By 1731 Walpole had made it clear that the government support which Berkeley needed would not be forthcoming. So in 1732 Berkeley gave the many books he had taken out with him for his new college to Yale College instead and returned to England, defeated. He never set foot on Bermuda.

In 1734 Berkeley was appointed Bishop of Cloyne in the south of Ireland. Unlike the Deanery of Derry, Berkeley did not regard the bishopric as a sinecure. He went straight to live in his diocese and remained there continuously until just before his death. He appears to have been a dutiful diocesan bishop with a particular interest in trying to promote harmony between the established Church of Ireland, to which he belonged, and the more numerous Catholics of that part of Ireland. One of his writings of the period is addressed to the Catholic clergy in most conciliatory terms asking for their support in improving the economic welfare of Ireland.

Berkeley was much exercised by the very poor economic state of Ireland compared with most continental countries and with

England. This backwardness he attributed partly to the laziness and ignorance of the peasant population, partly to the excessive number of absentee landlords who drained the country of its wealth while contributing nothing, and partly to an unnecessary excess of imports over exports. Berkeley exposed the facts and proposed some remedies in a work called the *Querist* which was published in three parts in 1735, 1736 and 1737. Unlike most of his writings the *Querist* makes laborious reading, especially since it takes the form of some six hundred separate numbered queries. Its intention was practical, but certain theoretical economic positions are implicit in Berkeley's criticisms and proposals, and it is thus his main contribution to economics.

The importance of work for wealth is one of Berkeley's main themes. It is to be found in the first query: 'Whether there ever was, is, or will be, an industrious nation poor or an idle rich?', and it recurs over and over again. Another main theme is that money is important only as an instrument of exchange and that gold and silver are of little value. 'Whether there be any virtue in gold or silver, other than as they set people at work, or create industry?', Berkeley asks, and 'Whether the denominations being retained, although the bullion were gone, things might not nevertheless be rated, bought and sold, industry promoted, and a circulation of commerce maintained?' (Queries 30, 26). But though he stressed the connection between labour and wealth, Berkeley was well aware of the importance of the market place for determining value. Query 24 runs: 'Whether the value or price of things be not a compounded proportion, directly as the demand, and reciprocally as the plenty?'

Berkeley was on the whole in favour of restricting foreign trade, largely because he thought it criminal to send abroad Irish food to import such things as French brandy when the peasants were starving. So he asks 'whether trade be not then on a right foot, when foreign commodities are imported in exchange only for domestic superfluities?' (Query 172). He goes on to ask 'whether there should not be published yearly schedules of our trade, containing an account of the imports and exports of the foregoing year?' (Query 179).

Berkeley was also much impressed with the importance of banks, thinking it 'the greatest help and spur to commerce that property can be so readily conveyed and so well secured by a *compte en banc*, that is, by only writing one man's name for another's in the bank-book' (Query 296). Banks promoted trade and he was convinced that it was necessary to establish a bank of Ireland, a national bank on the model of those in Venice, Hamburg and Amsterdam, cities whose wealth Berkeley attributed largely to their public banks. While it is hard to claim that Berkeley ranks with Hume and Adam Smith in importance as a philosophical economist, historians of that science regard him as a significant figure.

The two works for which Berkeley was best known in his own day were published while he was Bishop of Cloyne. We have considered *The Analyst* (1734) in the chapter on Berkeley's views on mathematics. In the following year he published replies to attacks on *The Analyst*, including the amusingly titled *Reasons for not Replying to Mr Walton's Full Answer*.

But something more must be said of *Siris: A Chain of Philosophical Reflexions and Inquiries concerning the Virtues of Tarwater, and divers other subjects connected together and arising one from another*, published in 1744. This was Berkeley's last published work apart from some letters about the virtues of tarwater and *Farther Thoughts on Tar-water*, published in 1752: the word *Siris*, derived from a Greek word meaning 'chain', is explained by the rest of the title. Starting from a consideration of the virtues of tar-water as a medicine and questions about its best method of manufacture, Berkeley goes on to consider more generally the nature of the physical universe, of the spiritual universe and, finally, of God. In the course of the discussions much curious learning is exhibited concerning Pythagoras, Plato, Aristotle, Theophrastus, Plotinus, Iamblichus and other ancient thinkers.

Berkeley believed that tar-water was a panacea. He had first come across it when in America, particularly as a remedy for smallpox. It was a concoction formed by boiling up in water the tar exuded from the incised bark of pine or fir trees; Berkeley directs that it should be drunk by the glassful. He tried the remedy on his local Irish population for smallpox, ulcers, consumptive cough, erysipelas, indigestion and asthma with uniformly beneficial results. The nerves constitute the inner garment of the soul, and thus the oil in tar-water can act beneficially on the mind also.

It was as providing a medical panacea that Berkeley's *Siris* attracted so much attention, though the medical fraternity appears not to have been unduly impressed. It is doubtful if much more of the work was read then, and few read any of it now; yet its editor A. C. Fraser calls it 'the consummation, on the basis of ancient philosophy, of Berkeley's conception of the concrete universe, past present and future, as in necessary dependence upon all-constitutive Intelligence'. Certainly there are passages, one or two of which have been quoted in earlier chapters, which do help to explain and enlarge Berkeley's analytic and metaphysical views of science. But though Berkeley certainly maintains the immaterialism of his earlier philosophy there is now a strain of speculative metaphysics which seems quite alien to the earlier Berkeley. Here is a specimen (S 171): 'The tunicle of the soul, whether it be called pure aether, or luciform vehicle, or animal spirit, seemeth to be that which acts upon the gross organs, as it is determined by the soul from which it immediately receives impression.' He goes on to say that 'some moderns have thought fit to deride all that is said of aetherial vehicles, as mere jargon or words without a meaning'. The early Berkeley who wrote: 'Mem. To be eternally banishing metaphysics, &c., and recalling men to Common Sense' (C 751) might have thought aetherial vehicles in no better condition than matter.

Berkeley continued to live in his diocese until 1752, when he retired to Oxford, where he had a son at Christ Church. He took a house in Holywell Street. On the evening of Sunday 14 January 1753, while listening to his wife reading from the Bible, he died suddenly. Perhaps he had a fear of being buried alive; he certainly expressed a wish in his will that he should not be buried until there were signs of bodily corruption. He was accordingly buried on the following Saturday. His grave can still be seen in the floor of the nave of Christ Church cathedral. There is a memorial tablet on a pillar close by; its eulogy of Berkeley's character and intellectual gifts is accurate; its dating of his birth is not.

9

Critical retrospect

THE aim of this book has been to describe the life and works of Berkeley, not to defend them or adversely criticise them, though there has been no rigorous avoidance of expressions of praise and agreement or of condemnation and disagreement. But since it has so often been said that Berkeley's views are impossible to accept and impossible to refute, the reader might welcome a final critical evaluation of his main position.

There are two main premises of Berkeley's philosophy. One of them is that all that is ever before the mind is ideas, ideas being taken to cover both perception and thought and to be mental images. The second is one of the many theses which have been called the principle of empiricism. Berkeley stated it at least twice in his notebooks; he said: 'Foolish in men to despise the senses. If it were not for them the mind could have no knowledge, no thought at all'; and again: 'I approve of this axiom of the Schoolmen, "Nihil est in intellectu quod non prius fuit in sensu" [Nothing is in the intellect which was not previously in sensation]' (C 539, 779).

It is surely clear that if both these premises of Berkeley are correct then his main contention that matter is unthinkable must also be correct. For the relevant concept of matter is of something that is never an object of the senses and so never in the intellect. If empiricism as Berkeley states it is correct then we can think only of the ideas that are the sole objects of the mind. So it does not matter much what we think of the detail of some of his argument, which varies in quality; we must either deny one or both of these premises or accept the conclusion.

It is far from clear that either of these premises is correct. Let us first consider briefly the premise that all objects of perception are ideas, thought of as mental images, caused by matter, according to Locke, or by God directly, according to Berkeley. Berkeley had claimed that Locke's ontology was inflated, and that this unintelligible matter was unnecessary; why should God use matter or any other instrument in his government of the world? So Locke requires God to create and control matter, matter to cause ideas, ideas to be the content of minds, and minds to receive them. Berkeley cuts out matter from the chain. Both are equally in disagreement with pre-philosophical common belief; for in most people's thought there is, maybe, God to create and sustain, there are physical bodies, and there are minds which observe the bodies. There is neither the matter which Berkeley rejected, nor the ideas of sense which he accepted. Certainly Berkeley does not deny that there are in some sense physical bodies, but they are hypothetical constructs and not the direct objects of perception.

It is by no means clear that the arguments against the common pre-philosophical beliefs are good ones. Berkeley relies principally on the so-called argument from illusion, on such facts as that water can feel hot to one hand and cold to another and that a penny will look a different shape from different angles. But it is not clear that these are good reasons for claiming that bodies are not directly perceived. It might be instructive for the reader to consider, if the facts of perspective tell against direct perception of objects, how a penny would have to look if it were directly perceived. Would it always look round, and, if so, how could he distinguish it visually from a sphere?

It is also not clear why, if we believe that we perceive physical bodies, we should think of matter as something distinct from them and lurking behind them. It might be thought that the scientific description of the world is an alternative description of the world we perceive rather than a description of another world. If it is an alternative description of the world we perceive it is not clear why we should think of ourselves as being obliged to ask whether the everyday description of the world or the scientific description is *the* correct one. There are many alternative and equally correct descriptions of each of us, for example, which vary only in their utility in various contexts. It is far from clear that when one says that a tomato is red one is saying anything which is in intention or in fact incompatible with scientific theories about matter, colour or anything else, so why need we choose one or the other?

So, while these few comments have obviously not refuted Berkeley's view that the sole objects of perception are ideas, we should at least not accept it without discussion or agree with him that, as he claims in the very first line of the *Principles*, it is evident that ideas are the sole objects of human knowledge.

It is also far from clear that the empiricist thesis as formulated by Berkeley is acceptable. It is not merely that there are some concepts, of traditional concern to philosophers, such as those of necessity, of matter, of God, of force or of goodness, which have often been regarded as examples of what must be treated as innate ideas or a priori concepts. This extreme empiricist doctrine seems to be unable to account for various plebeian concepts which it would be absurd to regard as a priori. Thus we might consider the concept of a trump, as it occurs in bridge. It seems clear that there is no sensible mark of being a trump which distinguishes it from other cards as there is a conspicuous mark of a spade which distinguishes it from other cards; so the concept of a trump cannot reach us from our senses as Berkeley claims is the case with all concepts. It is also very difficult to see how we could think about trumps in non-verbal ideas; we cannot concentrate our attention on any sensible feature in order to do so, for being a trump involves no distinctive sensible feature. It is easy to see that the same considerations apply to the concepts of an uncle, a felony, or of limited liability; with a little deeper thought it can be seen that the same applies to nearly all concepts.

So Berkeley has surely relied on a defective concept of empiricism in order to justify his claim that the concept of matter is unintelligible. It may well be that there is some other principle of empiricism which Berkeley could invoke to yield him the desired conclusion, but we cannot agree that Berkeley has clearly proved his contention.

But if Berkeley's arguments are not conclusive, they are by no means without value. Locke's views are very attractive to educated people with some knowledge of science; they swept Europe in the eighteenth century and they are probably held in some nebulous form by many people in the twentieth century. Locke was a less extreme empiricist than Berkeley, but possibly at the expense of some inconsistency, for at times he certainly seems to accept those empiricist premises that Berkeley accepted and whose self-evidence we have just called into question. It is a genuine question whether views like those of Locke are safe from the type of criticism that Berkeley had to offer.

But Berkeley was not merely destructive. In his own time, to Berkeley's intense indignation, his denial of matter was treated by most as a form of that scepticism which he claimed to demolish. There were indeed few in the eighteenth century who made any serious attempt to understand him. Hume (of whose work Berkeley appears to have been entirely ignorant) appreciated and understood him, but this is true of few others. Kant, without reading him, claimed to refute him in a 'Refutation of Idealism' which is a model of impenetrable obscurity, and it is typical of the attitude of the nineteenth century that in Ueberweg's monumental *History of Philosophy*, published at the end of the century, Berkeley is granted only a few words in the course of a chapter largely devoted to Locke.

But this view of Berkeley, based largely on ignorance, is quite wrong. His editor, A. C. Fraser, one of the first to appreciate his true worth, was surely right to place him with Hume and Kant as one of the three great philosophers of the eighteenth century. Unfortunately the view of Berkeley as merely a propounder of a paradoxical theory of perception has lingered on in the twentieth century. But his worth has been recognised more and more, and few who have read him with care would deny his importance in the philosophy of science or the brilliance of his many insights in other areas of philosophy. His position as one of the most gifted and most readable of philosophers is now secure.

Further reading

The Works of George Berkeley, Bishop of Cloyne, edited by A. A. Luce and T. E. Jessop, 9 vols. Nelson and Sons, Edinburgh, 1948–57, is the most complete and accurate presentation of all Berkeley's writings.

Berkeley's Complete Works, edited by A. C. Fraser, 4 vols, Oxford at the Clarendon Press, 1901, is not so complete but contains all the major works.

There are paperback editions of the *New Theory of Vision*, the *Principles* and the *Three Dialogues between Hylas and Philonous*, singly or in various combinations, in abundance.

Berkeley by George Pitcher, Routledge & Kegan Paul, London, 1977, is the best large-scale study of Berkeley available.

Berkeley by G. J. Warnock, Pelican, Harmondsworth, 1953, is a good shorter treatment concentrating on the main themes of the *Principles*.

Locke and Berkeley: A Collection of Critical Essays, edited by C. B. Martin and D. M. Armstrong, Macmillan, London, n.d., is a very useful collection which reprints some of the most important modern articles on Berkeley.

HUME

Preface

WITH the exception of the short biographical chapter, for which I am greatly indebted to Professor Ernest C. Mossner's excellent book *The Life of David Hume*, this book reproduces the text of the four Gilbert Ryle lectures which I delivered at Trent University, Ontario, in March 1979. I was all the more pleased to be invited to give these lectures, as Gilbert Ryle was my own tutor in philosophy, and I wish to express my gratitude not only to the sponsors of the lectures, the Machette Foundation and the Victoria and Grey Trust Company, but also to the members of the Department of Philosophy and many of their colleagues at Trent for the warmth of the hospitality which they showed to me.

In quoting from Hume's philosophical works, I have made use of the following texts, of which the first three are available in paperback.

A Treatise of Human Nature, edited by L. A. Selby-Bigge; second edition revised by P. H. Nidditch; including Hume's *Appendices* and *Abstract*. Oxford University Press, 1978.

Enquiries concerning Human Understanding and concerning the Principles of Morals, edited by L. A. Selby-Bigge; third edition revised by P. H. Nidditch. Oxford University Press, 1975.

Dialogues Concerning Natural Religion, edited with an introduction by Norman Kemp Smith, including Hume's *My Own Life* as a supplement. Bobbs-Merrill, 1977.

Essays Moral Political and Literary, Vol. II, edited by T. H. Green and T. H. Grose. Longmans, 1875.

At the wish of the Oxford University Press, I have put my references to these works within brackets in the text, identifying them by the letters T, E, D, and G respectively. The numerals following the letters refer to pages. My only other references of this sort are to pages of Mossner's book, identified by the letter M.

For all his other literary achievements, including his celebrated *History of England*, Hume was first and foremost a philosopher, and apart from the opening chapter, in which a sketch of his life is given, this book is entirely devoted to an exposition of his philosophy.

I owe thanks to Dr Henry Hardy of the Oxford University Press for commissioning this book from me, and once again to Mrs Guida Crowley for typing my manuscript and helping me to correct the proofs.

A. J. Ayer
10 Regent's Park Terrace, N.W.1.
18 April 1979

Contents

To Raymond Klibansky

1

Life and character

DAVID Hume, to my mind the greatest of all British philosophers, was born at Edinburgh on what, in the old calendar, was 26 April 1711. In his valedictory *My Own Life*, an autobiography running only to five pages, which Hume composed in April 1776, four months before his death, he showed pride in coming of good family, on both sides. His father, Joseph Home, combined the profession of law with the ownership of an estate at Ninewells in Berwickshire, which had belonged to the family since the sixteenth century, the family being, as Hume put it, 'a branch of the Earl of Home's or Hume's' (D 233), which was in our days to produce a Conservative Prime Minister; his mother, Katherine, was 'the daughter of Sir David Falconer, President of the College of Justice', and one of her brothers inherited a peerage. The couple had three children, of whom David was the youngest, his brother John being born in 1709 and his sister Katherine a year later.

Joseph Home died in 1713, while David was still an infant. The estate passed to the elder son and David was left with a patrimony of some £50 a year, which even in those days was not quite enough to make him financially independent. It was planned that he should follow his father's example and become a lawyer. Their mother, who did not remarry, managed the estate until John was old enough to take charge of it. By all accounts, David was devoted to her, as well as to his brother and sister. She was an ardent Calvinist, and brought her children up in the faith, which David rejected, together with all other forms of Christianity, in his teens. That this did not impair his relations with his mother suggests that he concealed it from her or at least did not obtrude it. Throughout his life he was of a peaceable disposition and averse from engaging in public as well as private controversy, though not at all lacking in the courage of his own convictions, however unorthodox, or reluctant to express them in print. The story of his mother's saying 'Our Davie's a fine good-natured crater, but uncommon wake-minded' is not supported by any documentary evidence. If it is true, it may be the expression of a feeling of exasperation at the time which it took him to become financially independent of the family estate.

In 1723, when David Hume was not quite twelve years old, he went with his elder brother to the University of Edinburgh. They were there for the best part of three years and left, as was quite common in those times, without taking a degree. The arts course, in which they were enrolled, comprised Greek, logic, metaphysics and natural philosophy, now better known as physics, as compulsory subjects. There were also elective courses in other subjects such as ethics and mathematics. The level of the lectures seems to have been fairly elementary, but it is probable that Hume gained some knowledge at this stage of the seminal work of Isaac Newton and John Locke. All that he himself says about his university studies is that he 'passed through the ordinary Course of Education with Success'.

Having returned to Ninewells, Hume tried to settle down to the study of law, but very soon gave up the attempt. The passion for literature, understood as including history and philosophy, to which he referred in his autobiography as 'the ruling Passion of my Life and the Great Source of my Enjoyments', proved too strong, to the point where, in his own words, he 'found an insurmountable Aversion to anything but the pursuits of Philosophy and General Learning' (D 233). Though he speaks of Cicero and Virgil as the authors whom he was 'secretly devouring', in place of the jurists whose works his family believed him to be studying, his thoughts ran chiefly on philosophy, and it was in 1729, when he was still only eighteen years of age, that there opened up to him 'the new scene of thought' which was to be displayed in his first and eventually most famous book, *A Treatise of Human Nature*.

The excitement of this discovery and the intensity with which he worked upon it combined to impair Hume's health. His disorder was psychosomatic and a course of regular physical exercise, supported by an ample diet, turned him within two years from a 'tall, lean and rawbon'd' youth into what he describes as the 'most sturdy, robust, healthful-like Fellow you have seen with a ruddy Complexion and a cheerful Countenance'. Nevertheless he remained subject to attacks of nervous depression, with physical symptoms such as palpitations of the heart, and the local physicians, to whom he frequently resorted, were unable to cure him. Eventually, he himself decided that he had better give up his studies, at least for the time being, in order to 'lead a more active life', and in February 1734 he left Scotland for Bristol, where he had been offered a post as clerk in a firm of sugar-merchants. His decision may have been influenced by the fact that he was shortly to be cited by a local servant-girl before an ecclesiastical court, presided over by his uncle, as the father of her illegitimate child. The charge was not considered proved against him and did not, even locally, damage his reputation. There is, indeed, later evidence that he remained susceptible to women, though he never married and was of too calm a temper, and too thoroughly immersed in intellectual pursuits, to qualify as an amorist.

Though he made some good friends in Bristol, it took Hume no more than four months to decide that the life of commerce did not suit him. It has been suggested that he was dismissed from his employment because of his insistence on criticising his employer's literary style (M 90). Whether this is true or not, there is no doubt that Hume was happy to be left free to concentrate on his philosophy. The most lasting result of his stay in Bristol was that he there changed the spelling of his name from Home to Hume, to accord with its pronunciation.

Having resolved to devote himself to the writing of his *Treatise*, Hume migrated to France, probably on the ground that he could manage better there on his small private income. After a short stay in Paris, where he obtained some useful introductions from a fellow Scotsman, the Chevalier Ramsay, he spent a year at Rheims and two years at the small town of La Flèche in Anjou, the site of the Jesuit College where Descartes had been educated. He made friends among the Jesuit Fathers and took advantage of their extensive library. By the autumn of 1737 the greater part of the book was written, and Hume returned to London to find a publisher for it.

This did not prove so easy as he had hoped. It was a year before he succeeded in making a contract with John Noon for an edition of a thousand copies of the first two 'books', entitled 'Of the Understanding' and 'Of the Passions', for which he received £50 and twelve bound copies. The work was published, anonymously, at a price of ten shillings, in January 1739, under the general title of *A Treatise of Human Nature: Being an Attempt to introduce the experimental Method of Reasoning into Moral Subjects*. The third 'book', 'Of Morals', was not yet ready for publication. Its appearance was delayed until November 1740, when it was published, this time by Mark Longman, at a price of four shillings.

The reception of the *Treatise* was a great disappointment to Hume. In his own words, 'Never Literary Attempt was more unfortunate than my Treatise. It fell *dead-born from the Press*, without reaching such distinction as even to excite a murmur among the zealots (D 234). This is not altogether accurate. It is true that not all the copies of Noon's edition were sold in Hume's lifetime, but the work was noticed in English and foreign journals, and obtained three reviews of considerable length. The trouble was that the tone of the reviews was predominantly hostile, and on occasion disdainful. Hume believed that the hostility arose largely from a misunderstanding of his views, and he sought to remedy this by publishing in 1740 an anonymous six-penny pamphlet, advertised as *An Abstract of a late Philosophical Performance, entitled* A TREATISE OF HUMAN NATURE, *&c. Wherein the chief Argument and Design of that Book, which has met with such Opposition, and been represented in so terrifying a Light, is further illustrated and explain'd*, but appearing under the less aggressive title of *An Abstract of a Book lately Published. Entituled, A Treatise of Human Nature, &c. Wherein The Chief Argument of that Book is further Illustrated and Explained*. This pamphlet fell into oblivion until a copy of it was discovered and identified in the late 1930s by Maynard Keynes, and published with an introduction by himself and Piero Sraffa under the title *An Abstract of a Treatise of Human Nature, 1740: A Pamphlet hitherto unknown by David Hume*. The abstract draws particular attention to Hume's theory of causation, which was, indeed, the feature of the *Treatise* for which it was later to become most celebrated.

Hume came to think himself largely responsible for the failure of the *Treatise*, because of its defects of presentation, and was later disposed to disown it. The first sign of this is to be found in the preface to the first of the two volumes of *Essays, Moral and Political*, published respectively in 1741 and 1742, in which, remaining anonymous, he is described as a 'new Author'. The essays, which were brought out by Andrew Kincaid in Edinburgh and numbered twenty-seven in all, were of varying degrees of seriousness, and covered a large range of topics, including criticism, manners, philosophy and politics. They were favourably received, especially the political essays on such subjects as 'The Liberty of the Press' and 'The first Principles of Government'. One that aroused particular interest was 'A character of Sir Robert Walpole', a harsher appraisal than Hume wanted to sustain when that statesman had fallen from power. For this reason, no doubt, he did not reprint the essay in later editions of the work. He also omitted several of the lighter pieces with such titles as 'Of Love and Marriage' and 'Of Impudence and Modesty'.

The publication of these essays not only made Hume some money, amounting perhaps to £200, but emboldened him to become a candidate for the Professorship of Ethics and Pneumatical Philosophy at Edinburgh University. The suggestion that he should apply was made to him in 1744 by his friend, John Coutts, the Lord Provost of Edinburgh. The holder of the Chair, Alexander Pringle, had been on leave for the past two years, serving abroad as an army doctor, and his appointment as Physician-General to the Forces in Flanders did not seem compatible with his remaining a professor in Edinburgh. There was then no overt opposition in the Town Council to the choice of Hume as his successor. Unfortunately, however, Pringle delayed his resignation till Coutts had ceased to be Lord Provost and the zealots, whom Hume had after all offended, had time to gather their forces. A pamphlet, entitled *A Letter from a Gentleman to his friend in Edinburgh*, which Hume published anonymously in 1745, denying that he had rejected, as opposed to explicating, the proposition 'that whatever begins to exist must have a cause', or that the argument of his *Treatise* led in any other way to atheism, failed to appease them. The Chair was offered in the same year to Hume's friend and mentor, Francis Hutcheson, who was Professor of Moral Philosophy at the University of Glasgow, and when Hutcheson declined it, the Council chose to promote the lecturer who had been doing Pringle's work.

Still lacking the financial security which the appointment would have given him, Hume accepted an offer of a salary of £300 a year to act as tutor to the Marquis of Annandale, an eccentric young nobleman, soon to be declared insane, who lived

near St Alban's at a convenient distance from London. In spite
of his employer's vagaries, and the ill-will shown him by an
influential member of the family, Hume was sufficiently contented with his position to be willing to consider retaining it at
a lower salary. No doubt the reason was that it allowed him
leisure to write. It was at this time that he began work on his
Philosophical Essays Concerning Human Understanding, later to be
entitled *An Enquiry concerning Human Understanding*, which was
designed to supersede the first book of the *Treatise*, and most
probably also wrote his *Three Essays, Moral and Political*. Both
works were published in 1748.

The *Enquiry* is, indeed, a much better written work than the
Treatise, from which it differs more in emphasis than in argument.
The central issue of causality is brought more into the fore-
ground, and it is less encumbered with what would now be
reckoned as psychology. There are also sections of the *Treatise*,
such as that on Space and Time, for which it has no counterpart.
On the other hand, it includes a chapter 'Of Miracles', which
Hume had omitted from the *Treatise* out of prudence. The central
argument of this chapter 'That no testimony is sufficient to
establish a miracle, unless the testimony be of such kind that its
falsehood would be more miraculous than the fact, which it
endeavours to establish' (E 115–16), with its iconoclastic implications, procured Hume more fame among his contemporaries
than anything else in his purely philosophical work.

Three Essays, Moral and Political, which appeared in February
1748, was the first of Hume's books to which he put his own
name, a practice he was thenceforward to continue. The essays
were prompted by the rebellion of the Young Pretender, and
Hume said of them, before their publication, that 'One is against
the original Contract, the system of the Whigs, another against
passive Obedience, the system of the Tories: A third upon the
Protestant Succession, where I suppose a Man to deliberate,
before the Establishment of that Succession, which Family he
should adhere to, and to weigh the Advantages and Disadvant-
ages of each.' In fact the essay on the Protestant Succession was
not published till 1752, and was replaced in the 1748 volume by
an essay on 'National Characters'. Hume was in no degree a
Jacobite, but he wrote a pamphlet in defence of his friend Lord
Provost Stewart, who was arraigned in 1747 for having surren-

dered Edinburgh to the rebels, though owing to the timidity of the printers the pamphlet was published only after Stewart's acquittal.

Hume's willingness to compromise over his tutorship availed him nothing, for in April 1746 he was dismissed, with a quarter's salary owing to him which he may, some fifteen years later, have succeeded in getting paid. He thought of returning to Scotland, to a home bereft of his mother, who to his great sorrow had died the year before, but was prevented by an offer from a distant kinsman, General St Clair, to act as his Secretary on an expedition which the General had been appointed to lead to Canada, with the intention of helping the English colonists to expel the French. While the expedition was waiting at Portsmouth for a favourable wind, Hume was promoted from his Secretaryship to be Judge-Advocate of all the forces under St Clair's command. The wind never did become favourable, and the expedition was diverted to Brittany, where it failed to take the town of L'Orient, abandoning the siege just at the moment when the French were deciding to surrender, and returned to England without having accomplished anything of note. General St Clair appears to have been more unlucky than culpable, and his conduct of the expedition was later to be defended by Hume in print against the ridicule of Voltaire. Once more Hume had to wait many years before he was able to extract from the Government the pay due to him as Judge-Advocate.

After the expedition was disbanded, Hume returned briefly to Ninewells, but early in 1747 he was back in London, having accepted an invitation from the General to serve as one of his Aides-de-camp 'in his military Embassy to the Court of Vienna and Turin'. He wore the uniform of an officer, which probably did not become him. According to an irreverent young witness 'the Corpulence of his whole Person was far better fitted to communicate the Idea of a Turtle-eating Alderman than of a refined Philosopher' (M 213–14). The same observer, though subsequently proud of his acquaintance with Hume, commented on the disparity between his mental powers and the vacancy of his countenance and sneered at his retention of 'the broadest and most vulgar Scottish accent' in speaking either English or French.

Hume remained at Turin until the end of 1748, so that he was absent from England during the period of the publication of the

Three Essays, the first volume of the *Enquiry*, and a reissue of *Essays, Moral and Political*, which laid the foundation of his literary reputation. The great French writer Montesquieu was so impressed with these *Essays* that he sent Hume a copy of his *L'Esprit des loix*, and the two men corresponded regularly for the remaining seven years of Montesquieu's life.

Hume himself was slow to realise that the tide was turning in his favour, at least if we are to believe his autobiography, in which he speaks of his mortification at finding on his return to England that neither the *Enquiry* nor the reissue of his *Essays* had achieved any great success. This was not however a discouragement but rather a stimulus to his literary ambition. Returning to Ninewells, he completed by 1751 the *Enquiry concerning the Principles of Morals*, designed to replace Book III of the *Treatise*, and considered by Hume 'of all my writings historical, philosophical or literary incomparably the best' (D 236). In the following year he published his *Political Discourses*, and during this period he also began work on his *Dialogues concerning Natural Religion* and engaged in research for his *History of England*. At the same time his work began to attract criticism. In his own words, 'Answers by Reverends and Right Reverends came out two or three a year' (D 235), but Hume maintained his fixed resolution 'never to reply to anybody'.

This hostility did not extend for the most part to the *Political Discourses*, though they did not escape being placed on the Roman Catholic Index, in 1761, along with all Hume's other works. The *Discourses*, described by Hume as 'the only work of mine that was successful on its first Publication', were originally twelve in number, of which only four were strictly political. One was concerned with the relative populousness of the ancient and modern worlds and the other seven were contributions to what is now called economics. Hume was a strong advocate of free trade, and his essays in some degree foreshadowed the theory developed by his young friend Adam Smith in his celebrated book *The Wealth of Nations*, the first volume of which was read with admiration by Hume a few months before his death.

In 1751, John Home married, and David and his sister set up house in Edinburgh, moving to slightly more luxurious quarters as his fortunes improved. Apart from his literary earnings, his appointments at Vienna and Turin had left him 'master of near a thousand Pound' and his sister had a small private income of £30 to add to his £50. Though he speaks of his frugality, he seems to have led an active social life, being frequently entertained by his numerous circle of friends, including many of the moderate clergy, and returning their hospitality. He was, however, prepared to move to Glasgow, if he had been able to secure the University Chair of Logic which Adam Smith vacated in 1752 to succeed to the Chair of Moral Philosophy, but though he had the support of other professors besides Adam Smith, the opposition of the zealots again prevented his appointment.

Hume was in some degree consoled for this failure by being made Librarian to the Faculty of Advocates at Edinburgh. The salary was only £40 a year and Hume refused to take it after 1754, when the Curators rejected, on the ground that they were indecent, three books that he had ordered, one of them being the *Contes* of La Fontaine. Hume did not resign till 1757, but compromised in the meantime by giving the money to his friend Blacklock, the blind poet. The advantage to Hume of the position was that, the library being exceptionally well-stocked, it gave him access to the books that he needed for the writing of his history. He appears still to have had access to the library after he had resigned its Keepership in favour of his friend the philosopher Adam Ferguson.

The six volumes of Hume's history appeared in an unusual order. It began with the Stuarts, the first volume, covering the reigns of James I and Charles I, and the second, which continued the story till the fall of James II, being published respectively in 1754 and 1756. The next two volumes, which came out in 1759, were devoted to the Tudors, and the work was completed by the publication in 1762 of two volumes spanning the centuries between the invasion of Julius Caesar and the accession of Henry VII. The first volume was a failure at the outset, partly because its attempt to be fair to both sides in the conflict between King and Parliament irritated the Whigs without satisfying the Tories, and partly, it would seem, because of a conspiracy into which the London booksellers entered against the Edinburgh firm to which Hume had entrusted it. Eventually this firm found it advisable to transfer its rights to Andrew Millar, Hume's usual publisher, who then brought out the subsequent volumes. These were much more successful, both critically and financially. The sums for which Hume sold the rights of the various volumes amounted in all to more than £3000, and the work came to be considered by Hume's contemporaries as an outstanding achievement, to the point where he was esteemed even more highly as a historian than as a philosopher. Thus Voltaire went so far as to say that 'nothing can be added to the fame of this *History*, perhaps the best ever written in any language' (M 318). A much later verdict of Lytton Strachey's, in an essay on Hume included in his *Portraits in Miniature*, that Hume's book, 'brilliant and weighty as it was, must be classed rather as a philosophical survey than a historical relation', comes nearer the mark, but the *History* remains very well worth reading, if only for its wit and the beauty of Hume's style.

In the course of publishing his *History* Hume brought out in 1757 another volume of essays entitled *Four Dissertations*. The most important of them was 'The Natural History of Religion'. The second, 'Of the Passions', was a condensation and revision of the second book of the *Treatise*. The third and fourth were 'Of Tragedy' and 'The Standard of Taste'. The essay on the standard of taste took the place of an essay on Geometry and Natural Philosophy which Hume was dissuaded from printing by his friend Lord Stanhope, who was a mathematician. Having discarded the mathematical essay, Hume planned to bring the number of Dissertations up to five by adding to the first three mentioned an essay 'Of Suicide' and one called 'Of the Immortality of the Soul', but his publisher, Millar, was afraid of the consequences of their being taken as a further affront to religion, and Hume withdrew them. Copies of the manuscripts were in private circulation, but the essays were never included in any authorised edition of Hume's works, though unauthorised versions appeared in 1777 and 1783, and they are to be found among 'Unpublished Essays' in the second volume of the Green and Grose edition of 1875.

In 1758 and again in 1761 Hume went to London to see the remaining volumes of his History through the press. On the first occasion he remained there for over a year, and had serious thoughts of settling there, before deciding that he preferred the atmosphere of Edinburgh. He was well received both in high society and in literary circles, though Boswell reports Dr Johnson's saying that he once left a company as soon as Hume joined it. Johnson's 'abhorrence' of Hume did not, however, prevent them on a later occasion from being fellow guests at dinner at the Royal Chaplain's without their coming into open conflict. Characteristically, Hume used his influence with Millar to ensure the publication of the *History of Scotland* written by his friend, the Reverend William Robertson, and to promote its sales, even to the possible detriment of those of his own work. He was, however, slightly annoyed when Robertson was appointed Historiographer Royal for Scotland, in preference to himself.

At the conclusion of the Seven Years War in 1763 the Earl of Hertford, a cousin of Horace Walpole's, was appointed British Ambassador to the court of France. Being supplied with an official secretary of whose character he did not approve, he decided to employ a personal secretary and offered the position to Hume, whom he had never met. Since he was himself a very pious man, this choice was surprising, but Hume had been strongly recommended to him, as one whose name carried great prestige in France. Hume at first declined the offer, but accepted when it was renewed. He liked both Lord and Lady Hertford when he met them in London, and in October 1763 he accompanied them to Paris.

From the moment of his arrival in Paris Hume enjoyed the most extraordinary social success. As Lytton Strachey put it, 'he was flattered by princes, worshipped by fine ladies, and treated as an oracle by the *philosophes*'. His closest friends among the *philosophes* were the *Encyclopédistes* Diderot and d'Alembert, and the materialist Baron d'Holbach. There is a story of his dining at Holbach's and saying that he had never met an atheist, whereupon Holbach told him that of the persons present fifteen were atheists and the other three had not made up their minds. Among the fine ladies his chief admirer was the Countess de Boufflers, who had made herself known to him by letter in 1761. Fourteen years younger than Hume, she was the mistress of the Prince de Conti, whom she had vain hopes of marrying when her husband died. Though she never lost sight of this primary objective, she appears for a time to have been in love with Hume, and there is stronger evidence from their correspondence that he was in love with her. Though they did not meet again after Hume left Paris in January 1766, they continued for the next ten years to write to one another. His last letter to her, commiserating with her on the death of the Prince de Conti and saying of himself 'I see death approach gradually, without any Anxiety or Regret. I salute you with great affection and regard, for the last time', was written within a week of his own death.

When Hume left Paris he took Jean-Jacques Rousseau with him. Rousseau had been living in Switzerland, but his heterodox religious views had made him enemies there, nor could he rely on being undisturbed in France. Hume was persuaded, mainly by their common friend Madame de Verdelin, to take Rousseau under his protection, though warned by the *philosophes* that Rousseau was not to be trusted. Rousseau's 'gouvernante', the illiterate Thérèse Le Vasseur, was to follow, escorted by Boswell, whom she seduced on the way. At first all went well. Hume and Rousseau liked and admired one another. There was some trouble in finding a place where Rousseau would consent to live, but he finally accepted an offer from Richard Davenport, a rich country gentleman, of a house in Staffordshire at a nominal rent. Hume also arranged for him to receive an offer of a pension of £200 from King George III. But then Rousseau's paranoia broke out. Horace Walpole had written a squib against him, which Rousseau attributed to Hume. There had been jokes about him in the English press. Thérèse made mischief. Rousseau became convinced that Hume had joined with the *philosophes* in a conspiracy against him. He refused the King's pension, became suspicious of Mr Davenport, and wrote bitter letters to his friends in France, to the English newspapers, and to Hume himself. Hume tried to persuade Rousseau of his innocence, and when he failed, became anxious for his own reputation. He sent d'Alembert an account of the whole affair, giving him leave to publish it, if he thought fit. D'Alembert did publish it, together with the letters that constituted the principal evidence, and an English translation of d'Alembert's pamphlet appeared a few months later. Rousseau remained in England till the spring of 1767 and then, without a word to Mr Davenport, returned with Thérèse precipitately to France. There was no doubt that Rousseau had behaved very badly to Hume, but some of Hume's friends thought that he should have made allowances for Rousseau's paranoia and that it would have been more dignified for him not to have publicised the quarrel.

For a few months in 1765, during the interval between Lord Hertford's departure for Ireland, where he had been appointed Lord Lieutenant, and the arrival of his successor, Hume had acted as Chargé d'Affaires in Paris and shown himself to be a capable diplomat. He refused Lord Hertford's invitation to serve with him in Ireland, but in 1767 accepted an offer from the Secretary of State, Lord Hertford's brother, General Conway, to serve in London as Under-Secretary for the Northern Department. He carried out the duties of this position very successfully for the following two years.

When Hume returned to Edinburgh in 1769, he had become so 'opulent' as to enjoy an income of £1000 a year. He built himself a house in the New Town in a street off St Andrew's Square, which came in his honour to be known as St David's Street. He resumed his active social life, took no public notice of the numerous attacks that were made on his philosophy, and occupied himself with the revision of his *Dialogues Concerning Natural Religion*. The work was posthumously published, most probably by Hume's nephew, in 1779. In the spring of 1775 he was, in his own words, 'struck with a disorder in my bowels, which at first gave me no Alarm, but has since, as I apprehend it, become mortal and incurable' (D 239). He suffered little pain and never 'a moment's Abatement of my Spirits'. Boswell characteristically intruded on him to see how he was facing the prospect of death, and was convinced by his assurance that he viewed it serenely. Equally characteristically, Dr Johnson insisted that Hume must have been lying. Death finally came to him on 25 August 1776.

Hume's life largely bears out his description of himself as 'a man of mild Dispositions, of Command of Temper, of an open, social, and cheerful Humour, capable of Attachment, but little susceptible of Enmity, and of great Moderation in all my passions' (D 239). There is no doubt that Adam Smith was sincere when he concluded his obituary portrait of his friend by saying 'Upon the whole, I have always considered him, both in his life-time, and since his death, as approaching as nearly to the idea of a perfectly wise and virtuous man, as perhaps the nature of human frailty will admit.'

2

Aims and methods

IN histories of philosophy, David Hume is most often represented as completing a movement which was started by John Locke in 1690, with the publication of his *Essay Concerning Human Understanding*, and continued by George Berkeley, whose *Principles of Human Knowledge* appeared in 1710, the year before Hume's birth. The main theme of this movement is that men can have no knowledge of the world but what they derive from Experience, and the lines of its development are that Experience consists, as Locke put it, of Sensation and Reflection, that the operations of the mind, which are the objects of Reflection, are directed only on to the material, or their own transformation of the material, provided by the senses, and that the material provided by the senses consists of atomic elements such as colours, tactile feelings, bodily sensations, sounds, smells and tastes.

According to this story, Locke made a valiant attempt to assemble on this basis a picture of the physical world which accorded with the scientific theories of Boyle and Newton. It largely depended on his adopting a theory of perception which divided the data or, as Locke called them, 'simple ideas' of sense into two categories: ideas, such as those of solidity, figure and extension, which were not only the effects of the actions of physical objects upon our minds, but also resembled these objects in character, and ideas, such as those of colour or taste, which were nothing more than effects. These were respectively termed ideas of primary and ideas of secondary qualities. In both cases, the qualities accrued to the objects in virtue of the nature and activity of their 'minute parts,' but whereas the primary qualities actually characterised the objects, the secondary qualities were only dispositional; they were merely powers which enabled the objects, under suitable conditions, to produce ideas in us.

Berkeley, according to the view which we are considering, is held to have refuted Locke by demolishing his theory of perception. He showed not only that Locke was unjustified in drawing his vital distinction between ideas of primary and secondary qualities but, even more damagingly, that he had no warrant, on his premises, for believing in the existence of physical objects at all, that is, so long as physical objects are conceived, in the manner of Newton and Locke, as existing independently of our perception of them, and not as being simply composed of ideas or 'sensible qualities', a view which Berkeley somewhat rashly claimed to be anyhow more in accord with common sense. There had to be minds to perceive ideas, and since only a small minority of our ideas were the products of our own fancy, they had in the mass to have some external cause. But for this there was no need, no warrant, and, as Berkeley reasoned, not even any coherent possibility of having recourse to matter. God would suffice not only to cause our ideas but also to keep things in being when they happened not to enter into the field of any human perception. He might have laid a smaller burden upon God if he had taken the course, which John Stuart Mill was later to pursue, of reducing physical objects to 'permanent possibilities of sensation', and there are passages where he seems to endorse this view. But Berkeley was an Anglican bishop, and it suited his religious interests to maximise the part played by God. In Newtonian physics, provision is made for a creator to bring the universe into being, but once the machinery is started, the creator can turn his back upon it: it runs securely on its own. In Berkeley's estimation, this gave encouragement to deism or worse. He, therefore, made sure that God was constantly on the watch.

The part assigned to Hume is that of undermining Berkeley in much the same way as Berkeley had undermined Locke. Berkeley had eliminated matter, at least as the physicists conceived it, but left minds intact. Hume, an avowed sceptic, showed that this favouritism was unjustified. We had as little reason for believing in the existence of minds, as beings maintaining their identity through time, as we had for believing in the existence of material substances. There was an equal want of any rational justification for believing in the existence of Berkeley's God. But Hume carried his scepticism further. Both Locke and Berkeley had taken the concept of causality on trust. They differed only in that Locke allowed relations of force to hold between physical particles, whereas Berkeley gave minds the monopoly of causal activity. Hume set himself to analyse the relation of cause and effect, and what emerged from his analysis was that the idea of force, or of causal activity, in its ordinary interpretation, was myth. There could be no necessary connection between distinct events. All that remains, then, is a series of fleeting 'perceptions' with no external object, no enduring subject to whom they could belong, and not themselves even bound to one another.

This was the outcome attributed to Hume by the ablest of his contemporary critics, the Reverend Thomas Reid, who succeeded Adam Smith as Professor of Moral Philosophy at Glasgow University. Reid was the founder of the Scottish school of common-sense philosophers who carried the tradition into the nineteenth century, and his *Inquiry into the Human Mind on the Principles of Common Sense*, published in 1764, set the fashion of regarding the first book of Hume's *Treatise*, which Hume himself had intended his own *Enquiry* to supersede, as the primary source of Hume's philosophical views. Reid gave Hume credit for taking Locke's premises to their logical conclusion. Since the result was patently absurd it followed that something had gone wrong at the start. The principal error, as Reid saw it, was the adoption by Locke and his followers of the theory of ideas: the assumption that what is immediately perceived, whether it be called an idea, as by Locke, or a sensible quality, or, as Hume preferred, an impression, is something that has no existence apart from the perceptual situation in which it figures. If we reject this assumption, as indeed most philosophers now do, and follow common sense both in taking for granted the existence of persons to whom perceptual acts can be attributed, and in taking these persons to be directly acquainted through their senses with one and the same world of physical objects, which exist independently of being perceived, then Hume's scepticism may not have been met in every detail, but at least its most outrageous features will have been obliterated.

The same conception of Hume, as the sceptic who brought the empiricism of Locke and Berkeley to grief, appears over a century later in the work of the Oxford philosopher T. H. Green, who published an edition of the *Treatise* with a long introduction, the main purpose of which was to demolish the work that he was editing. His line of attack, however, had next to nothing in common with that of Thomas Reid. By this time, in spite of the

rearguard action commanded by John Stuart Mill, the influence
of Kant and Hegel was belatedly extending itself over British
philosophy, increasingly to the detriment of common sense.
Green was one of the leaders of this fashion, and his main
objection to Hume was that he admitted no greater order into
the world than what could be supplied by the mere association
of ideas. Once again, Hume was held to be justified on the
principles which he had inherited from Locke and Berkeley, and
the moral drawn was that a new approach was needed. This had
been appreciated by Kant who, in his *Prolegomena*, gave Hume
credit for interrupting his 'dogmatic slumber' and giving his
'investigations in the field of speculative philosophy quite a new
direction'. At Oxford in the 1930s, and perhaps still to this day
in some places, the canonical view of Hume, as advanced for
instance by a former Master of Balliol, A. D. Lindsay, who
churned out the introductions to the handy Everyman editions
of required philosophical texts, was that for all his errors and
inconsistencies, which Green had relentlessly pinpointed, Hume
had still performed a considerable service to philosophy. By
showing on the one hand how an uncritical trust in reason had
foundered in dogmatism, and on the other by reducing pure
empiricism to absurdity, he had paved the way for Kant.

So far as I know, the first commentator to treat Hume neither
as an appendage to Locke and Berkeley nor as a forerunner of
Kant, but as a philosopher of original views which at least
deserved serious consideration, was Professor Norman Kemp
Smith, whose book *The Philosophy of David Hume: A Critical
Study of Its Origins and Central Doctrines* was published in 1941.
Kemp Smith's book is very long, and not always very lucid, but
it is sustained by careful and far-reaching scholarship and it has
the merit of paying close attention to what Hume actually said.
For example, he points out that if Hume's principal intention
had been to liquidate the estates of Locke and Berkeley, he would
have been unlikely to assert, as he does in the introduction to the
Treatise, that 'In pretending . . . to explain the principles of human
nature, we in effect propose a complete system of the sciences,
built on a foundation almost entirely new, and the only one upon
which they can stand with any security' (T xvi). He remarks also
that while Locke does figure in this introduction on the list of
'some late philosophers in England, who have begun to put the

science of man on a new footing', the others whom Hume men-
tions, 'my Lord Shaftesbury, Dr Mandeville, Mr Hutcheson, Dr
Butler' (T xvii), are all of them moral philosophers. This accords
with Kemp Smith's view that Hume's main concern was to as-
similate natural to moral philosophy. In moral philosophy, Hume
follows Francis Hutcheson in representing our moral judgements
as founded on the operations of a sovereign 'moral sense'. In
natural philosophy, comprising the study of the physical world,
the sovereignty passes to what Kemp Smith calls our 'natural
beliefs'. These are expressions of 'feeling', itself largely governed
by habit or custom and not subordinate to reason, in any strict
sense of the term. It is only in the limited field of what we now
call purely formal questions that reason holds sway. In sum,
Hume's celebrated dictum that 'Reason is, and ought only to be
the slave of the passions, and can never pretend to any other
office than to serve and obey them' (T 415) was intended, on
this view, to apply not merely, as has commonly been assumed,
to judgements of value but to all but the purely formal exercises
of our understanding. We shall have to consider later how far
Kemp Smith was justified in taking this overall view of Hume's
philosophy.

One point which does emerge from a careful scrutiny of the
texts is the extent of the gulf between Hume and Berkeley.
Admittedly, Hume speaks of Berkeley in the *Treatise* as 'a great
philosopher' (T 17), but this is primarily on account of Berkeley's
theory of abstract ideas, according to which 'all general ideas are
nothing but particular ones, annexed to a certain term, which
gives them a more extensive signification, and makes them recall
upon occasion other individuals, which are similar to them' (T
17). How far this theory deserves Hume's description of it as
'one of the greatest and most valuable discoveries that has been
made in late years in the republic of letters' is another question
which we shall have to consider. Hume is also at one with Berkeley in rejecting Locke's distinction between ideas of primary
and secondary qualities, and in the *Enquiry*, having dismissed the
opinion that 'the ideas of those primary qualities are attained by
Abstraction' as one 'which, if we examine it closely, we shall find
to be unintelligible, and even absurd' (E 154), he acknowledges
his debt to Berkeley for this sceptical argument. He then goes on
to say that 'most of the writings of that very ingenious author

form the best lessons of scepticism, which are to be found either among the ancient or modern philosophers, Bayle not excepted' (E 155). This is a remarkable assessment of Berkeley, and made even more so by the fact, abundantly documented by Kemp Smith, that Pierre Bayle's sceptical *Dictionnaire historique et critique*, which came out in 1697, was a primary source for Hume's own scepticism. Hume was quite well aware that Berkeley would not have owned to being a sceptic. On the contrary, he bracketed sceptics with atheists and free thinkers as the adversaries whom his system was meant to frustrate. If, in spite of this, Hume maintains that all Berkeley's arguments are 'merely sceptical', his reason is 'that they admit of no answer and produce no conviction. Their only effect is to cause that momentary amazement and irresolution, which is the result of scepticism'(E 155).

Did Hume take the same view of his own arguments? The evidence, as we shall see, is conflicting, even in the famous last chapter of the first book of the *Treatise*, where Hume claims to have shown 'that the understanding, when it acts alone, and according to its most general principles, entirely subverts itself and leaves not the lowest degree of evidence in any proposition, either in philosophy or common life' (T 267–8). I shall be arguing that Hume here greatly exaggerates the sceptical import of his reasoning, but the point I now want to make is that he recoils from the conclusion 'that no refined or elaborate reasoning is ever to be received' (T 268). He does indeed remark that 'nature herself suffices' to cure him of his 'philosophical melancholy' and that he finds himself 'absolutely and necessarily determin'd to live, and talk, and act like other people in the common affairs of life' (T 269). Even so, this does not imply a rejection of philosophy. Towards the end of the chapter Hume still permits himself the 'hope to establish a system or set of opinions which if not true (for that, perhaps, is too much to be hoped for), might at least be satisfactory to the human mind, and might stand the test of the most critical examination' (T 272). And in the *Enquiry*, which we must not forget was meant to supersede the *Treatise*, the sceptical note is scarcely struck. Moreover, where it does appear, its use is positive. It serves as a weapon against superstition.

Neither is it true that Hume regarded all of Berkeley's arguments as admitting of no answer. He may have thought that there was no detectable flaw in Berkeley's disproof of the existence of matter, though even this is doubtful, but he surely believed that he had an answer to Berkeley's attempted proof of the existence of God. The answer emerges in the *Enquiry* from Hume's reply to Malebranche, who had responded to Descartes by becoming one of those who 'pretend that those objects which are commonly denominated *causes*, are in reality nothing but *occasions*; and that the true and direct principle of every effect is not any power or force in nature, but a volition of the Supreme Being, who wills that such particular objects should for ever be conjoined with each other' (E 70). Hume's comment on this excursion into fairyland, which applies equally to Berkeley, is that if we cannot penetrate the secrets of physical forces, we are 'equally ignorant of the manner or force by which a mind, even the supreme mind, operates either on itself or on body' (E 72). If we have no consciousness of this power in ourselves, we explain nothing by attributing it to a Supreme Being of which we have no idea 'but what we learn from reflection on our own faculties' (E 72). Hume also teases Berkeley by remarking that 'it argues surely more power in the Deity to delegate a certain degree of power to inferior creatures than to produce every thing by his own immediate volition' (E 71).

Hume's gift for irony matches that of his fellow historian Edward Gibbon, and like Gibbon he is most ready to display it when he writes about religion. Thus in his essay 'On the Immortality of the Soul', which we have seen that he refrained from publishing during his lifetime, he remarks that 'Nothing could set in a fuller light the infinite obligations which mankind have to Divine revelation; since we find, that no other medium could ascertain this great and important truth' (G 406). More straightforwardly, he concludes the chapter of the *Enquiry* in which he has shown that there cannot be any justification for a belief in miracles, by asserting 'that the *Christian Religion* not only was at first attended with miracles, but even to this day cannot be believed by any reasonable person without one. Mere reason is insufficient to convince us of its veracity: And whoever is moved by *Faith* to assent to it, is conscious of a continued miracle in his own person, which subverts all the principles of his understanding and gives him a determination to believe what is most contrary to custom and experience' (E 131).

Hume is consistently hostile to Christianity, both on intellectual and on moral grounds. Thus in his essay 'The Natural

History of Religion', having conceded that 'the Roman Catholics are a very learned sect', he quotes with approval the verdict of 'Averroes, the famous Arabian', 'that of all religions, the most absurd and nonsensical is that, whose votaries eat, after having created, their deity' (G 343) and adds for his own part 'that there is no tenet in all paganism which would give so fair a scope to ridicule as that of the *real presence*; for it is so absurd, that it eludes the force of all argument' (G 343). Neither do the Calvinists fare any better. In their case Hume endorses the view of his friend, the Chevalier Ramsay, that their Jewish God 'is a most cruel, unjust, partial and fantastical being' (G 355). The proof of this proposition is given at some length and is taken to show that its adherents outdo the pagans in blasphemy. 'The grosser pagans contented themselves with divinizing lust, incest, and adultery; but the predestinarian doctors have divinized cruelty, wrath, fury, vengeance, and all the blackest vices' (G 356). This may be taken as a stricture only on the predestinarian doctors, but Hume had already argued in the *Enquiry* that since all human actions are determined, as much as any physical events, it follows that if they are traced back to a deity he must be 'the author of sin and moral turpitude', besides everything else. The Leibnizian idea that this is the best of all possible worlds, so that all the evil which it manifests is really a proof of God's goodness, seemed as preposterous to Hume as it did to Voltaire, though Hume lacked the temperament for writing a work of such savage irony as Voltaire's *Candide*.

In general, Hume is inclined to judge that believers in the unity of God, whether they have adopted a version of Christianity, or some other type of monotheism, have made an intellectual advance upon the polytheists who embraced religion in what he believes to have been its most primitive forms. On the other hand, the intolerance of the monotheists, continually resulting in active persecution of those who dissent from their religious views, has made them 'more pernicious to society' (G 338). Hume ascribes the origin of religious belief to men's ignorance of natural causes and to 'the incessant hopes and fears, which actuate the human mind' (G 315). For the satisfaction of these hopes and the allaying of these fears they looked to beings of a similar character to themselves but endowed with much greater powers. Their invention of these beings is explained by a 'universal tendency among mankind to conceive all beings like themselves, and to transfer to every object, those qualities, with which they are familiarly acquainted, and of which they are intimately conscious' (G 317). This tendency persists even when the beings rarely or never assume corporeal form, and their number is reduced to one.

Hume nowhere proclaims himself an atheist. On the contrary, in 'The Natural History of Religion' and elsewhere in his writings, he professes to accept the Argument from Design. 'The whole frame of nature', he writes, 'bespeaks an Intelligent Author; and no rational inquirer can, after serious reflection, suspend his belief a moment with regard to the primary principles of genuine Theism and Religion' (G 309). This remark is not patently insincere and I have to allow for my own prejudices in taking it to be ironical. The fact is, however, that in the superb *Dialogues Concerning Natural Religion*, on which Hume worked intermittently during the last twenty-five years of his life, the strongest arguments, as we shall see, are put into the mouth of Philo, whose part in the dialogue is to rebut the argument from design, and I agree with Kemp Smith, to whom we own an excellent edition of the *Dialogues*, that Hume, without ever openly displaying his hand, intended the discerning reader to conclude that he adopted Philo's position. In my view, indeed, the discrediting not only of the more superstitious types of theism but of any form of religious belief was one of the principal aims of Hume's philosophy.

In reviewing the work of any of the famous seventeenth- or early eighteenth-century philosophers, one must always bear in mind that they did not draw the distinction, which has more recently arisen, between philosophy and the natural or social sciences. This is not to say that they took philosophy itself to be a special science, but rather that they regarded every form of scientific enquiry as philosophical. For them, the main division was that between natural philosophy, which concentrated on the physical world, and moral philosophy, which Hume called 'the science of human nature'. It had to be admitted that natural philosophy had advanced much the further of the two. The moral philosophers had nothing of comparable importance to set against the progress in our understanding of the physical operations of nature that began with the work of Copernicus, Kepler and Galileo, and culminated in that of Boyle and Newton. Nevertheless there was a sense in which both Locke and Hume believed that moral philosophy was dominant. Their reason, as set out by Hume in his introduction to the *Treatise*, was that 'all the sciences have a relation, greater or less, to human nature and that, however wide any of them may seem to run from it, they still return back by one passage or another' (T xv). There are sciences like those of logic, morals, criticism and politics which have a closer connection with human nature than the others, but even mathematics and the physical sciences are dependent on man's cognitive powers. 'It is impossible', Hume says, 'to tell what changes and improvements we might make in these sciences were we thoroughly acquainted with the extent and force of human understanding, and could explain the nature of the ideas we employ and of the operations we perform in our reasonings' (T xv).

Hume, as did Locke before him, sets himself to fulfil these needs. He had a qualified respect for Locke, whom he reproaches, rightly, for his excessively loose employment of the term 'idea', and also, not quite so fairly, for being betrayed by the schoolmen into mishandling the question of innate ideas, and allowing 'a like ambiguity and circumlocution' to run through 'his reasoning on . . . most other subjects' (E 22); but he shared Locke's belief that the experimental method in reasoning, to which they both attributed the achievements of Newton and his predecessors, was applicable to the moral sciences. It was, however, Locke who had the deeper understanding of Newtonian theory. They both agreed that it depended upon 'experience and observation' (T xvi), but Locke noticed, as it would seem that Hume did not, that, in Newton's case, the dependence was indirect. He understood that Newton accounted for the behaviour of bodies in terms of the operations of their 'minute parts', which were not themselves observable; and it was his attempt to reconcile this fact with the restrictions which he laid upon the extent of our ideas, and our consequent capacity for knowledge, that led to much of the 'ambiguity and circumlocution' with which Hume reproaches him. Hume, on the other hand, speaks of Newton as though he did no more than practise straightforward induction. What Newton presumably meant by his disclaimer of hypotheses at the beginning of his *Principia*—the celebrated statement 'Hypotheses non fingo' ('I do not fashion hypotheses')—was that he advanced no propositions for which he lacked experimental evidence. What Hume apparently took him to have meant was that he abstained from any generalisation that was not directly founded upon observed instances. This historical error has some bearing upon Hume's treatment of causation, a feature of his system to which he himself rightly attached the greatest importance, but I shall try to show that it does not seriously diminish the force of his argument. It has no bearing upon his attempt to develop a science of the mind, since all that is at issue here is his ability to give an accurate description of different states of consciousness, and, remaining on the terrain of everyday observation, to hit upon generalisations which they can reasonably be supposed to satisfy.

On the face of it at least, the method which both Locke and Hume pursued was very simple. They asked two questions. What are the materials with which the mind is furnished, and what uses can it make of them? Hume's answer to the first question is that the material consists of perceptions, which he divides into the two categories of impressions and ideas. In the anonymous *Abstract* in which he extols the virtues of the *Treatise* he speaks of the author as calling 'a *perception* whatever can be present to the mind, whether we employ our senses, or are actuated with passion, or exercise our thought and reflection' (T 647). He goes on to say that a perception is to be called an *impression* 'when we feel a passion or emotion of any kind, or have the images of external objects conveyed by our senses' (T 647). '*Impressions*', he adds, 'are our lively and our strong perceptions.' It is implied that the reason why *ideas* are comparatively fainter and weaker is that they come into being 'when we reflect on a passion or an object which is not present' (T 647).

Except for the reference to external objects, which constitutes, as we shall see, a serious problem for Hume, this account of what he means by impressions is very similar to that given in the *Treatise*. He introduces them there as those perceptions which enter into our consciousness 'with most force and violence', and adds that he comprehends under the name 'all our sensations, passions and emotions, as they make their first appearance in the soul' (T 1). In the *Enquiry* he is content to say that what he means by the term *impression* is 'all our more lively perceptions, when we hear, or see, or feel, or love, or hate, or desire, or will' (E 18), but this definition is so compressed as to be misleading. The salient feature of impressions is not their force or vividness but their immediacy; this may in general have the effect of making them more lively than the images of memory or the creatures of fancy, which Hume included in the opposite camp of *ideas*, but the empirical evidence does not favour the assumption that this is always so.

Unlike Locke, Hume has no objection to saying that impressions are innate. He remarks that 'if by innate be meant, contemporary to our birth, the dispute seems to be frivolous; nor is it worth while to enquire at what time thinking begins' (E 22). In the *Enquiry*, where this passage occurs, he takes 'innate' to mean 'what is original or copied from no previous perception' and in the *Abstract*, what arises 'immediately from nature', and in both cases he concludes that all impressions are innate. This hardly seems true of our sense-impressions, according to the first definition, unless the word 'copied' is taken very narrowly. If we apply the second definition to them, we seem to have only a different way of making the point that they are the immediate contents of sense-perception. However, Hume's examples make it clear that he is concerned here chiefly with the passions. His contention is that such things as 'self-love, or the resentment of injuries, or the passion between the sexes' (E 22) are inherent in human nature.

There are passages in which Hume seems to imply that his distinction between impressions and ideas can be equated with that between feeling and thinking, but this does not mean that he is anticipating the distinction which Kant drew between intuitions and concepts. Not only do Hume's impressions enter the mind under concepts, but these concepts are guaranteed to apply to them. Hume's argument is that 'since all actions and sensations of the mind are known to us by consciousness, they must necessarily appear in every particular what they are, and be what they appear. Everything that enters the mind being in *reality* a perception, 'tis impossible that anything should to *feeling* appear different. This were to suppose, that even where we are most intimately conscious, we might be mistaken' (T 190). It is true that this statement appears in a context where Hume is concerned to deny that an impression could masquerade as an external object, but I think it sufficiently clear that he intends his assertion that 'all sensations are felt by the mind, such as they really are', to apply to our recognition of their qualities. Whether he is right on this point is an unresolved question. There is no doubt that we can honestly misdescribe our feelings, and the way things appear to us, but it can be argued that our mistakes are then purely verbal, that, as Bertrand Russell once put it, 'what I am believing is true, but my words are ill chosen'. The difficulty lies in there being cases where the line between factual and verbal error is not easily drawn. Fortunately, so far as Hume is concerned, the question can be left open. He is bound to hold that our estimates of the qualities of impressions run a relatively slight risk of error, but not that they are infallible. And indeed when it comes to our assessing the comparative proportions of spatially extended impressions, which he counts as complex, he admits the possibility of doubt and error. Our decisions as to whether they are 'greater, less, or equal' are 'sometimes infallible, but they are not always so' (T 47).

A more crucial element in Hume's account of impressions is his taking them all to be 'internal and perishing existences' (T 194). The arguments with which he supports this view are, as is frequently the case with Hume, a mixture of the logical and the experimental. The experiments which are supposed to 'convince us that our perceptions are not possessed of any independent existence' are those which typically figure in philosophical literature under the ill-chosen heading of 'the argument from illusion'. The opinion, for which there is factual evidence, 'that all our perceptions are dependent on our organs, and the disposition of our nerves and animal spirits . . . is confirm'd by the seeming encrease and diminution of objects, according to their distance; by the apparent alterations in their figure; by the changes in their colour and other qualities from our sickness and distempers; and by an infinite number of other experiments of the same kind' (T 211).

Quite apart from the question whether Hume is entitled, on his premises, to draw in this way upon physics and physiology, the argument is plainly not conclusive against opponents like Reid who take the common-sense view that in the normal exercise of sense-perception we are immediately presented with physical objects. It is not conclusive, because their position need not commit them either to denying that our perceptions are causally dependent upon a number of factors besides the existence of the object perceived, or to maintaining that we always perceive things as they really are. I think, therefore, that Hume would have done better to rely on his purely logical argument that it is self-contradictory to suppose that an entity which is defined as the content of a particular perception can lead a separate existence of its own. In short, impressions are made 'internal and fleeting' by fiat. In defiance of current fashion, I shall argue later that this, or at any rate something very like it, is a legitimate procedure, and that it can be made the basis of a tenable theory of perception.

For reasons which will soon become apparent, Hume's principal concern was with *ideas*, but the accounts which he gives of his use of the term *idea* are cursory and inadequate. In the *Treatise* he says that he means by *ideas* the 'faint images' of impressions 'in thinking and reasoning' (T 1). In the *Abstract* he says: 'When we reflect on a passion or an object which is not present, this perception is an *idea*. *Impressions*, therefore, are our lively and strong perceptions: *ideas* are the fainter and weaker' (T 647). Very much the same account is given in the *Enquiry*, except that the order of the explanations is reversed. The subject is introduced by the remark that 'we may divide all the perceptions of the mind into two classes or species, which are distinguished by their different degrees of force and vivacity' (E 18).

The reason why I said that these explanations are inadequate is not just that they carry the false assumption that the work of concepts, which is what ideas perform for Hume, is always carried out by images. It is rather that the emphasis is laid on the wrong factor. Let us consider, for the sake of argument, the case where the thought of some passion or sensation does take the form of an image. Now it may or may not be the case that the image is intrinsically less vivid than the passion or sensation was when it occurred. The point is that no degree of vividness or faintness can endow it with a reference beyond itself. To be an image *of* the passion or *of* the sensation, it has to be interpreted as a symbol; it has to give rise to a belief not in its own existence but in the existence of what it *represents*; and then the question of its own comparative intensity becomes irrelevant.

These points can be clearly illustrated by the example of memory. As it happens, Hume has very little to say about memory. He speaks of it as a faculty by which we repeat our impressions, though of course it is not possible, on his view, that any impression should literally be repeated, and says that what is reproduced in memory is something which, in respect of its vivacity, 'is somewhat betwixt an impression and an idea' (T 8). In general, he appears to take it for granted that memory is reliable, at least with respect to recent events. He puts the data of memory very much on a level with the immediate data of sense-perception, as sources of knowledge which serve as a basis for more venturesome inferences, and we shall see that it is with our right to make these more venturesome inferences that he is primarily concerned. What is of interest in the present context is the way in which Hume distinguishes between ideas of memory and ideas of the imagination. According to a fundamental principle of Hume's, which we shall presently examine, both must be derived from previous impressions, but whereas memory, so long as it is functioning properly, 'preserves the original form in which its objects were presented', as well as the order in which they originally occurred, the imagination, so long as it remains within the realm of past impressions, is free to arrange their counterparts in any order and combine them in any way it pleases, whether or not these combinations have actually occurred. There is, however, the difficulty, for the most part ignored by Hume, but mentioned once in passing, that we cannot return to our past impressions to discover where this difference obtains. Consequently, the only way we actually have of distinguishing memory from imagination 'lies in its superior force and vivacity' (T 85); the same terms as are used in the *Enquiry* to distinguish impressions from ideas. By comparison with the 'lively and strong' ideas of memory, the ideas of the imagination are 'faint and languid' (T 9).

This is clearly unacceptable. In the first place, it is perfectly possible to remember a past experience, say a conversation in which one took part, or one's feeling of disappointment when something went wrong, without the aid of any images at all. It is possible even to imagine that something is the case, and yet dispense with any actual image. Let us, however, consider only the cases where images do play a role. It is simply false that images which serve the imagination are always fainter and more languid than those that enter into memories. Indeed, Hume himself admits this in one of the sections of his Appendix to the

Treatise, and has to take refuge in saying that even if a poetical fiction paints the livelier picture, still the ideas it presents 'are different to the *feeling* from those which arise from the memory and judgement' (T 631). But this is really to concede that the whole question of relative vividness is beside the point. The distinctive feature of memory, whether it is served by images or not, is that it exhibits one's belief in something which one has learned: in the sense with which Hume is concerned, the belief is a belief in the occurrence of some past experience. The distinctive feature of the imagination, except in the sense in which to say that something is imaginary is to imply that it does not exist, is that it is neutral with regard to the existence of the states of affairs which it represents. Hume was right in so far as there is only a difference of 'tone' between one's memory of a past experience and one's imaginative reconstruction of an experience which one truly believes to have occurred, but he was mistaken if he took this to be the only or even the main point at issue.

I use the conditional because it is not clear that he always did so. Hume was not a consistent writer and in the Appendix to the *Treatise*, in a note on the section entitled 'Of the Nature of the Idea, or Belief', he says that in giving a philosophical account of belief 'we can do no more than assert, that it is something *felt* by the mind, which distinguishes the ideas of the judgement from the fictions of the imagination' (T 629). It is true that he does not explicitly include memories among the ideas of the judgement, but this can be put down to the context; and it is also true that he goes on to speak of the ideas to which we assent as being 'more strong, firm and vivid' than our reveries. But now it looks as if words like 'vivid' are being used in a technical sense which implies that the ideas which they qualify command assent.

The trouble was that Hume lacked an adequate theory of meaning and reference. Towards the end of his Appendix to the *Treatise* he admits to being dissatisfied with his treatment of belief. Since he associates belief primarily with inference, and assumes that all inferences must ultimately be based on some impression, he begins by defining belief as 'a lively idea related to or associated with a present impression' (T 96), but here again the word 'lively' is out of place unless it is simply cover for some such expression as 'assented to'. Hume did indeed make the valid point that belief cannot be a further idea, tacked on to the idea which gives the belief its content; for, as we should now put it, what a sentence is used to state remains the same, whether it is believed or not. Neither, Hume argues, can it be an impression, because it attaches to conclusions which consist only of ideas. He sometimes calls it a sentiment, without making it clear what he takes a sentiment to be if it is neither an impression nor an idea. In the end, he is reduced to saying in the *Enquiry* 'that belief consists not in the peculiar nature or order of ideas, but in the manner of their conception, and in their feeling to the mind' (E 49). This is scarcely illuminating, but in fairness to Hume it can be said that the problem of giving an analysis of belief which is neither trivial nor circular still awaits solution. Recent attempts to analyse it in terms of propensities to action have not, to my mind, been successful.

It might be thought that a theory of reference was contained in Hume's treatment of abstract ideas, but here, more than anywhere else, he is handicapped by his false assumption that the use of a concept consists in the framing of an image. This leads him to expend unnecessary labour in proving that images have determinate qualities, a proposition which he does not clearly distinguish from the proposition, for which he also argues, that images represent particular individuals which themselves have determinate qualities. I am not sure that the first of these propositions is true, but even if they are both true they are irrelevant, since the use of a general term need not be accompanied either by an image or by the thought of any particular individual. Hume is, indeed, right in welcoming Berkeley's 'discovery' that terms are made general not by their standing for an abstract entity, but by their use, but he has nothing more informative to say about their use than that 'individuals are collected together and placed under a general term with a view to that resemblance which they bear to each other' (T 23).

I referred earlier to a fundamental principle of Hume's concerning the derivation of ideas. This principle, as originally stated in the *Treatise*, is '*That all our simple ideas in their first appearance are derived from simple impressions, which are correspondent to them, and which they exactly represent*' (T 4). The extreme importance of this principle for Hume is that it provides him with a criterion of the legitimacy of ideas or concepts. As he puts it in the *Enquiry*, 'When we entertain any suspicion that a philosophical term is employed without any meaning or idea (as is but too frequent) we need but enquire, *from what impression is that supposed to be derived?*' (E 22).

Hume treats this as an empirical generalisation, to which, strangely enough, he at once suggests a counter-example. He envisages a case in which a man has been acquainted with various shades of colour, but has missed out one of them, and suggests, quite correctly, that the man could form an idea of the missing shade as being intermediate in hue between two of the others. Having devised this counter-example, Hume wantonly dismisses it, saying that it is too 'particular and singular' to oblige him to give up his general maxim; and indeed he continues to treat his maxim as though it held universally. He could have avoided this affront to logic if he had modified his principle so as to make it apply not to the origin but to the realisation of ideas. It would then require of an idea that it be capable of being satisfied by some impression. This principle can, I think, be defended if the word 'satisfied' is construed generously, so as to allow an idea to be satisfied if it enters into a theory which can be confirmed, at least indirectly, in sense-experience. This would, however, take us rather far from Hume. A modification which he might have accepted is that ideas must be capable of being instantiated by impressions, but this, though it accommodates his counter-example, is still too restrictive. In practice, Hume accepts such ideas as can be instantiated by bodies, which are themselves developed out of impressions by certain activities of the imagination. We shall be discussing the question how far this practice is at variance with his official theory.

Having fixed his attention on ideas, Hume proceeds to review the ways in which they are associated. In the *Treatise* he distinguishes seven different kinds of philosophical relation, which he divides into two groups according as they can or cannot be 'the objects of knowledge and certainty'. The four that can attain this mark, because they depend solely upon the intrinsic properties of ideas, are *resemblance, contrariety, degrees in quality* and *proportions in quantity or number*. The remaining three are *identity, relations of time and place*, and *causation*. Hume's reason for placing *identity* in the second group is that objects which are perfectly resemblant may still be numerically different if they do not coincide both in space and time. This confirms, what was already clear, that Hume's so-called relations between ideas are not merely such, but also extend to relations between the objects which fall under the ideas. Indeed, of all the relations which he lists, perhaps only that of *contrariety* is purely conceptual.

This division between relations prefigures the second of Hume's fundamental principles, which is that 'All the objects of human reason or enquiry may naturally be divided into two kinds, to wit, *Relations of Ideas*, and *Matters of Fact*' (E 25). In this proposition, which is taken from the *Enquiry*, affirmations concerning relations of ideas are treated as being purely conceptual, and consequently as being 'either intuitively or demonstratively certain'. They include the sciences of geometry, algebra and arithmetic. Hume has next to nothing to say about them, his own interest lying in our beliefs about matters of fact. This leads him, in the *Enquiry*, to reduce his list of relations to three, 'namely *Resemblance, Contiguity* in time and place, and *Cause and Effect*' (E 24). The first two are merely principles of association. The important relation is that of *Cause and Effect*, on which, as Hume puts it, all reasonings concerning matters of fact seem to be founded.

It is this relation, then, that Hume sets out to explore. It must, however, be noted that when he does explore it, in the domain of natural philosophy, he takes it as holding not between fleeting impressions but between enduring objects. This is shown by his examples, and indeed it is only if it is taken in this way that his analysis of causation can appear at all plausible. Equally, when it comes to moral philosophy, he relies on the existence of persistent selves. We must, therefore, begin by showing how he can arrive at these conceptions without too flagrant a display of inconsistency.

3

Bodies and selves

WHATEVER scepticism Hume may have professed, there is no doubt that he believed in the existence of what may be called the physical objects of common sense. Even if we assume that he left his philosophical self behind, as he in fact did not, when he wrote his volumes of history and his political essays, and, as he says he did, when he played backgammon and was merry with his friends, there is abundant evidence of such a belief in his philosophical writings themselves. He shows interest in the passions and emotions, which he enlists under the heading of 'secondary impressions', because they have a part to play in his moral theory, but neither in the first book of the *Treatise*, nor in the *Enquiry concerning Human Understanding*, does he pay very much attention to the original impressions of sense. He makes a number of remarks about them in general, referring, as we have seen, to the force and liveliness with which they are supposed to strike upon the mind, or to their being 'internal and perishing existences', but he has little to say about them in detail. When he adduces examples of matters of fact, he refers not to colours and shapes, but to the death of Caesar in the Senate-house at Rome, to the properties of mercury and gold, to the muscles and nerves of human bodies, to the sun and the planets, to flowers and trees, to the impact of billiard balls upon one another. It is on the constant conjunction of objects of this sort that, as we shall see, his analysis of causation depends. It would have been no use his applying his theory to impressions, as he must have done if he had really believed that there was nothing else available, for the very good reason that our actual impressions do not display the requisite regularity. To take a simple example, it may well be the case that roses planted in the spring habitually flower in the summer, but this is not to say that an impression of seeing a rose planted is habitually followed by an impression of seeing it come into flower. One may not be there at the later date, and even if one is there, one's attention may be otherwise occupied.

Let it be allowed, then, that Hume believed, and for his own philosophical purposes needed to believe, in the existence of bodies. In fact, at the beginning of the section of the *Treatise* entitled 'Of Scepticism with regard to the Senses', which supplies the main source for attributing to him a 'theory of the external world', he himself makes the cryptic statement 'We may well ask, *What causes induce us to believe in the existence of body?* but 'tis vain to ask. *Whether there be body or not?* That is a point, which we must take for granted in all our reasonings' (T 187). Even so a number of questions remain to be answered. We have seen that the bodies the existence of which Hume took for granted were such things as houses and books and trees and the bodies of animals and human beings, including their inner organs. How did he conceive of them? Like Locke, as the external causes of sensory impressions? Like Berkeley, as congeries of sensible qualities? Or after some fashion of his own? He has an answer for the causal question how we come to believe in the existence of body, but what does he mean by saying that it is vain to ask whether there be body or not? The most obvious interpretation to give to this statement would be that our belief in the existence of body is unquestionably true. Yet the upshot of Hume's investigation of the causes of this belief is that, whether it be considered in its vulgar or in what he calls its 'philosophical' form, it is not only not true but thoroughly confused. Admittedly, he does not expect this conclusion to carry any lasting conviction. 'Carelessness and in-attention', he said, 'alone can afford us any remedy. For this reason I rely entirely upon them: and take it for granted, whatever may be the reader's opinion at this present moment, that an hour hence he will be persuaded there is both an external and internal world' (T 218). Should we take this as confirming Kemp Smith's view that Hume intended our 'natural beliefs' to triumph over our understanding? But in what exactly were these natural beliefs supposed to consist?

Once more, the evidence is conflicting. There are passages which seem to imply that when Hume speaks of 'external' objects, he conceives of them, in Locke's way, as relatively enduring causes of our 'internal and fleeting' sense-impressions. For instance, we have already seen that, in the course of defining impressions in the *Abstract*, he speaks of our having images of external objects conveyed by our senses. Again, in the *Treatise*, at the beginning of the Book 'Of The Passions', where he makes his distinction between original and secondary impressions, he speaks of original impressions as 'Such as without any antecedent perception arise in the Soul, from the constitution of the body, from the animal spirits, or from the application of objects to the external organs' (T 276). In the chapter which he devotes to our ideas of space and time, in the first book of the *Treatise*, he says that 'we can never pretend to know body otherwise than by those external properties, which discover themselves to the senses' (T 64), and the implication that bodies have other properties, which lie beyond our knowledge, is confirmed by a note on the chapter, in one of the *Appendices*, where he speaks of the real nature of the position of bodies, which might or might not allow for a vacuum, as being unknown (T 639). He takes this to be implied by the 'Newtonian philosophy' which for the most part he does not contest. On the other hand, in the one place in which he examines its foundations, he does very firmly contest it; and he also implies that it is not what the carelessness and inattention of his reader will allow him to accept.

As is so often the case with Hume, the *Enquiry* summarises with greater elegance and clarity a position for which the arguments are developed in the *Treatise*. In this instance, we are told that

It seems evident, that men are carried, by a natural instinct or prepossession, to repose faith in their senses; and that, without any reasoning, or even almost before the use of reason, we always suppose an external universe, which depends not on our perception, but would exist, though we and every sensible creature were absent or annihilated. (E 151)

Hume goes on to ascribe this belief even to 'the animal creation'. He then adds:

It seems also evident, that, when men follow this blind and powerful instinct of nature, they always suppose the very images, presented by the senses, to be the external objects, and never entertain any suspicion, that the one are nothing but representations of the other. This very table, which we see white, and which we feel hard, is believed to exist, independent of our perception, and to be something external to our mind which perceives it. Our presence bestows not being on it: our absence does not annihilate it. It preserves its existence uniform and entire, independent of the situation of intelligent beings, who perceive or contemplate it. (E 151–2)

Unfortunately, in Hume's view, 'this universal and primary opinion of all men' does not withstand critical examination. It succumbs to 'the slightest philosophy' with the result that 'no man, who reflects, ever doubted that the existences, which we consider, when we say, *this house* and *that tree*, are nothing but perceptions in the mind, and fleeting copies or representations of other existences, which remain uniform and independent' (E 152). This would be all very well if we had any good reason to believe in the existence of these independent objects, but Hume maintains that we have not. The supposition that our perceptions are connected with external objects can evidently not be founded in experience and is also, Hume says, 'without any foundation in reasoning' (E 153). This leaves the sceptic in command of the field. Hume is not happy with this result, but does not look for any way of contesting it, such as searching for some flaw in the argument. What he does instead is simply to shrug it aside. We set the extreme sceptic at defiance by asking what purpose he thinks that his activity serves. He 'cannot expect, that his philosophy will have any constant influence on the mind: or if it had, that its influence would be beneficial to society' (E 160). On the contrary, it would be very harmful, since the inaction to which it would lead would put an end to men's existence. But 'Nature is too strong for principle.' The sceptic will be brought to confess that 'all his objections are mere amusement, and can have no other tendency than to show the whimsical condition of mankind, who must act and reason and believe' (E 160). Remarks of this sort do, indeed, lend support to Kemp Smith's theory that Hume was concerned to show that reason ought to give way to our natural beliefs, but I do not see them as establishing it decisively. If this had been Hume's intention, I do not think that he would have concluded the section on a sceptical note, stressing our inability to justify the assumptions on which we act or to remove the objections which may be raised against them. Neither does he explicitly assert that our natural beliefs are true.

There is, however, an important point on which I agree with Kemp Smith; and that is that it is possible to elicit from Hume's line of reasoning a theory of perception which does not dissolve into scepticism. It will mean parting company with Hume at one or two places, but the divergencies will not be so great as to prevent our arriving at a fair accommodation. They will consist for the most part in a re-evaluation rather than a rejection of his arguments. I shall try to show presently how I think that this can be done, but first I want to retrace the course that he actually pursues in the relevant sections of the *Treatise*, of which the most important for our present purpose is that 'Of Scepticism with regard to the Senses'.

The main questions which Hume sets out to answer in this section are 'Why we attribute a *continu'd* existence to objects even when they are not present to the senses; and why we suppose them to have an existence *distinct* from the mind and perception?' (T 188). He treats these questions as interdependent, in the sense that to answer either one of them would be to answer the other. He is right to the extent that if objects did have a continued existence, as he defines it, they would also have a distinct existence, but the converse need not hold. It might be and indeed has been maintained, for example by Bertrand Russell in *The Problems of Philosophy* and elsewhere, that the objects which are immediately present to the senses are distinct from the mind and yet have only a momentary existence, because of their causal dependence on the bodily state of the percipient.

On this point I side with Hume, with one important reservation. As we have noted earlier, Hume, while mainly relying on empirical arguments, including the reference to causal factors, shows some inclination to make it a truth of logic that sense-impressions are inseparable from the perceptual situations in which they occur. I remarked that the empirical arguments are not conclusive, though, as we shall see, they do present an obstacle to the currently bland acceptance of a position like Reid's, and I suggested that Hume should have been content to stand on his logical principle. My reservation is that this does not commit him to defining impressions from the outset as being dependent on the mind. In fact such a definition would be inconsistent with his own view, which we have yet to examine, that the self is nothing but a bundle of logically independent perceptions, from which he infers that a perception could exist apart from anything else. This is not, however, the point that I wish to stress, since he does not maintain that any perceptions actually do so. My point is rather that if impressions are to be taken as primitive in the order of knowledge, they cannot be accorded an initial dependence on either mind or body. At this stage neither minds nor bodies enter into the picture.

But is Hume entitled to take impressions as primitive? I maintain that he is, for the two following reasons. First, it is evident that one's ground for accepting any proposition concerning what Hume calls a matter of fact must finally depend on the truth of some judgement of perception. Secondly, it is easy to show that our ordinary judgements of perception assert more than is vouchsafed by the sense-experiences from which they issue. Though one is not normally conscious of making any inferences when one ventures on such a simple perceptual judgement as 'This is an ashtray' or 'That is a pencil', there is a sense in which they do embody inferences. But then these inferences must have some foundation. There must, in Bertrand Russell's terminology, be 'hard data' on which they are based. And Hume's impressions are simply these hard data, called by another name.

The second step in this argument has been contested, but to see that it is valid one needs only to be reminded of the very wide range of assumptions which our ordinary judgements of perception carry. For a start, there are the assumptions involved in characterising anything as a physical object of an observable kind. It has to be accessible to more than one sense and to any suitably equipped observer. It has to be capable of existing unperceived. It has to occupy a position or series of positions in three-dimensional space and to persist throughout some period of time. Neither are we normally committed only to these general assumptions. It is seldom that we are content to make so weak a claim as that we are perceiving a physical object of some sort or other. In the normal way, we identify it more specifically as an ashtray or a pencil or a table or whatever, and thereby commit ourselves to a set of further assumptions. These may relate to the object's origins, as when we claim to perceive some living thing, or to its physical constitution. In referring to an artefact, like a pencil, we make an assumption about its causal powers. Very often our description of an object which we claim to see or touch carries implications about its possible effects on the other senses, about the sound or taste or smell which we accord it the power to produce.

But now it is surely obvious that this whole wealth of theory cannot be extracted from any single occasion of sense-experience. I see what I do not hesitate to identify as a reading lamp on the table in front of me, but there is nothing in the visual pattern, considered on its own, from which to deduce that the object is tangible, that if any other observer were present he also would see it, that it will remain unperceived, most probably in the same position, that it is partly made of brass, that there is a socket for an electric bulb under its shade, and that this bulb can be made a source of light. What is present to my senses, so far as the lamp is concerned, is just a visual pattern, and all the rest is inference. This does not mean that I speak falsely when I say that I see the lamp or even that I am misusing the verb 'to see'. No doubt the assumptions which I am tacitly making are true in this instance, and it is common practice in the employment of perceptual verbs to take as their accusatives, not what I have called hard data, that is to say the actual contents of the sensory experiences in question, but the objects to the presence of which the hard data serve as sensory clues. But to overlook the hard data is not to abolish them, and the inferences are not removed by being unacknowledged. The common run of contemporary philosophers who are content to take the perception of physical objects as their starting-point need not be in error, since no one is obliged to embark on an analysis of perception. They fall into error only when they maintain, or imply, that no such analysis is possible.

The standard objection to the adoption of Hume's starting-point is that it imprisons the subject in a private world, from which he cannot ever escape. This objection would be serious if it were valid, but it is not valid. There is nothing private about the description of sensory patterns. It can be understood by anyone who has the requisite experiences. It is true that the patterns are made concrete by their occurrence in a particular sense-field at a particular time, and that this sense-field will in fact figure in the experience of only one person. It is equally true that a person's act of perceiving some physical object at a particular time is his and not anybody else's. The crucial point is that no reference to their ownership enters into the definition of impressions. As primitive elements, they are neutral in this and every other respect, except that of their intrinsic character. It remains to be seen whether we can find a passable route from them to physical objects, and whether we can then find a means of making a distinction between these physical objects and our perceptions of them. It may turn out in one case or the other that we shall come upon insurmountable obstacles, but this is certainly not a question that can be prejudged at the start.

For Hume the obstacles come very early. We have already seen that he takes it to be certain 'that almost all mankind, and even philosophers themselves, for the greatest part of their lives, take their perceptions to be their only objects, and suppose that the very being, which is intimately present to the mind, is the real body or material existence' (T 206). They must, however, be mistaken, since it is characteristic of what he here calls real bodies that they have a continued and distinct existence, whereas perceptions are 'dependent and fleeting'. Thus they are guilty of the contradiction of supposing that one and the same object both does and does not persist through time.

Before examining Hume's account of the way in which we are seduced into this error, it is worth remarking that, on his own showing, the contradiction is not so flagrant as it may at first sight appear. We have seen that he includes identity in his list of philosophical relations, but it now turns out to be a relation that no perception satisfies. This conclusion emerges from Hume's treatment of the question how we can come by the idea of identity. It cannot, he argues, be conveyed by one object, since the proposition 'an object is the same with itself' would be meaningless 'if the idea expressed by the word, *object*, were in no way distinguish'd from that meant by *itself*' (T 200). The idea which a single object conveys is not that of identity but that of unity. But if a single object cannot convey the idea of identity, it is even more obvious that a multiplicity of different objects cannot. Where then can the idea of identity come from? In what can it possibly consist?

Hume's answer to these questions is that the idea of identity is the product of a mistake into which we naturally fall when we think about time. He has previously argued that 'time, in a strict sense, implies succession, and that when we apply its idea to any unchangeable object, 'tis only by a fiction of the imagination, by which the unchangeable object is suppos'd to participate of the changes of the co-existent objects, and in particular of that of our perceptions' (T 200–1). We are, however, firmly addicted to this play of the imagination, which enables us to keep the idea of an object poised, as it were, between those of unity and number. So when we attribute identity to an object, what we must mean is 'that the object existent at one time is the same with itself existent at another' (T 201). Provided that they occurred in constantly changing circumstances, this could be true of at least some of our perceptions, if they themselves persisted unchanged. The trouble is that they do not.

How then do we come to think that they do? Hume's explanation, in his own words, is

that all those objects, to which we attribute a continu'd existence have a peculiar *constancy*, which distinguishes them from the impressions, whose existence depends upon our perception. Those mountains, and houses, and trees, which lie at present under my eye, have always appear'd to me in the same order: and when I lose sight of them by shutting my eyes or turning my head, I soon after find them return upon me without the least alteration. My bed and table, my books and papers present themselves in the same uniform manner and change not upon account of any interruption in my seeing or perceiving them. This is the case with all the impressions, whose objects are suppos'd to have an external existence; and is the case with no other impressions, whether gentle or violent, voluntary or involuntary. (T 194–5)

What this comes to is that the close resemblance between successive impressions and, what is equally important, their standing in apparently constant spatial relations to the members of series which exhibit the same internal resemblances, leads us to identify them with one another, and to ignore the interruptions which in fact occur between them. The result is that they are replaced in our imagination by a persistent thing, indifferently referred to by Hume as an object or a perception, which we conceive of as existing when it is not being perceived. Since Hume has shown some inclination, as we have seen, to make it a logical truth that impressions are internal and fleeting, it is something of a surprise to find him saying that 'the supposition of the continu'd existence of sensible objects or perceptions involves no contradiction' (T 208). His reason is not only that 'every perception is distinguishable from another, and may be considered as separately existent', with the consequence that 'there is no absurdity in separating any particular perception

from the mind' (T 209). He also concedes that 'the same continu'd and uninterrupted Being may be sometimes present to the
mind, and sometimes absent from it, without any real or essential
change in the Being itself' (T 207). I think that this concession
is genuine, and not just a description of the reach of our imagination, though I shall presently try to show that he did not need
to make it in this particular form. There is a way in which he
could have obtained what it gives him, while still making the
denial of a continued existence to any actual impression a matter
of logic rather than empirical fact. As it is, he holds it to be simply
false that any perception continues unperceived, and consequently false that interrupted perceptions can be identical. His ground
for this conclusion lies in his acceptance of the dubious argument
from illusion. He reasons correctly that if perceptions had a continued existence they would also have a distinct existence, but
then argues that a distinct existence is denied to them by experience. As given to sense, motion and solidity, colours, sounds, heat
and cold, pain and pleasure are all on the same footing. They are
'nothing but perceptions arising from the particular configurations
and motions of the parts of body' (T 192-3).

Hume accords the phenomenon of constancy the primary role
in causing the imagination to transform impressions into enduring objects, but he does not think it sufficient on its own. It is
aided in its work by what he calls coherence, of which he gives
two examples. The first example is that of his returning to his
room after an hour's absence to find that his fire is burning less
brightly. Since he has frequently witnessed the process of his
fire's dying down, his imagination fills the gap. The second
example is more complex. It is that of a porter bringing him a
letter from a friend two hundred leagues away. He hears the noise
of the door turning on its hinges but does not see it. He does not
see the porter climbing the stairs. Neither on this occasion has
he observed the action of the post and ferries which brought the
letter to him. Nevertheless he has come, through past experience,
to associate the creaking of the door with the sight of its opening;
he has learned that porters do not appear in his room without
having climbed the stairs to get there; experience has taught him
that letters do not arrive from distant places without being conveyed by observable means of transport. So once again his imagination fills in the gaps. It is, however, to be noted that his

imagination is here given far more work to do than in the previous example. It is no longer just a matter of its supplying the missing counterparts to the members of previous resemblant series. There may very well not have been any such series; for example, it is not very likely that Hume had ever actually witnessed the continuous movement of a letter over a distance of two hundred leagues. In this instance his imagination has not only extended the principle of constancy so as to supply itself with a sufficient stock of ordinary objects. It has also imposed, as Hume himself admits, a greater degree of coherence in their operation than has actually occurred in his past experience. What makes this procedure legitimate is its explanatory force.

Even so, Hume maintains that our imagination is deceiving us. The fact is that our percepts do not have a continued and distinct existence and that is that. Philosophers try to get over the difficulty by drawing a distinction between perceptions and objects, allowing the perceptions to be 'interrupted and perishing', and attributing to the objects 'a continued existence and identity'. But this 'new system' is a fraud. 'It contains all the difficulties of the vulgar system, with some others, that are peculiar to itself' (T 211). In the first place, it owes its appeal to the imagination entirely to the vulgar system. 'Were we fully convinced that our resembling perceptions are continu'd, and identical, and independent, we shou'd never run into this opinion of a double existence' (T 215), for it would then serve no purpose. Neither should we adopt it if we were fully convinced that our perceptions were dependent and interrupted, for our search for something to which to ascribe a continued existence would then lack any motive. It is the vacillation of our minds between two contrary hypotheses that leads philosophers to accept them both while trying to disguise the contradiction. Secondly, this hypothesis finds no support in reason, for we can have no rational ground for correlating our perceptions with objects which *ex hypothesi* are never themselves experienced. What the philosophers, who engage in this fraud, are really doing is to invent a second set of perceptions to which they attribute the continued and distinct existence which they would be attributing to our actual perceptions if their reason did not forbid it. In short, the philosophical system is 'loaded with this absurdity, that it at once denies and establishes the vulgar supposition' (T 218).

I am going to argue that Hume does less than justice to the philosophical system. It is untenable as it stands, but it does point the way to a solution of his difficulties. He is, however, justified in his onslaught on the Lockean version of it, which was presumably his actual target. Whatever distinction we end by drawing between things as they really are, and things as they appear to us, it cannot legitimately take the form of a multiplication of 'worlds'. Physical objects cannot enter the scene merely as the imperceptible causes of what one perceives, and if they could so enter it there would be no warrant for endowing them with any resemblance to their perceptible effects.

How then do we come by a warranted belief in the existence of physical objects having the perceptible properties with which we normally credit them? I suggest that Hume himself supplies the best answer. The phenomena of constancy and coherence, which he invokes to explain how we fall into the illusion of supposing our perceptions to have a continued and distinct existence, can be regarded instead as affording an adequate basis for an imaginative transformation of sense-impressions, or percepts, as, following Russell, I prefer to call them, into the constituents of the physical world of common sense. The only serious error that Hume made was to assume that the resulting objects were fictions. What there is depends in part on what our theories allow there to be, and the theory which can be developed out of percepts, on Hume's principles, contains acceptable criteria of existence. There is no reason, therefore, for denying that the objects which satisfy these criteria do in fact exist.

So far as I know, the first philosopher to make a serious attempt to legitimise the vulgar belief in physical objects, by the development of Hume's notions of constancy and coherence, was H. H. Price, whose book *Hume's Theory of the External World* was published in 1940. It is a characteristically thorough and ingenious work, which has not received the attention that it merits. Price borrows from Russell the term 'sensibilia' to refer to impressions which may not be actually sensed, and shows in convincing detail how the occurrence of gaps at different places in the various series of impressions that we take as emanating from the same physical object can sustain the conception of unsensed sensibilia as filling in these gaps. He does not think that Hume would have attached any meaning to the statement that these unsensed sen-

sibilia really existed, but he does think that Hume could consistently have adopted either the theory that when we refer to some
physical object we are asserting that our actual impressions are
such as they would be if the appropriate sensibilia existed, or the
more pragmatic theory that statements about physical objects
have no truth-value, but are to be construed as more or less
successful recipes for explaining and predicting the occurrence
of actual impressions. I think that a more realistic theory would
be preferable to either of these alternatives, though it may be that
Price's suggestions preserve a closer fidelity to Hume. My main
objection to Price's argument is that it represents physical objects
as what he calls 'families' of sensibilia, in a sense which allows
for a family, the various members of which have conflicting
properties, to occupy, or be as if it occupied, a particular place
at a particular time. He tries to avoid the contradiction by relati-
vising properties to points of view, so that a sensibile which is
elliptical from one point of view may be spatio-temporally coin-
cident with a sensibile, or an actual impression, which is round
from a different point of view, but this is a desperate device and
it may not even be coherent.

I think that we can arrive at a simpler as well as a more realistic
theory if we take advantage of the fact that visual and tactual
impressions occur in sense-fields which are spatially extended
and sensibly overlap in time. In other words, our hard data
include not only individualised patterns but the spatial and temporal relations which they bear to one another. This is a feature
of our experience to which Hume pays surprisingly little attention. He does, indeed, devote five of the six sections which
compose Part II of the first Book of the *Treatise* to the topic of
space and time, but they are mainly concerned with conceptual
difficulties which he might more profitably have left to the mathematicians, had he been already disposed to consign geometry to
them, and to maintain the sharp distinction which he was to draw
in the *Enquiry* between questions concerning relations of ideas
and those concerning matters of fact. As it is, he insists on too
simple a derivation of mathematical concepts from sensory impressions and is consequently driven to repudiate the notion of
infinite divisibility. He argues, instead, that the idea and therefore the impression of any finite extension must be compound,
consisting of the juxtaposition of a finite number of mathematical

points. These points are concrete objects, being either coloured or tangible, according as they are susceptible to sight or touch. They are *minima sensibilia*, not in virtue of being the smallest objects that we are capable of sensing, since the invention of more powerful microscopes might show that an impression which we had thought to be simple was really compound, but in virtue of the fact that they have no parts. From this Hume infers that every visual or tactual sense-field is a plenum, since we can have no idea of a spatial interval between two impressions except as something compounded out of these coloured, or tangible, indivisible points. What is true of space applies equally to time, with the same terms in each case and the substitution of immediate succession for temporary adjacency. Among other obvious difficulties, Hume's theory clearly falls foul of Zeno's paradoxes, but the theory of mathematical continuity was not properly developed until the nineteenth century, and Hume's troubles partly arose from his inability to see how an infinite number of parts could constitute anything less than an infinite whole. Even so it is strange that the only spatio-temporal relation which he was willing to acknowledge as given to sense was that of contiguity, for this is to impose a restriction upon our sense-experience to which it simply does not conform.

The spatio-temporal continuity which actually characterises most of our sense-experience, and in particular the sequence of our visual sense-fields, sustains the projection of spatial and temporal relations beyond the limits in which they are originally given. In this way successive sense-fields can come to be regarded as spatially adjacent. Then the facts which Hume summarises under his headings of constancy and coherence, the appearance of similar impressions in similar sensory surroundings, make it natural, as he remarked, for the observer to adopt a new measure of identity, according to which these corresponding impressions are not merely similar but identical. Our only difference from Hume at this point is that he represents the observer not as adopting a new measure of identity but as making an error of fact. In the same way, Hume's account of the process by which the fact that impressions are systematically 'recoverable' leads to their being thought of as persisting unsensed, should be taken, I suggest, not as the explanation of another error, but as a ground for extending the concept of identity. It is, on this view, an

entirely legitimate exercise of the imagination that visual impressions, which appear successively, should be conceived to exist
simultaneously and to occupy permanent positions in an indefinitely extended three-dimensional visual space.

At this point, however, we need to go a little beyond Hume.
The actual impressions, which we assign to the same object, are
not, as he wrongly says, exactly resemblant. Even if we make no
allowance, as yet, for changes in the object, there will be vari-
ations resulting from changes in the state or position of the
observer. What we must, therefore, imagine as persisting is not
any actual impression but what I have called elsewhere a 'standardised percept'.* This is a synthesis of what Price calls nuclear
sensibilia, that is, such as are obtainable from optimal points of
view. It serves as a model which actual impressions match more
or less closely. These standardised percepts may also be described as visual continuants. They can be regarded as under-
going qualitative changes when, under a variety of conditions,
the pattern appears to vary in one or more aspects, while the
remainder stay constant in a predominantly constant sensory
environment.

I can here only summarise the successive stages through which
the theory may now be supposed to pass. First, places are conceived in detachment from their occupants, which allows for the
possibility of movement. Then, for a variety of reasons, a set of
visual continuants is picked out as forming what we may call the
'central body', a term borrowed from the great American prag-
matist C. S. Peirce. This is, of course, the observer's own body,
though not yet characterised as such. Tactual space is constructed on much the same principle as visual space and grounds
are discovered for attributing tactual qualities to visual continuants. Sounds and smells and tastes are brought into the picture
by their being traced to their apparent sources. The observer
begins to make some simple causal correlations, which provide
him with an outline of the way things are. Most of his impressions
fit into this scheme but some do not. Self-consciousness arises
with the identification of other visuo-tactual continuants as resembling the central body in being the sources of signs. Most of
these signs can be interpreted as corroborating the main body of

* In *The Central Questions of Philosophy.*

the observer's experiences, but again some cannot. This is the source of the distinction between what is public and what is private. In the final stage, if I may quote my own account of it, the visuo-tactual continuants 'are cut loose from their moorings. The possibility of their existing at times when they are not perceived is extended to the point where it is unnecessary to their existence that they ever should be perceived, or even that there should be any observers to perceive them. Since the theory also requires that these objects do not change their perceptible qualities except as a result of some physical alteration in themselves, they come to be contrasted with the fluctuating impressions that different observers have of them. In this way the objects are severed from the actual percepts from which they have been abstracted and are even regarded as being causally responsible for them.'

In developing this theory of manifest objects, I think that I have succeeded in reconciling Hume's vulgar and philosophical systems, but there remains the problem of reconciling this outcome with the contemporary philosophical system, that is to say, the account of the physical world which is presented by contemporary physics. This problem has many ramifications, into which I cannot enter here. Briefly, what seems to have happened is that the perceptible 'constructs' which are needed for the conception of public space are dismissed into the private sector, and their places taken by imperceptible particles. Whether spatial relations can legitimately be severed in this way from their original terms is a debatable question, but it is not obvious to me that they cannot. What we must in any case avoid, as Hume said, is a system which puts physical objects, as they really are, in a duplicate space to which our senses give us no access. If we are to concede physics any pretensions to truth, our interpretation of it must be intelligible.

In the theory of the external world which I have foisted on Hume, personal identity is subordinated to bodily continuity. This was not Hume's own view, but it does no radical violence to his principles. On the contrary, in the section of the *Treatise* which he devotes to this topic, he claims it to be 'evident, the same method of reasoning must be continu'd, which has so successfully explain'd the identity of plants, and animals, and ships and houses, and of all the compounded and changeable productions either of art or nature' (T 259). The difference is just that Hume equates personal identity with the identity of the mind, and defines this without any reference to the body. When I say that he defines it, I allow for his saying that 'the identity, which we ascribe to the mind of man is only a fictitious one,' and like our other ascriptions of identity proceeds from the 'operation of the imagination' (T 259). I am, however, more influenced by the fact that it is vital to Hume's account of the passions, and also to his theory of morals, that one does have a genuine idea of oneself, and he is not so inconsistent as to free this idea from all dependence on impressions. What I therefore take him to mean by calling the identity of our minds 'fictitious' is that it is not what he calls a 'true' identity, that is, the identity of a single unchanging object, but one that can be resolved into a relation between perceptions. There is no implication, any more than in the case of perceptible bodies, that these relations do not really obtain.

There is, indeed, one passage, in the Book 'Of the Passions', in a section in which Hume expatiates on the nature of sympathy, as a factor in the love of fame, where he actually speaks of our having an impression of ourselves. ''Tis evident', he says, 'that the idea or rather impression of ourselves is always intimately with us, and that our consciousness gives us so lively a conception of our own person, that 'tis not possible to imagine, that any thing can in this particular go beyond it' (T 317). If this is not an oversight, the impression must be one of reflection, directed upon the idea of the self, for Hume consistently maintains elsewhere that since no impression is constant and invariable, one has no impression of oneself. He develops this point in a much quoted passage in the first Book of the *Treatise*. 'For my part,' he says, 'when I enter most intimately into what I call myself, I always stumble on some particular perception or other, of heat or cold, light or shade, love or hatred, pain or pleasure. I never can catch myself at any time without a perception, and never can observe anything but the perception.' He makes the apparent concession that some other person 'may, perhaps, perceive something simple and continu'd, which he calls *himself*', but shows this to be ironical by his assertion that 'setting aside some metaphysicians of this kind, I may venture to affirm of the rest of mankind that they are nothing but a bundle or collection of

different perceptions, which succeed each other with an inconceivable rapidity, and are in a perpetual flux and movement' (T
252). Hume's readiness to speak for the rest of mankind suggests
that his proposition is only disguised as an empirical generalisation. It is rather that he can conceive of nothing that he would
count as a pure awareness of oneself.

What then are the relations in virtue of which a bundle of
perceptions constitutes a self? Apart from a rather cursory reference to resemblance and causation and the remark that 'memory
does not so much produce as *discover* personal identity, by shewing us the relation of cause and effect among our different perceptions' (T 262), Hume barely attempts to give an answer, and
in one of the Appendices to the *Treatise*, he admits his failure to
find one, and indeed views the whole question of personal identity as posing a problem which he cannot solve. He upholds the
negative steps in his argument, that just as 'we have no idea of
external substance, distinct from the ideas of particular qualities',
so we have no notion of the mind 'distinct from the particular
perceptions', a conclusion sustained by the apparent matter of
fact that 'When I turn my reflexion on *myself*, I never can perceive
this *self* without one or more perceptions; nor can I perceive any
thing but the perceptions': that, consequently, it is the composition of perceptions 'which forms the self': that 'all perceptions
are distinct': that 'whatever is distinct is distinguishable: and
whatever is distinguishable is separable by the thought or imagination', with the result that perceptions 'may be conceived as
separately existent, and may exist separately, without any contradiction or absurdity' (T 634–5). But having thus 'loosened' our
perceptions he can find no means of binding them together. He
says that there are two principles which he cannot 'render consistent', though he believes each of them to be true. They are
respectively 'that all our distinct perceptions are distinct existences' and 'that the mind never perceives any real connexion
among distinct existences' (T 636).

This statement is puzzling. Evidently, these principles are not
inconsistent with one another. What Hume may have meant was
that they are collectively inconsistent with the proposition that
perceptions may be so 'composed' as to form a self. But even
this is not evident. It depends on what we understand by a 'real
connexion'. If what is meant is a logical connexion, then there is

no reason in logic why perceptions should not be distinct exist-ences, in the sense that we can consistently conceive of their separation, and yet stand, as a matter of fact, in such empirical relations to one another as are sufficient to constitute a self. This is the line taken by William James, who puts forward a Humean theory of the self in his major work, *The Principles of Psychology*, which has remained a classic since its first publication in 1890. The theory relies on what James takes to be the experienced relations of sensible compresence and sensible continuity.

Apart from a possible charge of circularity, the most serious objection to any theory of this type is that we are not continually conscious. We need, therefore, to find some means of linking the perceptions which lie on either side of an interval, say, of dream-less sleep, and there is at least no obvious candidate for this role, except their common relation, the nature of which itself presents a problem, to one and the same body. To be content to say that they belong to the same mind is unhelpful, if it is just a way of saying that they stand in whatever the relation we are looking for happens to be, and unintelligible if it refers them to the same underlying mental subject. As Hume succinctly puts it in his *Abstract* of the *Treatise*, 'the mind is not a substance in which the perceptions inhere' (T 658).

Neither is this the only difficulty. A point which oddly escapes Hume's sceptical notice is that one attributes identity to persons other than oneself, and that these attributions depend upon the identification of their bodies. It is not as if there were a common store of perceptions, which we could sort into the requisite bund-les, and then each light upon the particular bundle that con-stitutes himself.

We are not aware of the experiences of others in the way that we are aware of our own. This does not deter us from applying a psychological criterion of identity to other persons, or even to letting it override the physical criteria. One can imagine circum-stances in which one could attach a sense to saying that two or more persons were simultaneously housed in the same body or, as the result perhaps of a brain-transplant, if this were physically possible, that the same person occupied different bodies at dif-ferent times. Even so, the primary identification, from the point of view of others than the person or persons concerned, would still be that of the body, and if I am right in thinking that self-consciousness implies the discrimination of oneself from other conscious beings, there is a sense in which the factor of bodily continuity remains predominant.

This is not inconsistent with the view that bodies themselves are 'constructed' out of percepts. It is rather a striking illustration of the way in which the theory to which our impressions give rise, on Humean principles, 'takes over' its origins. The impressions are reinterpreted into the theory as states of an observer; and persons figure among the physical objects that the theory, to which we relate our assessments of existence, allows there to be.

4

Cause and effect

NO element of Hume's philosophy has had a greater and more lasting influence than his theory of causality. It has been frequently attacked, and frequently misunderstood. Not all the misunderstanding should be put down to the ill-will of Hume's critics. To some extent he courted it, though I agree with F. P. Ramsey, whose own theory, as set out in one of the Last Papers of *The Foundations of Mathematics*, is basically akin to Hume's, that Hume 'gave his readers credit for more intelligence than they display in their literal interpretations'. I shall argue that while Hume is vulnerable on many points of detail, partly because of his misguided insistence on tracing ideas to their origin, and partly because of his tendency to over-simplify the facts, his fundamental tenets not only admit of no answer but thoroughly deserve to carry conviction.

The first point to make clear is that when Hume speaks of 'the relation of cause and effect' he uses the term in a wider and looser sense than is now current. Whereas we are accustomed to distinguish between causal and functional laws, or between causal and statistical laws, or between events which are directly related as cause and effect and those which are related as the effects of a common cause or through their joint derivation from some overriding theory, Hume's usage is such that any law-like connection between matters of fact is characterised as causal. It is true that when he puts probability on a scale of evidence in which the first place is taken by knowledge, defined as 'the assurance arising from the comparison of ideas', and the second by 'proof', where the result of a causal argument is accepted without any of the uncertainty which attends probability (T 124), he goes on to distinguish the probability which is founded on *chance* from that which arises from *causes*; but there is no inconsistency here, since he maintains 'that there must always be a mixture of causes among the chances, in order to be the foundation of any reasoning' (T 126), and the very fact that he makes no provision for statistical laws except as probabilities founded on *causes* confirms the point that I have been making. Hume's usage can indeed be criticised as favouring the neglect of important distinctions, or even the adoption of an unsatisfactory account of probability, but we shall see that its defects do not vitiate the development of his essential argument.

Another unusual feature of Hume's terminology is that he most frequently speaks of the relation of causality as holding between objects, and indeed so defines it, though he is normally represented as taking it to be a relation between events. This emendation does him no disservice, as his references to objects in this connection can easily be rephrased as references to events, and his inclusion of mental elements, like feelings and volitions, among causes and effects is some justification for it. My own opinion is that his intentions are best represented by construing the relation, in his view of it, as holding between matters of fact, into which objects and events, actions and passions, states and processes, whether physical or mental, can be made to enter, according as the example makes one or other choice of terms appear more suitable. This course not only has the advantage of conforming to Hume's enlargement of the scope of the relation but, since matters of fact are correlative to true propositions, it also helps to bring out the point that Hume is concerned with the causal relation primarily as a ground for inference.

This point may be put more strongly. We have seen that Hume takes there to be three relations on which our association of ideas depends, those of resemblance, contiguity, and cause and effect, but there is a functional difference between the first two and the third. As good a way as any of expressing this difference would be to say that whereas the first two provide tracks for the movements of our attention, the third is the main source of supply for our factual beliefs. The impression or idea of an object is apt to arouse the idea of one that has been found to resemble it or has appeared contiguously to it, or contiguously to an object of a similar sort, but the process goes no further. It does not lead to any beliefs, beyond those that already lie within the domain of memory or the senses. Taken singly, or together, these relations do not persuade us of the existence of particular realities that have not yet come within our experience. For this we have to rely upon reasoning and, as Hume puts it in the Abstract, and similarly in the *Enquiry*:

'Tis evident, that all reasonings concerning *matters of fact* are founded on the relation of cause and effect, and that we can never infer the existence of one object from another, unless they be connected together, either mediately or immediately. In order therefore to understand these reasonings, we must be perfectly acquainted with the idea of a cause; and in order to that, must look about us to find something that is the cause of another. (T 649)

There is, however, more to the understanding of our reasonings concerning matters of fact than the analysis of the relation on which they are based. There is also the question of the support which the reasonings draw from the relation, and it is in the way it illuminates this second question that the importance of Hume's theory almost wholly lies.

This being said, we can begin with Hume's actual description of causality. His procedure is to distinguish the elements which enter into the common idea of the relation, and then look for the impressions from which they have been derived. Apart from the confusion of psychological with logical questions of which he is generally guilty, his method is open in this instance to a charge of circularity. As we have already remarked, the level at which he views causality in operation is that of physical objects and events, and in attaining this level he already needs to make use of factual inference. This circularity will not, however, appear to be vicious, and while his genetic approach does lead him to give too limited an account of the causal relation, especially in view of the amount of work with which he charges it, the harm which results does not go very deep. His principal theses are not affected by it.

In analysing our idea of the relation of cause and effect, Hume finds it to be compound. It essentially comprises the relations of priority, contiguity and what he calls necessary connexion. This turns out not to be a relation at all, in any straightforward sense of the term, but Hume at least begins by speaking of it as such. In the case of the first two relations the matching of ideas to impressions is allowed to be obvious. What does present a most serious problem for Hume is the discovery of an impression from which the idea of necessary connexion could possibly be derived.

Before we examine Hume's handling of this problem, which
leads to the nerve of his theory of causality, I should perhaps
say that I think it doubtful whether any of the three elements
which Hume takes to be essential to our idea of the causal
relation really is so. The reason he gives for making contiguity
essential is that

> tho' distant objects may sometimes seem productive of each other, they
> are commonly found upon examination to be link'd by a chain of causes,
> which are contiguous among themselves and to the distant objects; and
> where in any particular instance we cannot discover this connexion, we
> still presume it to exist. (T 75)

This may indeed have been true of the general opinion of Hume's
time, but there is nothing contradictory in the notion of action
at a distance, and a scientific theory which admitted it would not
now be rejected merely on that ground. Not only that, but
Hume himself allows causality to operate in a whole class of
cases where there is not just an absence of spatial contiguity,
but no question of there being any spatial relation at all. These
are the cases in which our thoughts and feelings have physical
causes and effects. For in Hume's view, only what was coloured
or tangible could literally be accorded spatial properties: he
queries our title to attribute spatial location to the data of the
other senses, even on the basis of their association with the
objects of sight and touch, and in the case of thoughts and
feelings, he holds that the maxim 'That an object may exist, and
yet be nowhere', is obviously satisfied. Whether he is right on
this point is debatable. I suppose that the popular answer might
turn out to be that our thoughts are inside our heads, but unless
we take what I still consider to be the unjustified step of identifying mental with cerebral events, this can hardly be taken as
literally true. And whatever reasons there may be for giving our
thoughts a figurative location, say by assigning them to some
area of the brain on which they are held to be causally dependent, this still will not yield the result that they are spatially
contiguous to their causes.

Hume does have an argument for insisting that causes must
precede their effects, in spite of what would appear to be the
possibility, in certain cases, of their being contemporaneous.

'Tis an established maxim [he says], both in natural and moral philosophy, that an object, which exists for any time in its full perfection
without producing another, is not its sole cause: but is assisted by some
other principle, which pushes it from its state of inactivity, and makes
it exert that energy, of which it was secretly possest. (T 76)

From this Hume infers that if any cause can be 'perfectly contemporary with its effect' all of them must be. The reasoning is
not made fully explicit, but appears to rest on the assumption
that every set of sufficient conditions produces its effect as soon
as possible, so that if it were possible for a cause, in this sense,
to produce a contemporaneous effect, any set of conditions which
failed to do so would not be sufficient. If we further assume
determinism, as we shall see that Hume does, so that every effect
is at least part of a further cause, we do away with succession
and so with time. For, as Hume puts it, 'if one cause was contemporary with its effect, and this effect with *its* effect, and so
on . . . all objects must be co-existent' (T 76).

Hume appears to have had some doubts about the validity of
this argument, but protected himself by adding that 'the affair is
of no great importance'. He was right on both counts. Nothing
in his further analysis of causality depends on causes' having to
precede their effects, and his argument *is* invalid. What its
premise entails is that there can be no interval of time between
the cause and the effect, but this does not exclude their overlap-
ping, and there is no reason why, if the overlap is partial in some
cases, it should not be complete in others. Neither is the premise
itself compelling. If, as Hume does, one is going to make the
concept of causality dependent on that of law, there is no logical
ground for excluding any interval of time between the states of
affairs which a law conjoins. We can admit the possibility of
action at a distance in time as well as in space.

I said earlier that I doubted whether the element of necessary
connexion was essentially comprised in the popular notion of
causality. This was partly out of charity, since I am going to argue
that unless it is given a very artificial interpretation, such as we
shall see that it receives from Hume, the term does not apply at
all to matters of fact, and I should prefer to avoid saddling the
public with such confusion of thought that its concept of causality
had no application. Even so, I should not be surprised if a social

survey revealed that most people associated with causality some vague idea of power, or force, or agency, and in that case I should preserve charity by severing these ideas from the description of the actual factors which make their causal judgements acceptable.

However this may be, the important point, at this stage of the argument, which Hume acknowledges, is that even if they were necessary, the relations of priority and contiguity are not sufficient for causality. Something more, or perhaps something wholly different, is required. What can it be? Hume offers an answer, but we shall find that the answer itself is of less consequence than the route which takes him to it, and that the splendour of the route owes less to what Hume asserts, as he pursues it, than to what he denies.

The first of his denials is that there is a logical relation between independent matters of fact. As he himself put it in the *Treatise*, we can rely on the principle 'That there is nothing in any object, considered in itself, which can afford us a reason for drawing a conclusion beyond it' (T 139). In the *Enquiry* he offers the further argument that 'Whatever is intelligible, and can be distinctly conceived, implies no contradiction, and can never be proved false by any demonstrative argument or abstract reasoning *a priori*' (E 35). He gives various examples: maintaining, for instance, that he can clearly and distinctly conceive that a body resembling snow in all other respects 'has yet the taste of salt or feeling of fire', that the proposition 'that all the trees will flourish in December and January, and decay in May and June' is perfectly intelligible (E 35); that from the sole premise that a billiard ball is moving in a straight line towards another, it would never be possible 'to infer motion in the second ball from the motion and impulse of the first' (T 650). If in each of these cases, or in the many other examples that he gives, we infer a contrary conclusion, it is because we are making projections from our past experience. So far as logic is concerned, anything may produce anything.

This step is undoubtedly valid, but some care is needed in setting the argument out. We must avoid being misled by the fact that it is common practice to describe objects in terms of their actual or possible relations to one another, and that very often, especially in the case of artefacts, our descriptions of them include a tacit or explicit reference to their causal properties. For instance, in calling something a pen we imply that it is designed to serve the purpose of producing legible marks; a looking-glass does not deserve its name unless it has the capacity of reflecting images; a match is something that, under specifiable conditions, produces flame when it is struck. Not only is there an enormous number of examples of this sort to be found in common usage, but we can take the process to any length we please. In any case in which we want to make the claim that two properties are invariably associated, we can guarantee their connexion by the simple device of reconstruing the predicate which has so far stood for only one of them in such a way that it comes to stand for their conjunction. Similarly, it is often in our power to reconstrue sentences which express empirical generalisations by framing a deductive theory in which they are treated as expressing definitions or their logical consequences.

It is, however, obvious that manœuvres of this sort afford no real protection against Hume's argument. The empirical questions which we apparently suppress by concealing them under definitions come to light again when we ask whether the definitions are satisfied. If we can manipulate predicates so as to establish logical connexions, we can equally reverse the process. A complex property can be resolved into its separate elements; and the predicates involved so construed as to make it an empirical question whether they are satisfied in common.

But may there not be limits to our power of dismantling a given structure of logically connected concepts? Hume's argument requires that every object be, as he puts it, 'consider'd in itself'. Is it quite certain that this is always possible? There does indeed, seem to be no difficulty so long as we are dealing with sensory qualities or even with particular impressions, but the matters of fact to which Hume applies his argument are not at this elementary level. They concern the behaviour of physical objects, and there is a ground for saying that these cannot be treated individually, as if nothing else existed. They are located in a spatio-temporal system, and this may be taken to entail that the identification of any individual object carries the presupposition that there are others to which it stands in some spatio-temporal relation. There is, however, a saving clause in that this reference to other objects is quite general. Within the whole range of objects to which the one that is being identified will be spatio-temporally related, there will be none in particular to which the identification need carry any reference. For this reason we can fulfil Hume's requirement that objects be considered in themselves, by taking it to imply that with regard to any two objects x and y we can identify either by a description which carries no reference to the other, and then, if this condition is satisfied, his conclusion that, from a statement which asserts the existence of x, under such a description, nothing whatsoever can be deduced about the existence or non-existence of y, emerges as the tautology that it anyhow needs to be.

It is well for Hume that he can avail himself of this tautology, since his other argument that the contrary of any matter of fact can be distinctly conceived is not conclusive. Its weakness lies in the assumption that what we find intelligible must be logically possible. A counter-example was put forward by Professor W. C. Kneale in his book *Probability and Induction*, published in 1949. It is generally though not universally held that a proposition of pure mathematics is necessarily true, if it is true at all. So if this is so, and if Hume were right, the contradictory of a true mathematical proposition should not be conceivable. But now consider Goldbach's conjecture that every even number greater than 2 is the sum of two primes. This has never been proved; neither has an exception been discovered. If we allow mathematical propositions to be true or false, independently of our having a proof or disproof of them, and if we insist on their necessity, then we must conclude that either Goldbach's conjecture or its negation is logically false. Yet each seems equally conceivable.

Even if one is not willing to make the assumptions which are needed to sustain this example, I think it should be conceded that the appeal to what we can imagine does not provide us with a foolproof criterion of logical possibility. Not all contradictions are immediately obvious, and conversely propositions which are logically possible, even propositions which are true, may defeat one's imagination. For instance, the curvature of space is something that we have been taught to believe in, but I suppose that before Einstein propounded his Theory of Relativity, most people would have found it inconceivable. I think, therefore, that while Hume's examples of changes in the usual course of nature have some force, it is on our ability to dissever the logical connections which our language forges between our descriptions of matters of fact that, as I said, his argument securely rests.

As it happens, the position which Kneale was trying to defend when he made use of Goldbach's conjecture was not that causal relations exemplify logical entailments, but rather that the laws of nature are what Kneale called Principles of Necessitation. This view is of especial interest, if only because it brings us to the second of Hume's important denials, which was that there could be any such thing as natural necessity, when this is taken to imply that there can be what Kant was to call synthetic relations between matters of fact, which are necessary even though their existence is not logically demonstrable.

Hume's argument is simply that no such relations are observable. If we take his favourite example of a game of billiards, we do indeed speak in 'forceful' terms of the cue being used to 'strike' the ball and of one ball 'cannoning' off another. But all that we actually observe is a series of changes in spatio-temporal relations. First there is a movement of the player's arm, coinciding with a movement of the cue, then an instant at which the cue and the ball are in spatial contact, then a period during which the ball is in motion, relatively to the objects in its neighbourhood, then an instant at which it is in spatial contact with a second ball, then a period in which both balls are in motion, and then, if the player achieves his cannon, an instant at which the first ball is in spatial contact with a third. In the whole of such a process there is no observable relation for which terms like 'power' or 'force' or 'necessary connexion' could be needed to provide a name. And the same applies to any other example that one might have chosen, whether it be a sequence of physical events, or a conjuction of physical properties. As Hume would put it, we are never furnished with an impression from which the idea of necessary connexion could be derived.

If one is looking for such an impression, the most obvious place to seek it is in one's own experience of action. Do we not find it in the exercise of our wills? Hume considers this suggestion in the *Enquiry* and raises three objections to it. The first is that we do not understand the principle of 'the union of soul with body', which we should do if volition gave us the impression of power: the second is that we cannot explain why we move some of our bodily organs and not others, whereas we should not be embarrassed by this question if we were conscious of a force operating only in favoured instances: the third is that 'we learn from anatomy' that strictly speaking we have no power to move our limbs at all, but only to set in motion nerves, or 'animal spirits', from which the motion of our limbs eventually results; and certainly we are not conscious of any relation of force between the exercise of our wills and the movements of these 'animal spirits' or anything like them (E 64–7).

I think that these arguments can be resisted. It has often been claimed that when we perform voluntary movements or handle objects in the various ways that we constantly do, we undergo an experience which fairly answers to the description of being the experience of bringing something about, and the fact that there are limits to what we can do in this way, and that we may be ignorant of the physical conditions which have to be satisfied if we are to accomplish anything of this sort at all, are not in themselves sufficient to make this description inapt. Indeed Hume himself speaks, in cases where we find ourselves trying to overcome physical resistance, of our experiencing an 'animal nisus', and acknowledges that it enters very much into the vulgar idea of power, even if this vulgar idea is neither precise nor accurate (E 67).

But now I must say that, whatever the rights or wrongs of this question may be, and however great its psychological interest, it is only peripheral to Hume's argument. What we must remember is that Hume is concerned with causality as the ground of factual inference; it has to supply the bridge which carries us safely from a true belief in one matter of fact to a true belief in another. And the consequence of this is that even if we do have experiences which are properly described as experiences of the exercise of power, they are nothing to the purpose. The reason for this is that they cannot be generalised. From the fact, if it be a fact, that a faithful description of some particular action of mine implies, either overtly or covertly, that I have undergone such an experience, it in no way follows that when I set myself to repeat the action, I shall have the same experience or indeed achieve the same result. There being no logical connection between the two performances, we can make our description of either one of them as elaborate as our psychological theories permit; it will still convey nothing about the nature of the other.

The same applies to the search for necessity in the physical world. Here again, Hume had failed to do full justice to his case by making it appear to rest upon an empirical generalisation, rather than a logical argument. If we return to his example of the billiard balls, I think that he is right in saying that no relations of force or power can be detected in the actual phenomena. The point which he overlooks is that it would not matter if they were detectable. For let us suppose that when the balls collided we did observe something which could fairly be described as the communication of force, and that we therefore included a reference to it in our description of the facts. So far as our right to make inferences goes, this complication leaves us exactly where we were. Let us call the two balls 'A' and 'B' and the supposedly forceful relation between them 'R'. Then, if there is any doubt whether the sequel to the spatial coincidence of A and B will be the same on a future occasion, there must be an equal, or indeed a stronger doubt, since more is being assumed, whether A will again stand in the relation R to B on a future occasion of their spatial coincidence, and whether there will be the same sequel. It may be objected that the doubt is settled in the second case by the very nature of the relation R. If A stands in relation R to B, it *must* impart motion to it, and this implies that under similar conditions it does so on all occasions. But this objection is simply fallacious. For either R is a merely phenomenal relation, that is to say, a relation such that an accurate observation of the phenomena is sufficient to establish its presence, or it is not. If it is, its existence will be entirely neutral with regard to what happens at any other place or time. If it is not, it can serve its intended purpose only if it comprises in its definition the clause that any terms which are related by it will always, under similar conditions, exhibit similar behaviour. But this makes the example just another case in which causal propositions are made true by fiat, and the same objections are fatal to it. Moreover, on this interpretation, what looked like the empirical proposition that necessary connexion is not detectable in any single instance of a conjunction of matters of fact, is promoted into a logical truth. For the relation is now defined in such a way that we have to examine every single instance of the phenomenon in question, in order to discover that it holds in any one of them.

There the matter of necessity might be allowed to rest, though much more would remain to be said about our grounds for making factual inferences. But assuming as he does that we have an idea of necessary connexion, Hume is driven by his principles to continue his search for the impression which could be the source of this idea. He sees that the mere multiplication of instances will not supply it. Having stated the principle, which we have already quoted, '*That there is nothing in any object, consider'd in itself, which can afford us a reason for drawing a conclusion beyond it*', he goes on to state the further principle, '*That even after the observation of the frequent or constant conjunction of objects, we have no reason to draw any inference concerning any object beyond those of which we have had experience*' (T 139), and if we are restricting ourselves, as Hume here does, to deductive inference, the truth of the second of these principles is no less evident than that of the first. Nevertheless it is in the multiplication of instances that Hume finds the clue that leads him to the end of his quest. His theory is that the observation of the frequent or constant conjunction of matters of fact of recurring types gives rise to a mental habit or custom of expecting this regularity to be repeated. The difference made by the multiplication of instances is, as Hume puts it in the *Enquiry*, that 'the mind is carried by habit, upon the appearance of one event, to expect its usual attendant, and to believe that it will exist' (E 75). It is, then, in 'this connexion which we *feel* in the mind, this customary transition of the imagination from one object to its usual attendant' that Hume discovers 'the sentiment or impression from which we form the idea of power or necessary connexion' (E 75). All that we have to go on is our past experience of regularity in nature; indeed there is nothing more there to be discovered. We become habituated to expecting that this regularity will be maintained. And this habit or custom is so firmly ingrained in us that we project the strength of the association into the phenomena themselves, and so succumb to the illusion that 'necessary connexion' is the name of a relation in which they actually stand to one another.

This leaves the way clear for Hume to define causality. Both in the *Treatise* and in the *Enquiry* he offers alternative definitions, according as the relation is considered as 'natural' or 'philosophical': that is to say, according as we attend only to the phenomena in which the relation is exhibited, or also take account of the light in which we view them. In the first case, a cause is defined in the *Treatise* as 'An object precedent and contiguous to another, and where all the objects resembling the former are plac'd in like relations of precedence and contiguity to those objects, that resemble the latter'. The alternative, 'philosophical' definition is that 'A cause is an object precedent and contiguous to another and so united with it, that the idea of the one determines the mind to form the idea of the other, and the impression of the one to form a more lively idea of the other' (T 170). The definitions given in the *Enquiry* are similar but more succinct. In its natural aspect a cause is said to be 'An object followed by another, and where all the objects similar to the first are followed by objects similar to the second', with the additional gloss, 'where, if the first object had not been, the second had never existed': when the contribution of the mind is brought in, a cause becomes 'an object followed by another, and whose appearance always conveys the thought to that other' (E 76–7).

It has often been pointed out, and hardly needs repeating, that these definitions are far from being adequate, as they stand. Apart from the infelicity, which we have already noted, of speaking of 'objects' as the terms of causal relations, and the unwarranted exclusion of action at a distance, they suffer from their failure to take account of the part played by theories in the derivation of what we take to be causal laws. It is doubtful, also, whether the conjunction need be entirely constant. We often make particular causal judgements, with no stronger general backing than a statement of tendency. Hume, indeed, makes some provision for cases of this sort when he speaks of 'the probability of causes'. He assumes, not altogether in accord with common usage, that a cause has to be a sufficient condition, and also unduly takes it for granted that there is never more than one sufficient condition for any given matter of fact. This would make a cause also a necessary condition, which is, indeed, what Hume describes it as being in the gloss to the first of his definitions in the *Enquiry*. He allows, however, for what he calls the contrariety of causes, which means that the presence of some other factor, or factors, prevents a given type of 'object' from being followed by its usual attendant. If we knew what these other factors were and how they operated we could make their absence part of our sufficient condition and regulate our expectations accordingly. As it is, we have often to be content with generalising from past frequencies. This account of our procedure is not objectionable in itself, so long as we admit the assumption of there not being a plurality of sufficient conditions. What it overlooks is the caveats which we impose on statistical inferences, and once more the extent to which statistical laws are derived from theories.

Conversely, not every constant conjunction is seen as warranting an ascription of causality. In cases where the examples are not numerous, or occur in what are thought to be exceptional circumstances, or do not fit in with our general picture of the way things happen, the conjunction may be deemed accidental, even though it has occurred without exception. This goes with the serious objection that Hume's use of words like 'similar' and 'resembling' in his definitions is too vague. Any two objects may be similar in some respect or other. We need to be told in some detail what kind or degree of similarity is required for the matters of fact which it groups to become suitable candidates for factual inference.

The charge of circularity is sometimes brought against the second of Hume's definitions in the *Treatise*, on the ground that he speaks of an object as 'determining' the mind to form the idea of another. This charge is unjustified. It is clear from the whole course of Hume's argument that no more is claimed here than that the mind in fact acquires the habit of associating the ideas in question. There is no implication that it is 'forced' to do so. On the other hand, it was a venial mistake on Hume's part to include a reference to the mind's propensity in what was supposed to be a definition of causality. In propounding causal judgements, we express our mental habits, but do not normally assert that we have them. An account of our mental habits does enter into the explanation of our ascriptions of causality: but this is not to say that when we attribute causal properties to some physical object, we are also making an assertion about ourselves.

Enough has been said to show that Hume's definitions are formally defective. The fact remains that they do bring out two points, the importance of which outweighs their defects. The first is that it is only the existence of the appropriate regularity in nature that can make a causal proposition true: and the second is that the difference between accidental and causal generalisations is not a difference in the ways they are satisfied, but a difference in our respective attitudes towards them. In the second class of cases we are willing to project accredited regularities on to imaginary or unknown instances; in the first we are not. Though he points the way to this distinction, Hume does not himself enquire into the principles which underlie it.

Instead, he raises the more general and fundamental question how we can ever be justified in making factual inferences which carry us beyond the evidence of our past and present observations. In raising this question, he posed what has come to be known to philosophers as the Problem of Induction. He approaches it by asking whether our procedure is governed by reason. If it were, he maintains that our reason 'would proceed upon that principle, *that instances of which we have had no experience, must resemble those, of which we have had experience, and that the course of nature continues always uniformly the same*' (T 89). But now we come to the next of his crucial denials. For he shows convincingly that the principle at issue can neither be demonstrated nor even lay claim to any probability. That the principle cannot be demonstrated follows evidently from the assumption, which we have seen that Hume is entitled to make, that the members of the two classes of instances are logically distinct. As for its being probable, we run up against the fact that the ascription of probability draws its force from past experience. In Hume's words, 'probability is founded on the presumption of a resemblance betwixt those objects, of which we have had experience, and those, of which we have had none; and therefore 'tis impossible this presumption can arise from probability' (T 90).

Does it follow that we have no good reason at all for trusting the outcome of any factual inference? From Hume's point of view, this would be a misleading way of stating what he has proved, since it suggests that we lack the good reasons we might conceivably have had. His own conclusion is rather that which Kemp Smith attributes to him: that reason has in such matters been ruled out of court. In a section of the *Treatise* in which he allows scepticism to invade the domain of reason, using the argument that the admitted possibility of our making mistakes in the demonstrative sciences entails that even in their case knowl-

edge degenerates into probability, with the surely fallacious rider
that, the judgement of probability itself not being certain, the doubts
successively mount up until even the probability is all taken away,
he remarks that the question whether he himself accepts the totally
sceptical conclusion, 'that our judgement is not in *any* thing possest
of *any* measure of truth and falsehood', is 'entirely superfluous',
since it is not an opinion that anyone can sincerely hold. If he has
developed the sceptic's case to its greatest extent, it is only to obtain
evidence for his hypothesis '*that all our reasonings concerning matters
of fact are deriv'd from nothing but custom: and that belief is more
properly an act of the sensitive, than of the cogitative part of our natures*'
(T 183). This echoes an earlier statement: 'Thus all probable reasoning is nothing but a species of sensation. 'Tis not only in poetry
and music, we must follow our taste and sentiment, but likewise in
philosophy' (T 103).

Does this mean that all factual reasoning is on the same footing;
that we are entitled to extrapolate from our past and present
experience in any way that suits our fancy? If Hume really thought
so, it is strange that he should have applied what he called 'the
experimental method' to the study of the passions or that he
should have laid down a set of 'Rules by which to judge of Causes
and Effects' (T 173ff.), such as that there must be a constant
union between them, and 'that the difference in the effects of two
resembling objects must proceed from that particular, in which
they differ'. Why is he so sure that 'there can be no such thing as
Chance in the world' (E 56), so that when we ascribe an event to
chance we are confessing our ignorance of its real cause, a question made all the more puzzling by his having been at considerable
pains to show (T 78ff.) that the generally received maxim that
'*whatever begins to exist, must have a cause of existence*' is neither
intuitively nor demonstrably certain, and to expose the fallacies
in the arguments by which various philosophers had sought to
prove it? The only explanation seems to be that the propositions
that 'every event has a cause' and that 'the course of nature
continues always uniformly the same' were regarded by Hume in
the light of natural beliefs. They cannot be proved, but nature is
so constituted that we cannot avoid accepting them.

But can we really not avoid it? It seems to me that we can, in
both instances, though I shall not here dwell upon the first. The
trouble with the second proposition is that it is not clear how it

is to be construed. If it is taken at its face value, as stating that the course of nature is entirely repetitious, then so far from its expressing a natural belief, it is very unlikely that anybody believes it. Our experience leads us to expect the occurrence of unforeseen events; at the most we may believe that they can subsequently be accounted for. On the other hand, if no more is being claimed than that past experience is, in some large measure, a reliable guide to the future, there is no question but that this is universally assumed. There still, however, remains the problem of explaining why not every instance of experienced conjunction is thought to be equally projectible.

This goes with the fact, which has been strangely overlooked by the many philosophers, starting with Kant, who have tried to rebut Hume by arguing for the necessity, or at least the probability, of some general principle of uniformity, that its very generality would prevent such a principle from doing the work required of it. I am not sure whether Hume believed that the adoption of the principle which he formulated would legitimise inductive arguments by making them deductive, but if he did, he was mistaken. This can easily be shown by considering any case in which a universal generalisation is inferred from an unexhausted series of wholly favourable instances. Suppose that a number of objects of the kind A have been observed and all found to have the property f. Then the suggestion is that by adding the premise that nature is uniform we can deduce that every A has f. But it still may happen that we come upon an A which lacks f. In that case we shall not only have suffered the not unprecedented setback of discovering that a generalisation which we had accepted is false. We shall have proved that nature is not uniform, since if the conclusion of a valid deductive argument is false, at least one of its premises must be false, and in view of the truth of the premise that all observed As have been f, the false premise has to be the principle of uniformity. But surely neither Hume, nor any other philosopher who has thought there to be a need for such a principle, can have seriously intended it to be so stringent that it succumbed to the discovery of a first exception to any generalisation for which there had been any positive support.

Let it be granted, then, that there is no such simple method of transforming inductive into deductive reasoning. It may still be held that the use of a general principle of uniformity, when combined with the evidence of previous observations, can serve to bestow a high measure of probability on some generalisations and still more upon our expectations of particular events. This was very much the line taken by John Stuart Mill, though it has been shown that he needed to make further assumptions for his methods to yield the results that he claimed for them. His position was, however, avowedly circular. The principle of uniformity was itself viewed as obtaining its support from the generalisations which it joined in supporting.

It has been suggested that the circle can be avoided by deriving a set of general principles from a combination of the deliverances of past experience with *a priori* relations of probability, themselves based on the mathematical calculus of chances. The short answer to this is that no such relations are available, for the reason which Hume already gave in his discussion 'of the probability of chances'.

Shou'd it be said [he remarks], that tho' in an opposition of chances 'tis impossible to determine with *certainty*, on which side the event will fall, yet we can pronounce with certainty, that 'tis more likely and probable, 'twill be on that side where there is a superior number of chances, than where there is an inferior: Shou'd this be said, I wou'd ask, what is here meant by *likelihood* and *probability*? The likelihood and probability of chances is a superior number of equal chances; and consequently when we say 'tis likely the event will fall on the side, which is superior, rather than on the inferior, we do no more than affirm, that where there is a superior number of chances there is actually a superior, and where there is an inferior there is an inferior; which are identical propositions and of no consequence. (T 127)

In short, the mathematical calculus is a purely formal system, and if we are to apply it to our estimates of what is actually likely to happen, we need to make some such empirical assumption as that where we have a set of mutually exclusive possibilities, like the coming uppermost of one or other of the six faces of a die, and no information which favours one outcome rather than any other, they can be expected to occur with approximately equal frequency. But then we are back in our circle, for we have no reason to make any assumption of this sort except on the basis of past experience. Mere ignorance does not establish any probability.

There are those who maintain that Hume, and his followers and opponents, have all been tilting at windmills, since scientists do not employ inductive reasoning. They advance hypotheses, submit them to the severest tests that they can devise, and adhere to them so long as they are not falsified. I doubt, for my own part, if this is a fully accurate account of scientific procedure, though it serves as a corrective to the mistaken view that the practice of science consists in nothing more than generalising from past observations. But in any case it does not entail that induction is or could be superfluous. For one thing, this suggestion overlooks the fact that an enormous amount of inductive reasoning is built into our language. In referring to physical objects of whatever sort, we are implying that properties which have hitherto been found in conjunction will continue to be so; in crediting these objects with causal powers, we are forecasting the repetition, under suitable conditions, of previous sequences of different sorts of events. Furthermore, there would seem to be no point in testing hypotheses unless their passing the test was thought to enhance their credibility: but that it does so enhance it is an inductive assumption.

A more promising line of argument was advanced long ago by C. S. Peirce. If there is no ascertainable generalisation to which a given set of facts conforms, there is nothing we can do about it; if there is such a generalisation then the reliance on past experience will eventually lead us to it. There is, however, the difficulty that there may be an infinite number of generalisations with which any limited set of observations might be consistent, and there is not much comfort in the assurance that we are bound to get the right result in an infinite time.

Even so, there is some point in remarking that any successful *method* of forming our expectations must be inductive, for the sufficient reason that it would not be a successful method unless it followed a pattern which corresponded to the pattern of events with which it dealt. The real trouble lies in the latitude which our observations allow us, so that we have to choose between a number of competing hypotheses which are equally well supported by our past experience. The question at issue is not so much *whether* the future will resemble the past, since if the world is to continue to be describable at all, it must resemble it in some way or other, but *how* it will resemble it. What we want and cannot obtain, except by circular argument, is a justification for our actual interpretation of the lessons of the past; a justification for adhering to a special corpus of beliefs. That we cannot obtain it is an insight which we owe to Hume. What he neither proved nor even sought to prove was that the consequence is that the beliefs should be abandoned.

5

Morals, politics and religion

CONSIDERING the relish with which Hume denies the necessity of the proposition that every event has a cause, we may be surprised to discover how firmly he accepts its truth. There is, indeed, a passage in the *Treatise* where, in the course of discussing the passions of fear and hope, he speaks of the probabilities which cause them as belonging to one or other of two kinds, according as the object is already certain but 'uncertain to our judgement' or 'when the object is really in itself uncertain, and to be determin'd by chance' (T 444), but this is a rare departure from his usual view that 'what the vulgar call chance is nothing but a secret and conceal'd cause' (T 130). Throughout his analysis of the passions, and his exploration of the foundations of morals and politics, his official position is that of a determinist.

In speaking of Hume as a determinist, we must, however, bear in mind that this does not in his case carry any pledge of allegiance to a reign of necessity in nature. The most to which it commits him, or any other determinist who understands what he is talking about, is the proposition that the concurrence and succession of matters of fact of different types exhibit perfect regularity. In accepting this proposition, Hume not only sets aside the doubts which he has raised about the validity of induction, but also discounts the fact that the regularities which our past experience has brought to light are far from being perfect. They do not cover all the accredited data and their level of generality allows for some unexplained latitude among the instances in which they are exemplified. Hume takes no notice of this second point, but he does acknowledge the first. He disposes of it by contrasting the opinion of 'the vulgar, who take things according to their first appearance', with that of philosophers who attribute any appearance of irregularity to 'the secret opposition of contrary causes' (E 86–7). The objection to this course is that it reduces the thesis of determinism to a convention. It survives in all circumstances if we are allowed to set aside any adverse evidence by an appeal to secret powers. To endow it with some interest, we need to break it down into a set of working theories which we then apply to different domains of fact. It is true that if our theories fail, we may retain the hope of finding replacements which will bring us success, but at least at any given stage the questions which we are asking will be empirical.

Though these considerations did not occur to Hume, there is no reason to think that he would have found them unwelcome. For the proposition which he wished to advance was not so much that the operations of bodies are strictly regulated as that there is no distinction in this respect between body and mind. The character of human nature is as constant as that of inanimate objects and what is more 'this regular conjunction has been universally acknowledged among mankind, and has never been the subject of dispute, either in philosophy or common life' (E 88). If we are startled to find this said of philosophy, we need to remind ourselves that the term, in Hume's usage of it, encompasses science; and what he is here maintaining is that the custom of drawing inferences from past to future experience, as well as the assumption of firmer regularities than we have actually discovered, occur no less in the social than in the natural sciences.

What [he asks] would become of *history*, had we not a dependence on the veracity of the historian, according to the experience which we have had of mankind? How could *politics* be a science, if laws and forms of government had not a uniform influence upon society? Where would be the foundation of *morals*, if particular characters had no certain or determinate powers to produce particular sentiments, and if these sentiments had no constant operation on actions? And with what pretence could we employ our *criticism* upon any poet or polite author, if we could not pronounce the conduct and sentiments of his actors either natural or unnatural to such characters, and in such circumstances? It seems almost impossible, therefore, to engage either in science or action of any kind without acknowledging the doctrine of necessity, and this *inference* from motives to voluntary actions, from characters to conduct. (E 90)

The conclusion which Hume drew from this is that no one seriously believes in the freedom of the will, if this is taken to imply that men's actions are uncaused. He admits that when it comes to one's own actions one has a tendency to claim this type of freedom. 'We feel, that our actions are subject to our will, on most occasions; and imagine that our will itself is subject to nothing' (E 94), partly because we do not suffer from any feeling of constraint. We may be ignorant of all the regularities to which we conform, and even when we discover them we may still fancy that we can elude their grasp. We may even prove this to our own satisfaction by choosing a different course of action in what we take to be the same circumstances, not seeing that there is a decisive difference in that

the fantastical desire of shewing liberty is now itself operating as a cause. What is more to the purpose is that, however we may imagine we feel a liberty within ourselves, a spectator can commonly infer our actions from our motives and character; and even where he cannot, he concludes, in general, that he might, were he perfectly acquainted with every circumstance of our situation and temper, and the most secret springs of our complexion and disposition. (E 94)

Since we are intended to side with the spectator, this last claim evidently begs the question, and to the extent that it does so, Hume fails to prove his point. But whatever other moral may be drawn from this failure, it does not strengthen the position of those who wish to maintain the usual association of free will with responsibility. From their point of view, as well as Hume's, the possibility of an overall reign of purely physical causes is ruled out of court. Let us suppose then that our actions do not proceed, with any high degree of regularity, from our character and motives. To what do we ascribe their waywardness? I see no other candidate but chance. But why should we be held responsible for actions which occur by chance, any more than for those that issue from our motives and characters, which may perhaps themselves be explained in terms of our genetic endowment, and the physical and mental stimuli to which we have responded from our infancy?

This is not to deny us any form of liberty. Hume defines it as 'a power of acting or not acting, according to the determinations of the will' (E 95), and this is something that we commonly possess. Not only that, but Hume is able to argue that it is liberty of this sort, rather than the freedom of the will to which we cannot properly lay claim, that is 'essential to morality'. His argument is that 'actions are objects of our moral sentiment, so far only as they are indications of the internal character, passions, and affections' (E 99). They cannot give rise to praise or blame when they are 'derived only from external violence', and equally there would be no point in the distribution of praise or blame, reward or punishment, unless it had an effect upon men's motives and characters, and consequently upon their actions. This does not debar us from praising or blaming the conduct of the dead, or that of persons whom for other reasons we have no actual power to influence, but this is chiefly another illustration of the force of custom. There being certain sorts of conduct that we find it possible and useful, in many cases, to promote or inhibit by the expression of praise or blame, we fall into the habit of reacting in the same way to all conduct of these sorts. It is also to be noted that even when the agents in question are beyond our reach, our evaluations of their actions may still have an effect on the behaviour of those who are inclined to follow their example.

On the question of free will, I think that Hume is right, except for his claim that his definition of liberty is one 'on which all men agree'. It would, I think, be generally agreed that he has laid down a necessary condition of liberty. I doubt, however, if it is commonly thought to be sufficient. It appears to me, rather, that not only our moral judgements but also many of our feelings about ourselves and other persons, such feelings as those of pride or gratitude, are partly governed by a notion of desert, which requires our wills to be free in a stronger sense than Hume's definition admits. In a muddled fashion, we credit ourselves and others with what has sometimes been described as a power of self-determination. The trouble is that even if there were something which answered to this description, we should not escape from Hume's dilemma. Either the exercise of this power would fit into a causal pattern, or it would occur at random, and in neither case would it appear to justify an ascription of responsibility. We could avoid the muddle, as in effect Hume proposes, by altering our notions of desert and responsibility so that they fitted into a purely utilitarian scheme, but whether we have such command over our sentiments as to be able to abide by such a policy, and whether it is wholly desirable that we should abide by it even if we could, are questions which are open to dispute.

A point of interest, which Hume slyly makes in passing, is that if determinism were valid and one assumed the existence of an omnipotent creator, another dilemma would arise for those who wished to maintain that the creator was benevolent. As Hume puts it, 'human actions... either can have no moral turpitude at all, as proceeding from so good a cause; or if they have any turpitude, they must involve our Creator in the same guilt, while he is acknowledged to be their ultimate cause and author' (E 100). One can escape through the horns of this dilemma by discarding the concept of guilt altogether, which it is arguable that we should do anyway in view of its dependence on the muddled concept of free will, but the escape is quickly followed by recapture, since the dilemma can be restated in terms of evil, with an even heavier burden placed on the creator, since not all the evil in the world results from deliberate human actions. In this case there is no escape, since evil can be taken as comprising a large amount of human and animal suffering, if nothing more, and it is not to be denied that such suffering occurs. It may be alleviated in some cases by the belief that it proceeds from a good cause, but quite apart from the fact that it is not clear how this could achieve any more than a diminution of the evil, such cases are exceptional. Having already rejected the preposterous suggestion that this is the best of all possible worlds, we are left with the conclusion that if there is an omnipotent creator, he is not benevolent.

Characteristically, Hume leaves it to the reader to draw this conclusion. Having presented his argument, he is content to remark that 'to defend absolute decrees, and yet free the Deity from being the author of sin, has been found hitherto to exceed all the power of philosophy' (E 103). Since the weakest link in Hume's argument is his assumption of determinism, it is worth remarking that its conclusion would scarcely be impaired if this assumption were relaxed. The moral standing of a creator would not be very much higher if he had willed only a considerable proportion of the world's evil and left the remainder to chance.

After making his ironical comment that the question of the Deity's involvement in sin has been found to exceed the power of philosophy, Hume recommends that the subject 'return, with suitable modesty, to her true and proper province, the examination of common life' (E 103), and this is the policy which he himself pursues in giving his philosophical account of human morality. Hume's moral philosophy, reviewed in all its detail, is subtle and complex, but it is derived from a small number of principles which can be clearly elicited. They are partly analytical and partly psychological. I shall first state and discuss them, and then consider the conclusions which Hume draws from them.

The principles are the following. No special importance should be attached to the order in which I have set them out.

1 Reason alone, being concerned only with the discovery of truth and falsehood, 'can never be the motive for any action of the will' (T 413). It is from this principle that Hume derives his celebrated dictum: 'Reason is and ought only to be the slave of the passions, and can never pretend to any other office than to serve and obey them' (T 415).

2 The passions by which we are motivated may be direct or indirect, calm or violent. The direct passions, such as those of joy, grief, hope or fear, arise either from natural instinct, or from our desire of good, which can here be equated with pleasure, or aversion from evil, which can here be equated with pain. The indirect passions, such as those of pride, humility, love or hatred, arise from a combination of these primitive motives with other factors. This distinction is independent of that between calmness and violence. It is because the motivation may be violent that 'men often act knowingly against their interest' and are not always influenced by 'their view of the greatest possible good' (T 418).

3 Sympathy for other creatures is a natural instinct. Its strength is such that although it is 'rare to meet with one, who loves any single person better than himself', it is equally 'rare to meet with one, in whom all the kind affections, taken together, do not over-balance all the selfish' (T 487). This natural instinct of sympathy or benevolence plays a large part in the formation of our moral and political attitudes.

4 'Since morals . . . have an influence on the actions and affections, it follows that they cannot be deriv'd from reason' (T 457). Accordingly, 'the rules of morality are not conclusions of our reason'.

5 Moral judgements are not descriptions of matters of fact. 'Take any action allow'd to be vicious: Wilful murder, for instance. Examine it in all lights, and see if you can find that matter

of fact, or real existence which you call *vice*. In whichever way you take it, you find only certain passions, motives, volitions and thoughts. There is no other matter of fact in the case' (T 468). Similarly, when 'instead of the usual copulations of propositions, *is*, and *is not*', one suddenly meets 'with no proposition that is not connected with an *ought*, or an *ought not*' (T 469), one is being tricked. It is not possible that 'this new relation can be a deduction from others, which are entirely different from it'.

6 'Vice and virtue may be compared to sounds, colours, heat and cold, which according to modern philosophy, are not qualities in the object, but perceptions in the mind' (T 469). Accordingly, 'when you pronounce any character to be vicious, you mean nothing, but that from the constitution of your nature, you have a feeling or sentiment of blame from the contemplation of it'. It is interesting to note that here and elsewhere in his writing about morals, Hume takes the Lockean view of secondary qualities, in spite of his previous rejection of it when he was writing about the understanding.

7 Though one speaks of virtuous or vicious actions, they derive their merit or demerit only from virtuous or vicious motives, and it is only as signs of such motives, or the character of the person who acts from them, that actions are subject to moral evaluation.

8 The sentiment of approbation, aroused by 'a mental action or quality' which we therefore call virtuous, is itself pleasing, and that of disapprobation, which is similarly related to vice, displeasing (E 289). We can therefore also take virtue to be 'the power of producing love or pride' and vice to be 'the power of producing humility or hatred' (T 575).

9 What arouses our approbation or disapprobation is the appraisal of qualities or motives as being respectively productive of a preponderance of pleasure or pain. These appraisals may also be characterised as judgements of utility.

10 'No action can be virtuous or morally good unless there is in human nature some motive to produce it, distinct from the sense of its morality' (T 479).

11 The sense of justice, on which both moral and political obligation depend, is derived not from any natural impressions of reflection but from impressions due to 'artifice and human conventions' (T 496).

Let us begin by examining the psychological principles. There may be some doubt whether the cases in which the kind affections do not overbalance the selfish are so rare as Hume supposes, but I can find no good reason to doubt that we do have a natural instinct of sympathy or benevolence. Attempts have been made to subordinate sympathy to self-love, but they appear to me perverse. Since there can be no reason *a priori* for assuming that every action has a selfish base, it is simpler and more sensible in this instance to accept what Hume calls 'the obvious appearance of things' (E 298).

Without entering into the niceties of Hume's distinctions between the direct and indirect or the calm and violent passions, I think that the following points should be accepted. First, that not all intentional action is motivated, in the sense that it proceeds from a desire to bring about some good either to oneself, or to others, or to society at large, and, secondly, that even when our actions are motivated in this way they may not conform to utilitarian principles. That they rarely conform to purely egoistic principles has already been conceded, but neither are they simply altruistic. Sympathy varies in degree, and its strength depends on a variety of other relations in which one may stand to its object; it is not simply proportionate to one's estimate of the object's worth or need. Thus, one may choose to confer benefit on a member of one's family, on a lover or a friend, at the cost not only of one's own interest but of what one believes to be the greater interest of a wider circle. In the cases where one's actions are not purposive, such emotions as those of pity or embarrassment or anger may lead us to behave, even consciously, in ways that do no good to any one at all. It might be argued that actions done out of pity or anger were purposive, since they implied a desire to do good or harm to the persons concerned, but the answer to this is that the desire proceeds from the emotions, not the other way around. Neither need it be the case, as Hume seems to imply, that actions in which one disregards the consequences proceed only from the violent passions. Very often they are due to inertia. One simply cannot be bothered to realise one's preferences, whether the preference consists in the procurement of pleasure or in getting out of a situation which one finds disagreeable. Again it can be argued that the disvalue which one attaches to making the effort is judged to outweigh the value which one expects to result from its outcome, but unless this account is made trivial by allowing the judgement to be unconscious and then equating inertia with it, I think that it is simply untrue to the facts.

To say that our motivated actions do not in general conform to utilitarian principles is not to deny that they should. It can still be maintained that it is only when they do so that we count them as virtuous. There is, indeed, the further psychological obstacle that not only do we not always do what we want, but even when we are doing what we want, our objectives are commonly more specific than the production of a state of pleasure or the abolition of a state of pain, though here again it could be held that it is only when they have these objectives that our actions are accounted virtuous. I think, however, that it would be a mistake to attribute this view to Hume. Admittedly, he says that 'every quality of the mind is denominated virtuous, which gives pleasure by the mere survey: as every quality, which produces pain, is called vicious' (T 591), adding that 'this pleasure and this pain may arise from four different sources', since 'we reap a pleasure from the view of a character, which is naturally fitted to be useful to others, or to the person himself, or which is agreeable to others, or to the person himself'. There are, however, two points which diminish the force of this quotation. One is that Hume does not think that the pleasure which we take in surveying a virtuous quality is always of the same kind; it varies according to the nature of the quality in question. The other is that when he speaks of a character as being fitted to be useful to others, he does not equate this utility with the maximisation of pleasure. It can consist in bringing about the satisfaction of whatever desires the persons affected happen to have.

In this context, it is also worth remarking that Hume is not a forerunner of utilitarians like Bentham and Mill. We shall see that he associates the conventional virtue of justice with regard to the public interest, but he by no means takes it to be a general feature of the objects of our moral approbation that they promote anything of the order of the greatest happiness of the greatest number.

It has been objected to Hume that there is no such thing as a moral sense, analogous to the physical senses, or a special feeling of moral approbation, which the view of virtuous qualities or characters invariably arouses. The answer to this is that he is not committed to saying that there is. Admittedly, as we have seen, he speaks of our having a feeling or sentiment of blame when we contemplate a character which we pronounce to be vicious, but the point which he is concerned to make is that in calling a character vicious we are not assigning it a special intrinsic property but expressing our reaction to the properties which it has. This reaction must, indeed, be adverse, but it need not take exactly the same form in every case. We do in fact have feelings of revulsion or moral indignation, but they need not always be present in every instance of moral condemnation. There is a large variety of states, dispositions and actions, not all of them infused with emotion, in which our attitudes of moral approval or disapproval may actually consist.

I believe also that some critics have been misled by Hume's use of the word 'mean' when he speaks of our meaning nothing by the use of moral predicates but that the contemplation of the actions or characters to which we apply them causes us to have favourable or hostile feelings. I do not think that Hume is advancing the thesis that a statement of the form 'X is good' is logically equivalent to the statement 'I have a feeling of moral approval in contemplating X' or yet to some such statement as 'The contemplation of X arouses a feeling of approval in most normal men' or 'in most of the members of such and such a society'. And the same applies to statements about the rightness of actions or the obligation to perform them. I do not credit Hume with the view that in making statements of either of these sorts we are covertly asserting something about ourselves or about other actual or possible critics. There is indeed a sense in which he is offering an analysis of our moral judgements, but the analysis is not intended to supply us with a recipe for translating the sentences which express them. It consists rather in an account of the circumstances in which we are induced to employ moral predicates, and of the purposes which their employment serves. Moreover, if we did insist on extracting from Hume a reformulation of our moral statements, we should come nearer the mark by crediting him with the modern 'emotive' theory that they serve to express our moral sentiments rather than with the theory that they are statements of fact about one's own or other people's mental condition.

It is not even clear that Hume is correctly described as a moral subjectivist, unless we are using the term 'subjectivist' in such a way that it is correct to say of Locke that he gave a subjectivist account of qualities like colour. But is it not one of Hume's principles that moral judgements are not descriptions of matters of fact? This is true, but what it means is that they lack the sort of factual content that is to be found in a description of a person's motives or in an account of what he actually did. From another point of view, it is as much a matter of fact that a motive or character of a given sort has the tendency to evoke certain responses in those who contemplate it, as it is a matter of fact that the responses are or tend to be produced. Neither is there any evidence in the texts that Hume wanted to deny this. What he did want to deny was that moral predicates stand for what Locke called primary qualities, or, in other words, that they stand for intrinsic features of the motives or characters or actions to which they are applied.

In this he is surely right. To take his own example of a case of wilful murder, the badness of the act is not an additional feature of it, ranking alongside the facts that the killer had such and such motives, or that he brought about the death of his victim in such and such a fashion. Neither is it manifested as a sort of glaze with which the conjunction of such facts is overlaid. My statement that it was a wrongful act may carry a descriptive content, if it is construed as presupposing my acceptance of some prevalent code of morals, which I can then be taken as asserting that the action violates, but it is not bound to any such presupposition. It would not be invalidated if my moral sentiments were at variance with those that prevailed in my community or indeed in any other. I could be argued out of them, in this or another instance, not only by its being shown to me that I was not properly or fully informed of the facts, but in a variety of other ways. For instance, I may be convinced on philosophical grounds that law-breakers should not be regarded otherwise than as sufferers from disease; I may attach importance to maintaining consistency in my moral attitudes, and may be persuaded that this case does not differ significantly from others of which I have taken a different view: I may be given cause to think that my view of the case is clouded by untoward features of my own experience and character. I may consequently decide that my original moral judgement was mistaken. I say 'mistaken' rather than 'false', because I think it conducive to clarity to assign a truth-value only to moral judgements which carry the presupposition of some code, so that it becomes a factual question whether the judgement accords with the rules of measurement which the code furnishes. Evidently this does not imply either that any one code is sacrosanct, or that all moral judgements are equally acceptable.

Hume's contention that 'ought' does not follow from 'is' has also been challenged. The favourite counter-example is that of promising. It has been argued that from the purely factual premise that, under specifiable conditions, a man utters a sentence of the form 'I promise to do X', it logically follows that, other things being equal, he ought to do X. But this is a fallacy. If the argument seems convincing, it is because it is situated within a moral climate in which provision is made for promising, that is, for the incurring of a moral obligation through the utterance, under the proper conditions, of certain sequences of words. But if we are dealing with a question of logical entailment, the existence of such a climate cannot legitimately be presupposed. It has to be stated as an extra premise, to the effect that the speaker belongs to a society in which it is an accepted principle that to utter such and such words is, in some range of circumstances, to assume a moral commitment. This is again a factual premise, but even when conjoined with the other, it does not entail the desired conclusion. We still need the moral premise that this rule of his society is one to which allegiance ought to be given.

A simple objection to Hume's theory is that it applies equally well to natural endowments or handicaps, such as good or ill looks, wit or dullness, a sociable or morose disposition, as to what are commonly reckoned as virtues or vices, like courage or cowardice, fidelity or fickleness, meanness or generosity. In an Appendix to the *Enquiry*, Hume acknowledges the fact and dismisses it as of no importance, appealing on this point to the authority of Cicero, whom he frequently takes as a model, and also to that of Aristotle, who 'ranks courage, temperance, magnificence, modesty, prudence and a manly openness, among the virtues, as well as justice and friendship' (E 319). This fails to account for the distinction that we ordinarily make, though I suspect that Hume is right in claiming that it is not based on any consistent principle. Possibly, we tend to confine moral epithets to those amiable or unamiable qualities which require more cultivation to become habitual, or depend to a greater extent upon the presence or absence of self-discipline. This would still allow good manners to count among the virtues, but I do not find this unacceptable.

To anyone who has studied Kant, who notoriously held that an action is moral only when it is done from a sense of duty, it may come as a shock to find Hume saying that an action must proceed from some motive other than a sense of its morality if it is to be morally good. Hume does not deny that men can and do act out of a sense of duty. What he denies is that this in itself confers any merit on an action. A man who is of a miserly disposition may grow ashamed of it and so force himself to perform acts of generosity. In time his initial reluctance to perform them may or may not be overcome. It is not, however, necessary that it should be overcome in order for his actions to be morally good. Their goodness depends on their conforming to a habitual practice of generosity, and so long as this is true it makes no moral difference whether the agent has generous feelings, whether he thinks it profitable to himself to display a generosity which goes against his inclinations, or whether he acts against his inclinations because he thinks that generosity ought to be practised. We must, therefore, avoid being misled by Hume's saying that actions are morally good only as being signs of a good motive or a good character. It does not mean that he conceives of characters or motives as being good in themselves. They owe their goodness only to the fact that they *habitually* give rise to actions which are morally approved. It is the consequences that call the tune: and motives are brought to the fore only because they can be counted upon regularly to produce beneficent actions. To have a sense of duty as one's primary motive for behaving well is rather to be deprecated, since this suggests that one is deficient in natural benevolence.

In fact the opposition between Hume and Kant on this issue goes deeper, since Kant's ground for tying morality to the sense of duty was that an action could have moral worth only if it was performed freely, and that it was only when they were done from a sense of duty that actions were free in the requisite form. It is not at all clear what this form of freedom was supposed to be but in any case there seems to be no warrant for drawing a distinction on this basis between the sense of duty and any other motive.

The principle that reason alone can never be the motive for any action, though it may appear psychological, is defended by Hume in a way that makes it analytic. It is a straightforward consequence of his confining what he counts as reason to the drawing of inferences and the appraisal of truth and falsehood, and his semantic assumption that operative motives cannot significantly be characterised as true or false. Reason has control over the passions, in so far as it can be used to discover that a passion is based on a false judgement, as for example when the object of one's fear is proved not to exist, or that the means chosen to procure some end are insufficient for the purpose. A third instance, which Hume failed to notice, is that in which reason shows us that the achievement of a desired end will probably result in the occurrence of something which we have a greater desire to avoid. The dramatic statement that reason is and ought only to be the slave of the passions amounts only to what is, for Hume, the truism that reason enters into the sphere of action only when we have been motivated to aim at some end. The phrase 'ought only to be' is merely a rhetorical flourish, since the choice of ends has been put outside the sphere of reason. Similarly, Hume's startling assertion that it is 'not contrary to reason to prefer the destruction of the whole world to the scratching of my finger' or 'to choose my total ruin, to prevent the least uneasiness of an *Indian* or person wholly unknown to me' or 'to prefer even my own acknowledg'd lesser good to my greater' (T 416) is no more than a consequence of the scarcely controversial assumption that one's preferences, however eccentric, are not themselves the bearers of truth-values and need not be the outcome of any erroneous inferences.

The supporting argument that morals cannot be derived from reason, since they have an influence on our actions and affections is, on the other hand, invalid. Even on Hume's own showing, our actions and affections may be influenced by the truth or falsehood of our judgements or the soundness of our inferences; it is only our objectives, when not considered as means to further ends, that are not susceptible to this influence. Nevertheless the deduction that 'the rules of morality are not conclusions of our reason' holds good independently, since what it rightly claims is that the rules of morality do not come within the province of

'Relations of Ideas'.

The main objection to be faced is that we do have a conception of the rationality of ends as well as means. Hume avoids it by suggesting that we mistake calm passions for 'the determinations of reason' but this is not a sufficient answer. It is true that we speak of a person as behaving irrationally when he rushes into a course of action without thinking about the consequences, but we also consider some rankings of ends, such as those that occur in Hume's examples, as being irrational in their own right. I think that what we mean by this is that they are choices which no sensible man would make. There is an obvious risk of circularity here, since his choice of ends enters into our conception of what constitutes a sensible man. A possible way of escape is just to take it as a matter of fact that a person who habitually chooses ends of a certain type arouses in the average spectator an impression of folly. We can then define the irrationality of ends in terms of the behaviour of such a person, and their rationality as its opposite.

There remains the question whether the sense of justice, in which Hume discovers the source of our obligations, is natural or artificial. Hume's ground for saying that it is artificial is that there are no natural motives to supply it. With very rare exceptions, men do not have any such passion as the love of mankind, and their natural feelings of benevolence towards a limited number of persons would favour injustice, in that it would lead them to promote the interest of these persons at the public cost. Neither can the sense of justice arise directly from man's selfishness, though Hume's explanation of it does relate it indirectly to self-interest.

His explanation runs as follows. Because of his physical weakness, a man can survive and prosper only as a member of a group, even if in the first instance it is so small a group as that of the family. As groups intermingle, they tend to prey on one another. 'There are three different species of goods, which we are possess'd of; the internal satisfactions of our mind, the external advantages of our body, and the enjoyment of such possessions as we have acquir'd by our industry and good fortune' (T 487). It is the third of these goods that is chiefly at risk, on the one hand because of men's avidity and the limited extent of their benevolence, and on the other because of the niggardliness of nature. If men had always lived in an environment of such abundance that all their material appetites, however luxurious, could easily be satisfied, 'the cautious jealous virtue of justice would never once have been dreamed of' (E 184). As things are, different groups have to compete for the relatively scarce quantity of goods that are or can be made available. If this competition were unrestrained, no man could ever count on 'the peaceable enjoyment of what he may acquire by his fortune and industry' (T 489). To avoid such a calamity men have found it in their interest to subscribe to a set of conventions which establish rights to property and also lay down the conditions in which its transfer from one man to another is legitimate. These conventions are not promises. On the contrary, promises are themselves based on a convention, the purpose of which is to give men security of each other's future conduct. It is on the three 'laws' of the stability of possession, its transference by consent, and the performance of promises 'that the peace and security of human society entirely depend' (T 526).

So far it is only a question of self-interest. Morality comes into the picture both naturally, because we sympathise with the victims of injustice, either through our affection for them, or, in cases which this does not cover, through putting ourselves imaginatively in their place, and artificially, because those who educate and govern us see it as their business to train us to apply eulogistic epithets to conformity with the rules of justice and dyslogistic epithets to their breach, thereby arousing and fortifying the moral sentiments with which the use of these epithets is associated.

The justification of these rules is that their observance conduces to the public interest. This is, however, true only in general and may be false in some particular instances. An example which Hume gives is that in which 'a man of a beneficent disposition, restores a great fortune to a miser or a seditious bigot'; the man 'has acted justly and laudably, but the public is a real sufferer' (T 497). Even so, Hume maintains, in agreement with many present-day utilitarians, that we should always stick to the general rule. He offers no argument for this beyond saying that it is 'impossible to separate the good from the ill. Property must be stable, and must be fix'd by general rules. Tho' in one instance the public be a sufferer, this momentary ill is amply compensated by the steady prosecution of the rule, and by the peace and order, which it establishes in society' (T 497). But why should the public be required to suffer at all? Only, it would seem, because toleration of exceptions would weaken respect for the general rule, with a resulting disutility that would outweigh the utility of the exceptions. But even if we accept this line of reasoning, it does not cover the cases where there is no serious probability that the choice of an action which went counter to the rule would become generally known. Why should we then adhere to the rule when the purpose of the rule would be better served by our departing from it? I do not believe that those who uphold what is currently known as rule-utilitarianism have a satisfactory answer to this question.

Another objection to Hume's account of justice is that it is tied too closely to the institution of property. For instance, the only provision that it makes for the value of equality is that we are equally bound to comply with the rules that our conventions establish. This is, however, a defect that is easily remedied, since the conventions can always be adjusted to suit any ranking of their interests that the members of a society can be induced to accept.

Though justice is necessary for the maintenance of society, government, in Hume's view, is not. A primitive uncultivated society can subsist without it. Only, when it is successful in war, a period of government will be needed to regulate the partition of the spoils. The warrior chief is then likely to become the civil arbiter. It is for this reason, according to Hume, that 'all governments are at first monarchical'.

In more developed societies, government is needful because men are naturally disposed to sacrifice their long-term to their short-term objectives, and it is in their interest to be restrained from doing so. It therefore pays them to submit to rulers, whose short-term interests include the retention of their privileges, which in turn depend upon the enforcement of law and order. There is, indeed, the possibility of the rulers' becoming so tyrannical that their subjects would be better off without them, in which case they are at liberty to remove them if they have the power to do so. Such action is not, however, to be undertaken lightly, in view of the disturbance which it creates, and it is also true that the habit of civil obedience leads men to put up with tyranny for longer than would be the case if they strictly attended to their interest. There are various ways, including succession, conquest, and the operation of constitutional laws, in which particular governments may be instituted. What is more important is the tenure of power. No matter how a system of government comes into being, its mere persistence will generally be sufficient for its being regarded as legitimate. There is a sense, then, in which government rests on the consent of the governed, but it does not follow from this that we have to invent a social contract as the moral justification for political obedience. Since the rules of justice are necessary for the validity of contracts and also sufficient to account for political obligation, even a genuine contract would, as Hume rightly argues, have no part to play in this case, let alone the philosophical fictions which writers on politics have tried to pass off as contracts. The suggestion has been made that we incur an obligation to obey a government by choosing to remain subject to it, but apart from any other objection this presupposes that we have a serious alternative, which is very often not the case. Otherwise, as Hume remarks in his essay 'Of the Original Contract', it is like telling a man who has been shanghaied aboard a ship that he is free to leap into the sea and perish.

Hume makes no attempt to connect morals with religion, no doubt because he saw that morals cannot be grounded on any form of authority, however powerful, though religious belief may operate as a sanction through its effect on the passions. In any case Hume was less interested in the utility of religious belief than in its pretension to truth. We have seen that he rejected Christianity. By examining his *Dialogues Concerning Natural Religion*, I shall now try to justify my claim that he also rejected deism.

The three participants in the *Dialogues* are Demea, who believes that the existence of God can be demonstrated *a priori*, though we are incapable of penetrating the mystery of his nature; Cleanthes, who argues that there can be no other proof of God's existence than what we can extract from our observations of the world, and consequently bases his theism upon what is commonly called the argument from design; and the sceptical Philo, who agrees with Cleanthes that the argument from design is the only one worth considering, and devotes himself to showing what a very poor argument it is. This does not lead him into any profession of atheism. He even goes so far at one point as to assert that 'when reasonable men treat these subjects, the question can never be concerning the *being*, but only the *nature* of the Deity' (D 142), but in the light of his general argument this remark appears ironical. In the management of the *Dialogues*, Philo is given by far the most to say, and this is one reason for concluding that he speaks for Hume.

Demea's argument is that nothing can exist without a cause, that the idea of an infinite regress of causes is absurd, and that the regress can be brought to an end only by there being an ultimate cause who necessarily exists. This is the Deity, 'who carries the *Reason* of existence in himself; and who cannot be supposed not to exist without an express contradiction' (D 189). Cleanthes's rebuttal of this argument is that the existence of a deity is supposed to be a matter of fact, and that no matter of fact is demonstrable *a priori*. Moreover, if we were entitled to speak of a necessary being, it might just as well be the universe itself. Demea makes no attempt to reply to this objection, with which Philo concurs, and his part in the remainder of the *Dialogues* is pretty well limited to an occasional pious protest against Cleanthes's failure to make a sufficiently large distinction between the qualities and powers of human beings and those of their supposed creator.

While he gives numerous examples, accepted by Philo, of the adaptation of means to ends in nature, Cleanthes's position is summarised in one powerful statement of the argument from design.

Look round the world [he says]: Contemplate the whole and every part of it: You will find it to be nothing but one great machine, subdivided into an infinite number of lesser machines, which again admit of subdivisions, to a degree beyond what human senses and faculties can trace and explain. All these various machines, and even their most minute parts, are adjusted to each other with an accuracy, which ravishes into admiration all men, who have ever contemplated them. The curious adapting of means to ends, throughout all nature, resembles exactly, though it much exceeds, the productions of human contrivance; of human design, thought, wisdom, and intelligence. Since therefore the effects resemble each other, we are led to infer, by all the rules of analogy, that the causes also resemble; and that the Author of nature is somewhat similar to the mind of man: though possessed of much larger faculties, proportioned to the grandeur of the work, which he has executed. By this argument *a posteriori*, and by this argument alone, we do prove at once the existence of a Deity, and his similarity to human mind and intelligence. (D 143)

Philo's rejoinder to this argument is the principal theme of the Dialogues as a whole, but his main objections to it can be concisely summarised.

1 Causal arguments are based on experienced regularities. They are not available in this case since we are not acquainted with a multiplicity of worlds. Cleanthes can appeal only to analogy, which is a weaker form of reasoning.

2 If we press the analogy, on the assumption that like effects have like causes, we have no warrant for concluding that the universe was planned by an infinite, eternal, incorporeal Being. We have no experience of anything of this sort. Machines are constructed by mortal human beings who have bodies, belong to one or other sex, work in co-operation, proceed by trial and error, make blunders and correct them, improve on their designs. By what right therefore can we deprive the universal planner of body and sex? Why should we not conclude that the world is due to the combined efforts of many gods? Why should it not be 'the first rude essay of some infant deity, who afterwards abandoned it' or 'the production of old age and dotage in some superannuated Deity' (D 169) whose death left it to its own devices? Why should not many worlds 'have been botched and bungled, throughout an eternity, ere this system was struck out' (D 167)?

3 If this is to make the analogy too strong to suit Cleanthes, it is also in fact too weak. The world does contain many human artefacts, and many natural objects which resemble these artefacts at least to the extent that they or their parts serve some function, to which they are more or less well adapted. It does not follow, however, that the universe as a whole is a machine or anything like one; or that there is any purpose which it serves. It is no more like a machine than it is like an animal or vegetable organism. It would be no 'less intelligent, or less conformable to experience to say, that the world arose from vegetation from a seed shed by another world, than to say that it arose from a divine reason or contrivance' (D 178).

4 If we are tracing the universe of objects into 'a similar

universe of ideas' (D 162), why should we stop there? If the order in ideas needs no further explanation, why should the order that we find in matter?

5 Our experience of the world shows that 'matter can preserve that perpetual agitation, which seems essential to it, and yet maintain a constancy in the forms, which it produces' (D 183). Why should we not be content to credit matter with a force which enables it to develop out of what we may suppose to have been an original chaos into an order accounting among other things 'for all the appearing wisdom and contrivance which is in the universe' (D 184)? Surely this theory is to be preferred to the unverifiable and practically useless hypothesis of a supernatural agency.

6 Not only is the argument from design exposed to all these objections, but even if they are waived it achieves next to nothing. The most that a man who accepts it is entitled to conclude is 'that the universe, sometime, arose from something like design: But beyond this position he cannot ascertain one single circumstance, and is left afterwards to fix every point of his theology, by the utmost licence of fancy and hypothesis' (D 169).

Probably the last point was, in Hume's eyes, the most important of all. He was, as I have tried to show, campaigning on many fronts against religious belief, but above all he wished to preserve philosophy from the 'licence of fancy and hypothesis' into which theology falls. We have seen that he was not a model of consistency, but he was at least consistent in his naturalism, his insistence that every branch of science be anchored in experience. His main interests were too broad to be captured in a paragraph, but his general outlook can perhaps be summarised, and I can see no better way of doing so than by quoting the famous passage with which he concludes the first *Enquiry*:

When we run over libraries, persuaded of these principles, what havoc must we make? If we take in our hand any volume; of divinity or school metaphysics, for instance; let us ask, *Does it contain any abstract reasoning concerning quantity or number?* No. *Does it contain any experimental reasoning concerning matter of fact and existence?* No. Commit it then to the flames: for it can contain nothing but sophistry and illusion. (E 165)

Bibliographical note

THE editions of Hume's works from which I have quoted are listed in the Preface. The original dates of publication of these, and of other works by Hume to which I refer, are as follows:

A Treatise of Human Nature 1739–40

An Abstract of the Treatise of Human Nature 1740 (published anonymously)

Essays, Moral and Political 1741–2

Three Essays ('Of Natural Character', 'Of the Original Contract' and 'Of Passive Obedience') 1748

Enquiry concerning Human Understanding 1748 (first published as *Philosophical Essays concerning Human Understanding*)

Enquiry concerning the Principles of Morals 1751

Political Discourses 1752

History of Great Britain from the Invasion of Julius Caesar to the Revolution of 1688 (6 vols) 1754–62

Four Dissertations ('The Natural History of Religion', 'Of the Passions', 'Of Tragedy' and 'Of the Standard of Taste') 1757

Two Essays ('Of Suicide' and 'Of the Immortality of the Soul') 1777

My Own Life 1777 (first published as *The Life of David Hume, Esq., Written by Himself*)

Dialogues concerning Natural Religion 1779

A large collection of Hume's letters was edited by J. Y. T. Greig in two volumes and published in 1932 under the title *The Letters of David Hume* by the Oxford University Press. In 1954 the same publishers brought out a collection entitled *New Letters of David Hume*, the product of extensive research by its editors, Raymond Klibansky and Ernest C. Mossner. Of the many books written about Hume's philosophy, the two which I should especially wish to recommend are *The Philosophy of David Hume* by Norman Kemp Smith, which was published by Macmillan in 1941, and *Hume's Theory of The External World* by H. H. Price, which was published by the

Oxford University Press in 1940. The points for which I am indebted to these works are indicated in the text.

Index

OXFORD

MORE OXFORD PAPERBACKS

This book is just one of nearly 1000 Oxford Paperbacks currently in print. If you would like details of other Oxford Paperbacks, including titles in the World's Classics, Oxford Reference, Oxford Books, OPUS, Past Masters, Oxford Authors, and Oxford Shakespeare series, please write to:

UK and Europe: Oxford Paperbacks Publicity Manager, Arts and Reference Publicity Department, Oxford University Press, Walton Street, Oxford OX2 6DP.

Customers in UK and Europe will find Oxford Paperbacks available in all good bookshops. But in case of difficulty please send orders to the Cash-with-Order Department, Oxford University Press Distribution Services, Saxon Way West, Corby, Northants NN18 9ES. Tel: 0536 741519; Fax: 0536 746337. Please send a cheque for the total cost of the books, plus £1.75 postage and packing for orders under £20; £2.75 for orders over £20. Customers outside the UK should add 10% of the cost of the books for postage and packing.

USA: Oxford Paperbacks Marketing Manager, Oxford University Press, Inc., 200 Madison Avenue, New York, N.Y. 10016.

Canada: Trade Department, Oxford University Press, 70 Wynford Drive, Don Mills, Ontario M3C 1J9.

Australia: Trade Marketing Manager, Oxford University Press, G.P.O. Box 2784Y, Melbourne 3001, Victoria.

South Africa: Oxford University Press, P.O. Box 1141, Cape Town 8000.

PHILOSOPHY IN OXFORD PAPERBACKS

Ranging from authoritative introductions in the Past Masters and OPUS series to in-depth studies of classical and modern thought, the Oxford Paperbacks' philosophy list is one of the most provocative and challenging available.

THE GREAT PHILOSOPHERS
Bryan Magee

Beginning with the death of Socrates in 399, and following the story through the centuries to recent figures such as Bertrand Russell and Wittgenstein, Bryan Magee and fifteen contemporary writers and philosophers provide an accessible and exciting introduction to Western philosophy and its greatest thinkers.

Bryan Magee in conversation with:

A. J. Ayer
Michael Ayers
Miles Burnyeat
Frederick Copleston
Hubert Dreyfus
Anthony Kenny
Sidney Morgenbesser
Martha Nussbaum

John Passmore
Anthony Quinton
John Searle
Peter Singer
J. P. Stern
Geoffrey Warnock
Bernard Williams

'Magee is to be congratulated . . . anyone who sees the programmes or reads the book will be left in no danger of believing philosophical thinking is unpractical and uninteresting.' Ronald Hayman, *Times Educational Supplement*

'one of the liveliest, fast-paced introductions to philosophy, ancient and modern that one could wish for' *Universe*

Also by Bryan Magee in Oxford Paperbacks:

Men of Ideas
Aspects of Wagner 2/e

POLITICS IN OXFORD PAPERBACKS

Oxford Paperbacks offers incisive and provocative studies of the political ideologies and institutions that have shaped the modern world since 1945.

GOD SAVE ULSTER!

The Religion and Politics of Paisleyism

Steve Bruce

Ian Paisley is the only modern Western leader to have founded his own Church and political party, and his enduring popularity and success mirror the complicated issues which continue to plague Northern Ireland. This book is the first serious analysis of his religious and political careers and a unique insight into Unionist politics and religion in Northern Ireland today.

Since it was founded in 1951, the Free Presbyterian Church of Ulster has grown steadily; it now comprises some 14,000 members in fifty congregations in Ulster and ten branches overseas. The Democratic Unionist Party, formed in 1971, now speaks for about half of the Unionist voters in Northern Ireland, and the personal standing of the man who leads both these movements was confirmed in 1979 when Ian R. K. Paisley received more votes than any other member of the European Parliament. While not neglecting Paisley's 'charismatic' qualities, Steve Bruce argues that the key to his success has been his ability to embody and represent traditional evangelical Protestantism and traditional Ulster Unionism.

'original and profound . . . I cannot praise this book too highly.'
Bernard Crick, *New Society*

Also in Oxford Paperbacks:

Freedom Under Thatcher   Keith Ewing and Conor Gearty
Strong Leadership   Graham Little
The Thatcher Effect   Dennis Kavanagh and Anthony Seldon

PAST MASTERS

General Editor: Keith Thomas

The *Past Masters* series offers students and general readers alike concise introductions to the lives and works of the world's greatest literary figures, composers, philosophers, religious leaders, scientists, and social and political thinkers.

'Put end to end, this series will constitute a noble encyclopaedia of the history of ideas.' Mary Warnock

HOBBES

Richard Tuck

Thomas Hobbes (1588–1679) was the first great English political philosopher, and his book *Leviathan* was one of the first truly modern works of philosophy. He has long had the reputation of being a pessimistic atheist, who saw human nature as inevitably evil, and who proposed a totalitarian state to subdue human failings. In this new study, Richard Tuck shows that while Hobbes may indeed have been an atheist, he was far from pessimistic about human nature, nor did he advocate totalitarianism. By locating him against the context of his age, Dr Tuck reveals Hobbs to have been passionately concerned with the refutation of scepticism in both science and ethics, and to have developed a theory of knowledge which rivalled that of Descartes in its importance for the formation of modern philosophy.

Also available in Past Masters:

Spinoza   Roger Scruton
Bach   Denis Arnold
Machiavelli   Quentin Skinner
Darwin   Jonathan Howard

PAST MASTERS

General Editor: Keith Thomas

Past Masters is a series of concise, lucid, and authoritative introductions to the thought of leading intellectual figures of the past whose ideas still affect the way we think today.

'One begins to wonder whether any intelligent person can afford not to possess the whole series.' *Expository Times*

FREUD

Anthony Storr

Sigmund Freud (1865–1939) revolutionized the way in which we think about ourselves. From its beginnings as a theory of neurosis, Freud developed psycho-analysis into a general psychology which became widely accepted as the predominant mode of discussing personality and interpersonal relationships.

From its inception, the psycho-analytic movement has always aroused controversy. Some have accepted Freud's views uncritically: others have dismissed psycho-analysis as unscientific without appreciating its positive contributions. Fifty years have passed since Freud's death, so it is now possible to assess his ideas objectively. Anthony Storr, psychotherapist and writer, takes a new, critical look at Freud's major theories and at Freud himself in a book which both specialists and newcomers to Freud's work will find refreshing.

Also available in Past Masters:

HISTORY IN OXFORD PAPERBACKS

Oxford Paperbacks' superb history list offers books on a wide range of topics from ancient to modern times, whether general period studies or assessments of particular events, movements, or personalities.

THE STRUGGLE FOR
THE MASTERY OF EUROPE 1848–1918

A. J. P. Taylor

The fall of Metternich in the revolutions of 1848 heralded an era of unprecedented nationalism in Europe, culminating in the collapse of the Hapsburg, Romanov, and Hohenzollern dynasties at the end of the First World War. In the intervening seventy years the boundaries of Europe changed dramatically from those established at Vienna in 1815. Cavour championed the cause of *Risorgimento* in Italy; Bismarck's three wars brought about the unification of Germany; Serbia and Bulgaria gained their independence courtesy of the decline of Turkey—'the sick man of Europe'; while the great powers scrambled for places in the sun in Africa. However, with America's entry into the war and President Wilson's adherence to idealistic internationalist principles, Europe ceased to be the centre of the world, although its problems, still primarily revolving around nationalist aspirations, were to smash the Treaty of Versailles and plunge the world into war once more.

A. J. P. Taylor has drawn the material for his account of this turbulent period from the many volumes of diplomatic documents which have been published in the five major European languages. By using vivid language and forceful characterization, he has produced a book that is as much a work of literature as a contribution to scientific history.

'One of the glories of twentieth-century writing.' *Observer*

Also in Oxford Paperbacks:

Portrait of an Age: Victorian England   G. M. Young
Germany 1866–1945   Gorden A. Craig
The Russian Revolution 1917–1932   Sheila Fitzpatrick
France 1848–1945   Theodore Zeldin